John Blanchard grew up in southwest London, UK. While at school and university he had temporary jobs in London, Bremen and Frankfurt, in a chandlery, the Royal Mail, an electric hammer factory, a department store, a coffee factory and teaching English. Then, as a school teacher, he focused on how language can be used to help people teach and learn better. He worked with colleagues in higher education, and continued doing so as an education consultant. Along the way he has learned from those he has met in conversation, through reading, viewing visual media and, perhaps most powerfully, by studying and working together.

For everyone who wants to help us live well.

John Blanchard

To Make a Better Future:
What Must We Do?

AUSTIN MACAULEY PUBLISHERS™
LONDON * CAMBRIDGE * NEW YORK * SHARJAH

Copyright © John Blanchard 2023

The right of John Blanchard to be identified as author of this work has been asserted by the author in accordance with sections 77 and 78 of the Copyright, Designs and Patents Act 1988.

All rights reserved. No part of this publication may be reproduced, stored in a retrieval system, or transmitted in any form or by any means, electronic, mechanical, photocopying, recording, or otherwise, without the prior permission of the publishers.

Any person who commits any unauthorised act in relation to this publication may be liable to criminal prosecution and civil claims for damages.

A CIP catalogue record for this title is available from the British Library.

ISBN 9781398458246 (Paperback)
ISBN 9781398458253 (ePub e-book)

www.austinmacauley.com

First Published 2023
Austin Macauley Publishers Ltd®
1 Canada Square
Canary Wharf
London
E14 5AA

Whenever I think about how communities and organisations work, I remember Keith Robertson, Tyrrell Burgess and Bill Brookes who were my mentors.

Heartfelt thanks to my wife Jacky Blanchard for insights and much discussion.

I owe a great deal also to the following for their comments and suggestions on drafts: Fiona Carnie, Peter Hains, Gerald Hewitson, Stephen Monsell, Frank Newhofer, Steve Parker, Janet Reibstein, Andy Robertson, David Salinger, Norman Schamroth, Nick Symes and Amanda Worrell.

Over many and recent years, each of the following has been a powerful example and encouragement: Albert Bandura, Richard Bentall, Brian Boyd, Patricia Broadfoot, Stephen Brookfield, Nick Brown, Madeleine Bunting, Jennifer Charteris, Patrick Condren, Antonio Damasio, Andrea Etherington, Michael Fielding, Chris Frith, Carolyn Godfrey, Mike Golby, A. C. Grayling, Woody Harding, Jonathan Hawksley, Kevin Laland, Luigi Luisi, Chris Marsden, Iain McGilchrist, Ray Ockenden, Cailin O'Connor, Dick Passingham, Adam Phillips, Lord Martin Rees, Michael Rutter, Royce Sadler, Ingrid Sidmouth, Phil Silvester, Iram Siraj, Stuart Twiss, Margaret Welsh, Maryanne Wolf, Liz Worthen, Maulfry Worthington and Patrick Yarker.

Table of Contents

Introduction	11
1: Beginning	13
2: Origins	36
3: Us and Them	58
4: Learning	78
5: Trying to Think	87
6: Helping One Another Learn	101
7: Knowing and Not Knowing	112
8: Trusting	134
9: Finding Satisfactions	149
10: Doing the Right Thing	167
11: Taking Responsibility	185
12: Leading	204
13: Deciding	224
14: Living Well	237
Abbreviations	239

Introduction

Do you want us to live better than we do now?

Do you want to help make a better future for generations to come?

If your answer is yes to both questions, this book is for you.

I offer you other people's stories and reflections along with some of my own. Speaking to us through these pages are researchers, entertainers, writers and working people who have helped me.

We have different ideas about how to fund and run our lives. Some of us don't like to admit that on our own we aren't able to look after ourselves. As the historian and author Rutger Bregman (2019)[1] wrote, 'A better world doesn't begin with me, but with all of us'; and his book points to how we can do it: 'our main task is to build different institutions'. Alongside our instinctive, spontaneous ways of behaving, we need coordinated expertise committed to our safety and well-being.

We interact at a distance and virtually, and what each of us feels, thinks and does affects what the rest of us feel, think and do. Unique and resourceful as we are, we need one another. In *Lean on Me*, the singer-songwriter Bill Withers (1972)[2] told us:

> 'Sometimes in our lives
> We all have pain
> We all have sorrow …
> Lean on me when you're not strong
> And I'll be your friend
> I'll help you carry on
> For it won't be long
> 'Til I'm gonna need
> Somebody to lean on.'

Cooperating with one another on a grand scale is probably the greatest challenge we face. We are now facing graver risks than ever before. We have reason to be afraid. If we don't find different ways to live, any of these—or, more likely, a combination of these—will destroy us:

> our planet's damaged ecosystem and loss of biodiversity
> wildfires, rising sea levels and extreme weather
> wealth and income inequalities
> pandemics
> obesity, starvation and malnutrition
> industrial, technological and institutional mistakes
> genocide and nuclear, chemical, biological or cyber warfare.

Such dangers need the attention of more than lone individuals, groups or communities. Cooperating with one another on a grand scale is probably the greatest challenge we face. We can take courage from the fact that we're not alone: sharing our hopes and fears prompts us to aspire, learn and use our imaginations and intellects for the good of us all.

---

[1] See Rutger Bregman's (2019) *Humankind: A Hopeful History*, translated from the Dutch by Elizabeth Manton and Erica Moore, published in London, UK, by Bloomsbury, p 383.

[2] See or listen to Bill Withers' (1972) *Lean on Me*, on the album *Still Bill*, co-produced by Ray Jackson, Melvin Dunlap and James Gadson in Los Angeles, CA, on The Record Plant label.

1 Beginning

The people we hear from in this chapter include Susie Orbach; Donald Winnicott; Patricia Crittenden; Daniel Wilcox and Clark Baim; Julia Samuel; Suzanne O'Sullivan Adam Phillips; Ankhi Mukherjee; Lisa Feldman Barrett; Carol Dweck; Shankar Vedantam and Bill Mesler; and Michio Kaku.

How do we become who we are?

From the Outset

I wonder what you think makes the greatest difference to who we become.

The psychotherapist and psychoanalyst Susie Orbach (2000)[1] wrote about how we start by needing to be held: 'what the child is pre-wired with is the capacity to announce her presence, to enunciate in whatever ways she can her physical agency and to develop agency', How she 'is held, how she is rocked, how she is changed, how she is fed, how she is sung to and how her physical expressions are interpreted are of tremendous significance'.

The bonding between a mother or mother-figure and her infant is assisted by glands which produce the hormones oxytocin and vasopressin. The biologist Robert Sapolsky (2018)[2] explained that these signalling molecules 'decrease anxiety and stress, enhance trust and social affiliation, and make [us] more cooperative and generous'. How well infants are cared for adds up to their sense of themselves, and decides whether or not they feel safe in their body. The sculptor Antony Gormley said our body is 'our first dwelling'—a sanctuary, a point of departure and a source of strength.

It's troubling not to be well cared for. Just as troubling is when we are too well cared for. When our main carer depends on us for her or his identity and well-being, we develop a false or damaging sense of our worth and purpose[3].

Then, we don't feel secure or adventurous enough to broaden our horizons and make our own world.

The paediatrician and psychoanalyst Donald Winnicott (1964)[4] understood that how we behave towards children transfers to how they feel about themselves and their world, and so to how they behave: 'good enough environmental provision' brings 'forward development', along with more or less successful transitions to fruitful experiences and relationships.

Our basic needs are to be held, to have water, food and sleep, to excrete waste fluids and solids and to have a balanced physiology. When these needs are attended to, we're in a position to meet our more complex needs and have them met with others' involvement. Then, when things go well enough, we are accepted and appreciated, and so may rely on:

> Safety, stability and order
> Affectionate, caring relationships
> Having a sense of possibility and direction.

Meeting these needs and fulfilling these capacities enable us to:

> Bond and belong
> Love and be loved
> Be autonomous and live well together.

When we benefit from having healthy ties, attachments and coalitions—and sometimes miraculously without them—we want to make the most of whatever happens. We learn how to follow our instincts and interests. And when the people who lead our communities and institutions have developed secure feelings of attachment, affirmation and cooperation, we all benefit.

Balancing What You Want with What's Available

The psychologist Patricia Crittenden's (1992)[5] understanding of the role that attachment plays in your life is as follows. From your first experiences, you use information about things you notice around you, such as whether or not your main caregiver is present, and whether what you feel is pleasure, contentment, discomfort or alarm. This leads you to express yourself and respond to your caregiver's cues. In other words, you use what you feel to achieve a balance between what you want and what's actually available.

You can't always be conscious of these strategies. Part of your response is to have fears and hopes which become the source and stuff of undercurrents in your experiences. Another response is to keep your anxiety and negative emotions beneath the surface, pretend you're ok and thereby avoid antagonising or alienating whoever you depend on. To begin with and periodically for ever afterwards, how you *feel* is all you *know*.

Your attachment to your first care-giver gives you a mistaken assurance that she or he knows everything there is to know about you. For a while at least, and then intermittently, you can't help feeling that what you're wanting and expressing is automatically understood by others. You may carry this sense into later life too and, as Orbach wrote, you may 'endow [your] partners with magical powers, as though they can know [you] and see [you] and help [you] without your telling them'.

Your imagination invests other people with great power or authority, so you tend to be surprised, and/or relieved, to realise that no one always or wholly reads your mind. You probably have your first inkling of this when you tell a lie and get away with it. It's quite a discovery: you can hide what you feel, think and do. Later you realise that other people do these things too. When you glimpse that other people don't reveal everything they feel and think, you may become disillusioned and so learn that you have little option but to come to terms with some things you can't change, at least in the present.

You adapt your behaviour to suit your situation. Much of what you do is a kind of performance, including doing things to move or placate others. You also put up a front and choose to act in calculated and contrived ways. You experiment with personas and roles. You pretend, for example imitating other people's behaviours and characteristics. All kinds of playing—and watching other people playing—give you mental space and time to ask questions and look at things differently.

It's easier, and in the short term deceptively comforting, to stay bound by what you know and repeat what's habitual or expected of you. You dismiss or repress feelings and thoughts that can't be integrated, though this may involve splitting off parts of yourself. Orbach wrote about Winnicott's (1960) understanding that this is a 'problem of internal alienation': you contrive false selves to compensate for your undeveloped or partially impaired true and better self.

Kinds of Attachment

The clinical and forensic psychologist Daniel Wilcox and psychotherapist Clark Baim (2015)[6] described two kinds of attachment.

In one case, care provided is 'predictable but not attuned', which is to say that the baby is consistently handled and treated, but in ways that do not meet her or his actual needs and wants. When she or he cries, she or he is regularly ignored, handled roughly or even physically abused. This baby adapts by withholding expression of feelings, because crying only increases the distress. She or he learns that 'When I feel bad, no one helps, and when I cry I feel worse.' Cared for in this way, she or he learns that what she or he does makes certain things happen. She or he realises that adjusting her or his reactions brings some protection and comfort, whereas acting on bad feelings brings more trouble and can be dangerous. She or he begins to distrust her or his own emotions. Still, emotions boil away under the surface and then burst through in bouts of distress, desperate comfort-seeking, aggression and/or sexualised behaviour. She or he finds ways to distance herself or himself from her or his feelings. This toddler develops strategies that help her or him get close to a parent who ignores or neglects her or him, or she or he develops ways of appeasing people close to her or him, complying with their demands or ingratiating herself with them. From puberty onwards, in order to avoid the risk of being hurt, the child loses sight of her or his needs and wants and becomes isolated, self-reliant and/or becomes promiscuous.

In a different case, the baby's care is 'unpredictable and inconsistently attuned'. The caregiver is not consistently attentive and may often or easily be distracted, misuse alcohol or drugs, be psychologically unwell, behave violently and/or suffer violence. Inconsistent care is confusing if not disturbing and damaging for the baby. This baby learns to organise her or his responses to get what she or he can out of the precarious situation and have some control. As a result, she or he feels inconsolably sad and expresses anger in temper tantrums. The child acts out to gain the carer's attention. This confuses the carer, who can't understand that being inconsistent doesn't help. She or he learns to exaggerate feelings of sadness, fear or anger, and then keep changing her or his tactics. As time passes, both carer and child share a bond in misery. The child's strategies evolve in subtlety and complexity: aggressive outbursts alternate with disarming displays of helplessness or coyness. This has the effect of keeping the attachment figure locked in an irresolvable struggle, as the child continually switches between anger-aggression and appeasement-comfort. From puberty onwards, the young person may develop behaviours such as exacting revenge, punishing would-be carers and/or seeking to be rescued. And these feelings and responses transfer to many other figures: family members, friends, neighbours, partners, teachers, caring professionals, colleagues …

The writer, director, podcaster, singer and former actress Jennette McCurdy's memoir (2022)[7] *I'm Glad My Mom Died* described her attachment to her narcissist mother—an example of the attachment brought about by predictable-but-not-attuned caring. When people who lead our communities and institutions have developed flawed patterns in their relationships and behaviours, we are in trouble. Narcissism is a compulsion to manipulate and control one or more people. As a form of political programme it is totalitarianism.

Hardships, Challenges

Constructive, satisfying attachments are microcosms of vital, productive partnerships and coalitions. Our adaptations and initiatives are meant to help us to feel safe and content. But if, early on and subsequently, we can't off-set our poor or harmful attachments, we feel that we have little or no worth. Hurt and shame make us bereft and rootless. We fail to hold onto or we drive away the people we need and want. We may sense we're at fault. We make 'false selves' to hide behind or make up for what we feel is missing. We blame and punish others. We become ill and harm ourselves.

Growing up may expose children to extreme experiences. Post-Traumatic Stress Disorder (PTSD), for example, was first recognised as a condition in 1983, and Complex Post-Traumatic Stress Disorder (C-PTSD) in 1994. For an individual, C-PTSD2 grows out of emotional neglect, humiliation, bullying, disrupted childhood attachment, violence and anger. On a social, political or industrial scale, its causes include dictatorship, civil war, human rights violations and economic deprivation[8]. Symptoms include that you feel unsafe; you don't relax; your sleep is disrupted; you hate who you are; you are drawn to unavailable or disturbed people; you often lose your temper and are worried much of the time; you are paranoid; you feel safer alone; you find your life exhausting and unpleasant; you are rarely spontaneous; you bury or burn yourself up by overworking and engaging in extreme or obsessive pursuits.

The psychiatrist Patricia Crittenden and surgeon and specialist in child neuropsychiatry and psychotherapy Andrea Landini (2011)[9] focused on what it can mean to be traumatised by physically or emotionally threatening circumstances. These are experiences that can't automatically or straightforwardly be processed and learned from. Children are especially vulnerable because they have only just begun 'to store, retrieve, and integrate' the meanings they construct: they are novices in the face of harm and danger.

Caregivers are a vital part of your environment. Growing up with denial or ambivalence of affection leads to your absorbing and then projecting negativity and lack of trust, so that you tend to treat others as you have been treated—at least some of the time and especially when stressed or tired. Deprivation is followed by desperation and/or determination to escape, compensate or fight back. You learn to deal with challenges by pushing forwards or dominating others. Breaking down may be the only other option you know.

You have to work through your experiences, and you help yourself when you compare your view of your world with how others see theirs. The advantages of discovering you have things in common with all sorts of people are that you're helped to explore affiliations, tastes and choices. Receiving good enough attention, you grow up feeling open to new experiences because you trust how you've been cared for. Just as physical objects and toys can be 'left around' for you to learn from, so too do encouragements and opportunities lead you to want to explore and find your place in your world.

From the beginning, healthy development gives you an ever-widening circle of situations and challenges. Constructive experiences give you space and time to explore and experiment, whereas ill-intentioned and negative experiences lead you to contrive make-do and emergency responses.

Grieving

An absence is as upsetting as a harmful presence. You feel this acutely, for example if the parenting you receive is interrupted or negligent. You don't simply 'move on' from neglect, hurt and loss: these never quite disappear. Trauma is extreme adversity and becomes part of who you are.

Griefs resurface and revive your healing. The psychotherapist Julia Samuel (2017)[10] wrote that 'The paradox of grief is that finding a way to live with the pain is what enables [you] to heal… Pain is the agent of change', as it is of birth. But because 'It is often the behaviours [you] use to avoid pain that harm [you] the most', it takes a conscious effort to do the apparently impossible and combine 'holding on' with 'letting go'. What applies to grief applies to all your struggles with conflict and pain. Actual or anticipated pain alerts you to what you might do differently: the negative points to the positive, if you can be open to it.

You need to make sense of things. It helps to try new ways of looking at your past and towards possible futures. This is how you learn to try new ways of responding, experimenting and taking initiatives. As the professor of bioengineering, psychiatry and behavioural sciences Karl Deisseroth (2021)[11] explained, the 'steady progression of experience clarifies patterns and buries structural threads'. Provided your basic needs are met, your genetic make-up, combined with healthy and empowering relationships, enables you to grow and discover directions you enjoy taking and thrive by. Shocks and insults are mitigated as your instincts and latent capacities are ignited. Then, you avoid losing confidence in yourself and avoid relying too much on others. At first unconsciously and involuntarily, you develop a sense of your true and better self.

Your 'immunity' to adversity grows when you resist, counteract and transform events and situations that test, deprive and shock you[12]. Mental immunity depends on your absorbing and drawing on the equivalent of biochemical antibodies that protect and defend you physically. But if you're over-protected, it's likely that your natural resilience will be weakened and progressively disabled. Your true and better self can only mature and thrive if it's healthy enough and nurtured to find ways to do what's really good for you and those around you.

Entering Your World

To begin with, you and your world are one: there is no 'I' separate from 'you' or 'them'. You take your encounters with people and the world into yourself. It is 'through the internalisation of a relationship' that you come to speak[13] and, without being aware of it, you meet your needs and fulfil your capabilities with others' help. At this stage you are egocentric. It may be that narcissists are stuck in their egocentrism.

Whatever your age, you're unlikely to be aware of much of what your brain and body actually do. Your automatic actions give you the impression you're managing external things. The psychologist Chris Frith (2007)[14] wrote that 'because [your] brain suppresses the bodily sensations it can predict, [you] feel most in control when [you] do not feel anything'. Yet being confirmed and confident in ties of nurturing affection helps you realise that you depend on others and they on you. So you alternate reaching out to and moving away from those who care for and about you[15]. Narcissists, like sociopaths and psychopaths, can't do this.

Being cared for enables you to care for yourself and about others. Being healthy and secure, you grow through curiosity, adventure and challenge and find your own path as well as paths you share with others. You cope with and grow through the disturbances of change, absence and loss. In this way, time is your friend as well as your enemy.

You learn about your carers' and others' feelings and about the causes and consequences of feelings and the actions they give rise to. Orbach (2016)[16] wrote that the best of all possible relationships are ones in which you are curious about 'the why of the other's feelings'. How well you learn to interpret your world and express yourself shapes who you become. The language that surrounds you and that you start to use helps you construct, interpret and regulate your emotions. It is perhaps the most sophisticated aspect of being human that language enables you to penetrate others' feelings and thoughts, and it is through words, thoughts and deeds that you affect and change others and they are affected and changed by you—for good *and* ill.

As time goes by, words shape your feelings and thoughts about yourself 'in a world of other selves'. If the words you hear are kind and constructive, you are helped to bond and grow. Then you may accept being apart, separate and different. Words are crucial to developing a working view of yourself, of others and of everything that attracts and deserves your attention. If things go well, your experience expands and deepens your initial sense of 'I' offering many forms of 'we'. What each of us feels, thinks and does is subjective *and* inter-subjective. Objective is what is *out there*, beyond *I* and then beyond *we*. When you're aware of *your* world, you have begun to co-construct objectivity.

Looking for objectivity doesn't come naturally and requires effort, both imaginatively and intellectually. Everyone is bound to make their own sense and version of what they feel. Learning to live well with other people depends on everyone's coming to terms with what they agree their situation is and what should be done to protect and enhance it. When you begin to engage with and use objectivity, you extend and enrich what is subjective. Objectivity grows out of everyone's subjectivities and is enhanced by their cooperation.

What Words Do

Several of the schools I've known for children and young people with moderate, profound and multiple learning difficulties and disabilities have routines that encourage learning about how we need and affect each other. Regularly at the start of a session or periodically, everyone in the class chooses a word to say how they're feeling. Words for many different emotions are displayed and added to over time. Doing this, everyone expands their vocabularies and gains insight into possible responses to events and prospects. Incidents, issues, fears and hopes are brought to light and may be addressed there and then, or attended to later. And the class is better prepared for what lies ahead.

Words spark and support your wondering, but also fend it off and snuff it out. You use words to share and develop what's inside you, but also to hide and stifle it. Who you are is made up of your consciousness and unconsciousness— a dynamic amalgam of how you see and feel about yourself and how others see and feel about you. You may picture your unconscious as a source of your feelings and a repository for things you daren't or can't face or own, at least not without effort and/or help[17]—revealed, for example, in your dreams and by the slips of your tongue[18].

Orbach (2016) wrote that in therapy 'the act of saying something out loud makes conscious something one may be acting on but not yet thought about ... [Then] what was previously unknown and as yet unconsidered enters into awareness, enabling the capacity to think about what was under the surface'. We might treat consciousness as multi-layered—ranging from feelings and thoughts that remain latent to feelings and thoughts that become considered and deliberate.

Your passive as well as your active communication moves and moulds you: you're led to ideas and actions you don't fully conceive for yourself. Language is rarely a private possession: you share it and evolve it with others. As the psychoanalyst Adam Phillips (2021)[19] observed, 'We think of ourselves as doing things with words, while language does things to us'. Because you need to be cared for, supported and challenged, your life is bound up with others' lives. This extends as people further and further afield affect you, for example, via community, culture, technology, institutions and systems.

You have potential and, when you join with others, everyone's potential is exponentially greater. When things go well, you develop ways of exploring what you're not used to: you try others' perspectives and put yourself in their shoes. You are helped when those who are close to you tell you stories[20]: they wonder and help you wonder how and why things turn out as they do. You may respond more readily to allusiveness than to literalness; stories may enrich your understanding more often than matter-of-fact accounts.

How You Feel

Your genes work with whatever your environment offers and throws at you. You grow healthily when you enjoy sound relationships *and* when you assert yourself and tackle or bypass what looks forbidding.

The neurologist Suzanne O'Sullivan (2015)[21] wrote that 'The body has a multitude of ways through which it can express emotion', including blushing, palpitations, tiredness, weakness and fainting. Any of your bodily functions can go awry or break down. Cells can overgrow and tumours form or stop growing—you may suddenly lose hair, for example. Chemicals can be overproduced; your thyroid gland may become overactive or underactive; sometimes, your organs overreact: 'When that happens, something that was normal is no longer so and illness occurs.'

Your body's responses to emotion and stress produce physical symptoms. O'Sullivan made this distinction crucial to her practice: 'Psychosomatic disorders are not neurological disorders... [They] are physical symptoms that mask emotional distress', as in paralysis or hearing loss. For attentive doctors, 'behaviour surrounding the symptom is key, not the symptom itself... If illness seems to be helping solve the problem of loneliness, then treat the loneliness and the illness will disappear. Or find out where the gain lies and address that.' Or, if the problem lies in maladaptive responses to the messages the body sends and receives, these can be worked on. If there's a specific trauma triggering illness, it may be traced and addressed. With help, you can alter or break a pattern that stops you growing healthily.

Between the ages of around 12 to 25, your plastic brain is quick and receptive[22]. In adolescence, your capacity for remembering is at its most powerful. It's also the case that during those years you're likely to take more risks in the company of peers. This has advantages as well as disadvantages. So it is that adolescents, boys especially, jump off piers and cliffs, drive fast and play with danger.

Healthy or otherwise, there's little that is one-dimensional or monochrome about human beings. Phillips (2013)[23] saw that 'A good life … involves making the messes you need'. There's happiness that comes from abiding by the rules, being safe and feeling protected, and there's a kind of happiness that comes from breaking rules, feeling guilty and making amends. Being bad can be as alluring as being good.

Becoming a Person

As Orbach and Winnicott explained, it can happen, for example, that 'when the main parent, usually the mother, is unable to see and respond to what the child needs and wants, the child's True Self goes underground'. This enables her or him to find within himself or herself things—such as acquiescent smiles—that the mother can respond to: 'This makes the mother feel good in what she is then able to give and the child feels good that he or she has mother's approval and attention. As this pattern of pleasing continues, the True Self fails to come alive'. This child copes as best she or he can in a second-best kind of way which tends, over time, to undermine steady gains in healthy self-confidence.

To help yourself cope with rebuffs, deprivation and desolation, you cry. Later you sulk, feel angry, displace your upset, blame others and fight. In the same way that you're unwell when you lack proteins, vitamins and minerals, you're unwell when your needs aren't met well enough for you to feel yourself—alive, belonging and effective. Then discontent may turn inward, for example giving rise to psychosomatic illness. Later, other manifestations are physical self-harming, such as cutting, punching walls or other people and finding toxic outlets or salves for tensions that can't be sublimated, channelled or resolved.

The theatre practitioner, playwright and poet Bertolt Brecht[24] made use of alienation as a device to prompt his audiences to distance themselves from what they were seeing and hearing, feeling and thinking. His play *The Good Woman of Szechwan* (1943, 1953) is the story of Shen Te who can't help being generous to others, but who is taken advantage of and oppressed by individuals and social systems. She is an example of how many of us might need sometimes to invent a proactive, protective, false self. It became impossible for Shen Te to manage being her true and better self, so she divided herself in two. She adopted a ruthlessly pragmatic *alter ego*, Shui Ta.

Brecht showed the advantages of an approach to life that includes having sometimes to be unnaturally calculating and self-interested because the world isn't one-dimensional or consistent: we can't expect always to be treated fairly. There aren't many situations and events that don't have downsides as well as upsides. Most of our challenges require us to minimise the ill-effects of our initiatives and responses while maximising their potential benefits. This inescapable state of affairs means we have constantly to deal with ambiguities, anomalies, contradictions and complexities. We find this difficult because we'd prefer our world and our life to be simpler and more straightforward.

To Be At One with Yourself

The better you understand your own and others' needs and wants, the better you may be understood, and the better we all may live. Crucial to this is your becoming accustomed to and interested in how things look to other people—their opinions, wants, needs and suggestions. This curiosity leads you to new or better nuanced ways of doing things and expecting there will be puzzles, snags and upsets as well as enlightenment and rewards along the way. Sometimes, though, you fight shy of tackling complexity and conflict.

You have been primed by evolution to make spontaneous and deliberate forecasts and run mental simulations about how things could turn out. This is part of your response to uncertainties you are bound to have to contend with. It's how you learn to make corrections in the light of what happens next and thereafter. These processes are metabolically more efficient than just reacting to events as though they were just one thing after another.

The psychologist and brain researcher Lisa Feldman Barrett (2018)[25] explained that your brain translates 'all the sensations from your internal organs and tissues, the hormones in your blood, and your immune system' and produces 'a spectrum of basic feeling from pleasant to unpleasant, from calm to jittery, and even neutral… If you want to feel good, then your brain's predictions about your heart rate, breathing, blood pressure, temperature, hormones, metabolism, and so on, must be calibrated to your body's actual needs'. When that doesn't happen, 'your body budget gets out of whack', and you feel bad 'no matter what self-help tips you follow'.

Your all-round health affects how well your brain functions. You help yourself by having up to 18 hours' fasting most days, though your lifestyle may lead you to have snacks in between two or three substantial meals a day. Barrett noted, 'Modern culture, unfortunately, is engineered to screw up your body budget. Many of the products sold in supermarkets and chain restaurants are pseudo-food loaded with budget-warping refined sugar and bad fats'. This disrupts your 'eating healthfully, exercising and getting enough sleep'.

Have there been times when you have felt especially healthy and at ease with yourself?

What factors helped you?

You maintain a healthy balance between risk and safety by drawing on your instincts, reflecting honestly on your experience and taking note of recent, well-grounded science. You help yourself and others by giving and receiving. Taking turns helps you feel good, which boosts your all-round health. Getting involved in other people's stories—through talk, shared imagining, performance, film and reading—is restorative and stimulating. So is looking after plants and natural environments. You are helped by being given regular massage, which 'limits inflammation and promotes faster healing of the tiny tears that result from exercise', and by spending time, if not living, in surroundings that are green and light.

Phillips (2002)[26] observed that, from the start and forever after, your 'fundamental need … is to be able to live in a way that enables [your] needs to come to light… to be known, penetrated, affirmed, recognised, nurtured'. Other people who have roles in your life affect your well-being and prospects. Some might not find you wholly appealing, some might want to abuse or exploit you, but, if you're lucky, there are some who do their best for you, just as you do your best for them.

Becoming Resilient

To live well, we have to come to terms with things within and around us. It takes commitment, adaptability and perseverance to help ourselves and others be introspective *and* outward-looking. We have therefore to try not to underestimate how hard it is to pause, step back and consider other people and alternative courses of action. We have to give ourselves space and time to do these things and look for other people's involvement. We help ourselves when we use diverse sources of information and evidence to check how reliable and valid our feelings, thoughts and calculations are. Gradually, through our own efforts and with others' example and encouragement, we become increasingly aware, reflective, confident and resourceful.

The more segmented, stratified and divided our relationships and societies are, the more complex and challenging our lives are likely to be. The specialist in Victorian and Modern English literature, critical theory and postcolonial and world literature Ankhi Mukherjee (2021)[27] has written about the urban poor in cities across the world. In a talk (2018)[28], she spoke about how the disenfranchised and dispossessed are helped both by their own strength and resilience and by 'free clinics' and 'guerrilla volunteers' using psychoanalysis in the service of poverty alleviation.

From the beginning, you want more than anything else to be held, then absorbed—to 'forget yourself'[29]—for example through physical and emotional commitment, endeavour and intimacy. When you're happy and creative, it is as though you're temporarily in a state of suspension or harmonious motion. The psychologist Mihaly Csikszentmihalyi (1991)[30] wrote about this in terms of having a sense of 'flow'—a healthier, more reliable and less expensive option than using artificial stimulants, alcohol or drugs. This depends on resolving tensions and conflicts in your feelings, thoughts and actions. You are helped by supportive interactions and constructive relationships with other people, starting with those closest to you.

All being well, you want to make sense of your experiences, opportunities and challenges because sound sense tends to help you and those around you. How you express yourself plays a part in shaping who you become. It is good to notice and try out new words to see if they fit how you feel: 'Words seed your concepts, concepts drive your predictions, predictions regulate your body budget, and your body budget determines how you feel'. Barrett recommended you work on developing your 'emotional intelligence'.

Working towards worthwhile goals helps you rethink feelings you may have that you should simply put up with the way things are and shy away from challenges for fear of failing or upsetting other people. Then you want to act in your own and joint interests, you're uninhibited by embarrassment or fear and you give your energies fully to what you do. But positive feelings are punctured by unkind criticism.

You're not helped by others who want to control you, have you placate or please them and misuse you for their own selfish purposes. You live better and longer when your purposes are integral to who you feel you truly can be. Then you tend to tackle activities that invite and reward your commitment and concentration. Then you tend to do well as you try to control what is controllable. This equates to self-efficacy[31]. It confirms resilience, gives confidence and promotes self-esteem. It is the opposite of and a remedy for dysfunctionality and ill-health. It brings you dignity and recognition.

The New Zealand Rugby All Blacks mental resilience coach Gilbert Enoka said, 'In the end, you need only three bones to be successful: a wish bone, a back bone and a funny bone.'

Getting Back on Track

'Brief' or 'solution-focused' therapy[32] is an approach to your becoming responsible for your well-being using these strategies:

> Describe what's concerning or troubling you
> Notice what you've done well so far and what obstacles and difficulties you've overcome on the way
> Picture what things would look like if a specific aspect of your life were much better than it currently is; and give yourself a score out of 10 for how close you are right now to that better state of affairs—0 for nowhere near, 10 for you're there
> Decide what you'll try to do to get one or two points closer to how you want to be

Do that thing, and repeat the process until you're happy with your progress.

A part of this can be to answer a 'miracle question': what would things look like if whatever is troubling you were no longer there? Then consider what would need to happen for that change to happen. This prompts you to address your present situation and decide what to do about it.

You are well when you feel whole, balanced and resilient. Well-being confirms you're changing, enjoying the benefits and rising to the challenges. The psychologist Carol Dweck (2000)[33] studied this. She reported that humans have contrasting assumptions and beliefs about their chances of success. There's a spectrum and you move along it according to your genetic endowment, your start in life and your ongoing experiences. If your mindset tends to the 'fixed' end of the spectrum, you feel less able to use your resources to be well and do well. Nor does feeling entitled or bound to succeed do you any favours. But if your mindset tends to the 'growth' end of the spectrum, you feel you can rise to the occasion and carry on developing your abilities through effort and with support. Resilience is a bridge to confidence.

Mindsets, though, are not permanent, and other people can help you realise you are evolving and growing. As Dweck (2006)[34] observed, 'This is the process we want [learners] to appreciate: hard work, trying new strategies, and seeking input from others; … once we acknowledge that we all have recurrent fixed mindsets, we can talk to one another openly. We can talk about our fixed-mindset personas, when they show up, how they affect us, and how we're learning to deal with them'. We can learn, and we can help one another see, that we can change and together change aspects of our world.

Resilience and self-esteem are neither innate nor fixed. They are undermined by lack of confidence and by complacency. Lack of confidence leads you to expect that, whatever you do, you won't do well. Complacency is believing you'll always be well and do well, whether or not you extend yourself, whether or not others help you. When you're properly confident, you expect to do better when you try hard, focus your efforts and are open to support and challenge.

To be confident is to have a rudder. To be resilient is to find your rudder when things get difficult. Your rudder is what you know and can do, which includes knowing there are things you currently neither know nor can do. Feeling confident and resilient, you face difficulties and emerge intact, enriched and strengthened if not triumphant.

What sorts of things have been your rudder?

Becoming Confident

The physicist, futurist and populariser of science Michio Kaku (2021)[35] advised that 'the bedrock of [your] understanding of the world is science. Which is ultimately based on things that are testable, reproducible and falsifiable'. Science is rigorous, collaborative learning from experience. He added a caution, though, that 'scientists are often reluctant to admit that there are some things beyond the realm of science. For example, it is impossible to prove a negative'. Some things are beyond everyone's—even scientists'—proofs.

This is the opposite of believing that success is a gift and comes from fate or magic or status. Resilience and confidence are healthy alternatives to 'false positivity'[36]. Valuing yourself and recovering quickly are ways of experiencing challenges; they're not characteristics you're born with or without, or which depend on powers or influences you can't affect, or which work simply because you believe they will. When you value yourself and are resilient, you trust yourself enough to know that, with luck, making mistakes and failing don't destroy you or make you worthless.

The journalist, writer and science correspondent Shankar Vedantam and science writer Bill Mesler (2021)[37] observed that you don't always check the accuracy of what you see, hear or read, even when you want help to cope with difficulties in life: sometimes you 'choose the hope of lies over the despair of truth'.

Can you think of occasions when you have, or someone you know has, believed something that is untrue or inaccurate?

Can you see why you or they did that?

How did things work out?

Vedantam's and Mesler's reading was that, according to recent psychologists and neuroscientists, 'the human brain is designed to make a number of errors in perception and judgement. These "bugs"—distortions, shortcuts and other cognitive cross-wiring—produce slanted pictures of reality'. This is evolutionary, and evolution isn't primarily interested in 'helping us perceive reality accurately': its mission is fitness, and its method is to promote whatever helps pass on genes. That means we act on whims and fantasies as well as reliable information.

Our biochemistry and neurology give us 'a greater likelihood of survival and reproduction': jumping to conclusions and believing fabrications have sometimes been advantageous to our ancestors and will probably continue to help us, albeit unpredictably.

We have a 'self-deceiving brain': 'As a species, humans are not the strongest or fastest. We don't have sharp claws or teeth. Our muscles are puny compared to many other creatures. But what we do have is each other. This is why the self-deceiving brain prompts us to band together, fight for one another, defend each other. It regularly overrules the logic of mere self-preservation because, in our evolutionary past, standing with the tribe increased the odds our genes would survive'. We can imagine this served humans well when we lived in cohesive tribes. But as we have become more distant from and less familiar with the numbers of people affecting us, it is less clear what we should do.

So sometimes we put too much trust in what we see or hear without checking. We also share and hold onto beliefs to help us cope in the very short term. And we are 'easily deceived by those with whom we have formed emotional attachments'—parents, carers, friends, and charismatic, fanatical, cult, community and gang leaders—and so we come to be deceived by what others believe and their misleading sources. Many of us find pictures, symbols, rumour, gossip, fashionable views, songs, poems, stories, mimes, dramas and films are more accessible and more appealing than advice, analyses, arguments, lectures, essays, TED Talks, reports and recommendations: 'Evolution has given us minds that are alert to stories and suggestion, to imagination and self-deception, because, through many thousands of years of natural selection, minds that can attend to stories have been more successful at passing on their owners' genes'.

Being Yourself, Helping Others

You're bound to mislead and be misled, not least because you mis-read situations and one another. You may gain by and enjoy misleading other people. Misleading others without realising you're doing it can be forgiven, especially if you later realise what you've done and say you're sorry or make amends.

You help yourself and other people by sharing perceptions and trying to be truthful. You also help yourself by accepting you are sometimes uncertain. When you predict events—privately or letting others know—you expose yourself to the possibility of being proved wrong.

It is more beneficial to predict than merely to expect, and more effective to pause, think and simulate than merely to predict events. Doubts prompt you to check how confident you are of your predictions and simulations, and how satisfied you can then be that they have served you well. Doubting, imagining and reviewing outcomes help you test your beliefs and thereby learn to be flexible and critical. To be critical is to be grounded in verifiable evidence and committed to envisaging possibilities. It is the opposite of being negative or opinionated or blown by prevailing winds. It engenders and strengthens collective intelligence—a spirit of cooperative, enlightened decision-making and action. This is how a group or community becomes more and better than the sum of its parts.

We aren't helped by people, ideas or movements that want us to stay as we are—which usually means doing or being what someone else wants us to do or be. We can help ourselves *and* welcome others' help. Kaku (2021) emphasised the effort this entails: 'Everything that has meaning is the result of struggle and sacrifice, and is worth fighting for'. Something we need to struggle and fight for is developing trust in our interdependence. That is how we come to understand our own and others' needs and wants, and so come to live better lives.

The stand-up comedian, actor and writer Eddie Izzard (2017)[38] described his way of dealing with feeling unconfident: 'I'll just borrow confidence from a future version of myself… I will go to the bank manager of confidence, in some part of my brain, and I will borrow that confidence from the future, and then I can wear it like a cloak'. It's helpful to make what we have achieved into a reserve that we draw on. Our borrowing is repaid by what we go on to accomplish. If we hear yourselves or someone else saying 'I can't', we might say, 'Yes, you can. Borrow from your bank of confidence. It'll back you to succeed.'

Through our interactions, we can learn to enjoy being interdependent. That is how individuals and communities survive and evolve. As Rutger Bregman (2019)[39] wrote, 'Human beings crave togetherness and interaction. Our spirits yearn for connection just as our bodies hunger for food'. Institutions formalise our interconnectedness by providing forums and processes which harness all of our goodwill, determination and talents, and so enable us all to share leadership, be free, act together as equals and thereby overcome difficulties and flourish.

Sometimes, it is a combination of spontaneous combination of courage, inventiveness and determination that enables human beings to achieve the apparently impossible, prompted by the willingness to take calculated risks and be supported by soundly based and well organised expertise. Ron Howard's film (2022)[40] *Thirteen Lives* documents individuals' and teams' imagination, expertise, cooperation and endurance. Over 17 days in June and July 2018 in the Tham Luang Nang Non cave, northern Thailand, around five thousand people, including four volunteer cavers, an anaesthetist, Navy Seals, a water engineer, villagers, farmers, an elder with extensive knowledge of the locality, emergency services personnel, a regional governor and a government minister saved the lives of 12 boys and their football coach trapped in caves flooded by early monsoon rains. Throughout, they managed to reconcile their having doubts with trusting they could and should attempt things no one had ever done before. They felt free to act as equals.

Summing Up

To be confident is to have a rudder. To be resilient is to find your rudder when you need it.

We have a 'self-deceiving brain'. We also have each other.

The better we learn to make clear what we want, then organise and cooperate, the more capable everyone becomes.

Benevolent institutions formalise our interconnectedness by harnessing all our goodwill, determination and talents.

Chapter 1
1 See Orbach (2000) *The Impossibility of Sex: Stories of the Intimate Relationship Between Therapist and Patient*, p 234.
2 See Sapolsky's (2018) *Behave: The Biology of Humans at Our Best and Worst*, p 135.
3 See the psychologist, psychoanalyst and philosopher Alice Miller's (1995) *The Drama of Being a Child: The Search for the True Self*, and (1991) *Breaking down the walls of silence*.
4 See Winnicott's (1964) *The Child, the Family, and the Outside World*, pp 17, 44, 86-87 and 194; also (1963) essay 'Morals and Education', pp 96- 99.
5 See Crittenden's (1992b) 'Children's strategies for coping with adverse home environments', *Child Abuse & Neglect*, 16: 329-343. Doi: 10.1016/0145-

2134(92)9oo43-q. Also her (2008) *Raising Parents: Attachment, Parenting and Child Safety*.

[6] See Daniel T. Wilcox's and Clark Baim's (2015) 'Applications of the Dynamic-Maturational Model of Attachment with Children Involved in Care and Family Proceedings', *Child Abuse Review*.

[7] Jennette McCurdy's (2022) memoir was published in New York, NY, by Simon and Schuster.

[8] Information about C-PTSD is available from the School of Life, a global organisation based in London, UK, dedicated to helping people to lead more resilient and fulfilled lives. Visit the schooloflife.com website and view 12 signs you might be suffering from PTSD via https://www.youtube.com/watch?v=qOibW5LXt3w.

[9] See Patricia Crittenden's and Andrea Landini's (2011) *Assessing Adult Attachment: A Dynamic-Maturational Approach to Discourse Analysis*, published in New York, NY, by W.W. Norton, p 250.

[10] See Julia Samuel's (2017) *Grief Works: Stories of Life, Death and Surviving*, published in London, UK, by Penguin Random House, pp xviii-xx.

[11] See Karl Deisseroth's (2021) *Connections: The Story of Human Feeling*, published in London, UK, by Viking/Penguin, p 205.

[12] The developmental psychopathologist and consultant psychiatrist Michael Rutter wrote about this in *Maternal Deprivation Reassessed* (1981), published in Harmondsworth, UK, by Penguin. He spoke to the theoretical physicist, author and broadcaster Jim Al-Khalili on BBC Radio 4's programme *The Life Scientific* (3 June 2014) about the part played by children's growing capacity to respond to disappointment, neglect, abandonment or abuse and so become autonomous. He gave child adoption as an example: we wouldn't generally recommend children be adopted, but if 'you come from an abusive, neglectful family, then adoption is protective'.

[13] See Susie Orbach (2000), pp 231-232.

[14] See Chris Frith's (2007), *Making up the Mind: How the Brain Creates our Mental World*, published in London, UK, by Viking, Penguin USA, pp 92 and 105. For his explanation of how we perceive things, pp 126-127 and 138.

[15] In *Child Care and the Growth of Love*, the psychologists Mary Ainsworth and John Bowlby (1965), published in London, UK, by Penguin Books, saw our developing attachments to stable caregivers as a necessary channel for vital affection and nurture during infancy and into childhood.

[16] See Susie Orbach's (2016) *In Therapy: The Unfolding Story*, published in London, UK, by Profile Books, p 147; then about the unconscious, pp 216 and 220; about splitting off parts of our self, p 226; and about Winnicott's notion of the True and False Self, referred to in the 'Resisting Othering' section of chapter 3. He explained this in his (1960) 'Ego distortion in terms of true and false self' in *The Maturational Process and*

the Facilitating Environment: Studies in the Theory of Emotional Development, published in New York, NY, by International Universities Press, Inc., pp 140-157.

[17] See Adam Phillips' (2013) *One Way and Another: New and Selected Essays*, published in London, UK, by Hamish Hamilton, pp 140-157: 'The idea of an unconscious is, among other things, a way of describing the fact that there are things we didn't know we could say'.

[18] See Sigmund Freud's (1914) *Zur Psychopathologie des Alltagslebens: Über Vergessen, Versprechen, Vergreifen, Aberglaube Und Irrtum*, published in Berlin, Germany, by S. Karger, and (1914) translated from the German by A. A. Brill as *The Psychopathology of Everyday Life*, published in New York, NY, by The Macmillan Company. And Freud's (1899) *Die Traumdeutung*, published in Leipzig, Germany, and Vienna, Austria, by Franz Deuticke, and (1913) translated from the German by A. A. Brill as *The Interpretation of Dreams*, published in New York, NY, by The Macmillan Company.

[19] See Adam Phillips' (2021) *On Wanting to Change*, published in London, UK, by Penguin Random House UK, p 18.

[20] See the professor of applied linguistics and education Gordon Wells' (1986) *The Meaning Makers: Children learning language and using language to learn*, published in Portsmouth, NH, by Heinemann Educational Books, which illuminated how crucial children's hearing, reading, constructing and reconstructing stories are to their meaning-making.

[21] See Blakemore (2019).

[22] See the cognitive neuroscientist Sarah-Jayne Blakemore's (2019, 2020) *Inventing Ourselves: The Secret Life of a Teenage Brain*, published in New York, NY, by Public Affairs/Perseus Books, pp 201, 73 and 196.

[23] See Adam Phillips' (2013), pp 323-324 and 125.

[24] See Bertolt Brecht's play *The Good Woman of Szechwan* (from the German *Der gute Mensch von Sezuan*, produced in 1943, then translated and edited by Eric Bentley and published in 2007 in London, UK, by Penguin.

[25] See Lisa Feldman Barrett's (2018) *How Emotions Are Made: The Secret Life of the Brain*, pp 56 and 176-181, published in Basingstoke, UK, by Macmillan.

[26] See Adam Phillips' (2002) *Equals*, published in London, UK, by Faber & Faber, p 140.

[27] See Ankhi Mukherjee's (2021) *Unseen City: Travelling Psychoanalysis and the Urban Poor*, published in Cambridge, UK, by Cambridge University Press.

[28] Listen to Ankhi Mukherjee's talk *The psychic life of the poor* at https://www.youtube.com/watch?v=2q T1Bqvu1Bc.

[29] See Phillips (2013), p 339.

[30] See Mihaly Csikszentmihalyi's (1991) *Flow: The Psychology of Optimal Experience*, published in New York NY, by Harper Collins, which gave an extensive review of research into happiness and creativity.

[31] See Albert Bandura's (1997) *Self-Efficacy: The Exercise of Control*, published in New York, NY, by W. H. Freeman and Co., which is explored here in the 'Self-Efficacy' section of chapter 5.

[32] See the therapist and Director of Training for Focus on Solutions Limited in Birmingham, UK, Bill O'Connell's (2012) *Solution Focused Therapy*, published in Thousand Oaks, CA, by Sage Publications.

[33] See Carol Dweck's (2000) *Self-Theories: Their Role in Motivation, Personality, and Development*, published in Philadelphia, PA, by Psychology Press, p 128.

[34] See Carol Dweck's (2006) *Mindset: Changing the way you think to fulfil your potential*, published in London, UK, by Robinson/Random House, pp 215 and 218.

[35] See Michio Kaku's (2021) *The God Equation: The Quest for a Theory of Everything*, published in New York, NY, by Doubleday/Random House, pp 194 and 189.

[36] See the journalist Oliver Burkeman's (2012) *The Antidote: Happiness for People Who Can't Stand Positive Thinking*, published in London, UK, by Faber & Faber.

[37] See Shankar Vedantam's and Bill Mesler's *Useful Delusions: The Power & Paradox of the Self-Deceiving Brain*, published in New York, NY, by W. W. Norton, pp 27, 58, 65-66, 95, 135 147 and 152.

[38] See Eddie Izzard's (2017) *Believe Me: A Memoir of Love, Death and Jazz Chickens*, written with Laura Zigman, published in London, UK, by Penguin Michael Joseph.

[39] See Rutger Bregman (2019), p 74.

[40] See Ron Howard's film (2022) *Thirteen Lives*, written by Don Macpherson and William Nicholson, and released by United Artists Releasing and streamed by Amazon Prime Video.

2 Origins

The people we hear from here include Merlin Sheldrake; Fritjof Capra and Pier Luigi Luisi; Robin Dunbar; Brian Boyd; Peter Godfrey-Smith; Oliver Sacks; Yuval Noah Harari; Chris Frith; Robert Sapolsky; Antonio Damasio; A. C. Grayling; Jamie Metzl; and Karl Deisseroth.

How do we flourish?

Evolving

4.5 billion years ago, gravity, gas and dust formed the Earth. Fossils in the oldest rocks show that 3.5 billion years ago living things appeared. These single-cell organisms contained genes whose molecules carried instructions for making proteins which sustained and developed life.

The first organisms evolved biochemical looping mechanisms which made sensing, signalling and interacting possible, first inside cells and then, 800 million years ago, between cells[1]. Clusters of specialised interactive cells became the first animals.

600 million years ago, cell-to-cell connections evolved further, creating multi-cellular animals with nervous systems which made two-way signalling and cooperation possible. Symbiosis is a special kind of interdependence whereby one organism provides or becomes what another organism needs but can't make or do for itself. It is evident in a mother's or mother-figure's nurturing.

Symbiosis is 'a ubiquitous feature of life' at the heart of the biologist Merlin Sheldrake's (2020)[2] work: each of us has 40 trillion or more microbes living in and on our body which give rise to coalitions that 'allow us to digest food and produce minerals that nourish us… They guide the development of our bodies and immune systems and influence our behaviour. If not kept in check, they can cause illnesses, and even kill us'.

Organisms evolve through processes of acquiring, changing and passing on their traits, in an environment that consists of their own molecular biology, other organisms and their abiotic surroundings. Genetic material is affected and altered by its interactions. When genomes mutate, it is not according to any permanent blue-print, so variations occur, modifying offspring's inheritance. The naturalist, geologist, biologist and botanist Charles Darwin (1859)[3] gave the name 'natural selection' to these dynamics. He saw how individuals, groups and species with certain traits survive and reproduce more successfully than those lacking such traits.

The physicist and systems theorist Fritjof Capra and natural scientist Pier Luigi Luisi (2014)[4] explained what is now understood about these complex processes. In Capra's (2019) talk *Mind, Matter, and Life*[5], he described 'networks as the basic pattern of organisation for all living systems': ecosystems are food-webs which are networks of organisms, organisms are networks of cells and cells are networks of molecules. Cellular networks produce, repair and regenerate themselves by 'transforming or replacing their components'. So stability and change are key characteristics of life.

Humans emerged between 7 and 5 million years ago in Africa, living as foragers in small nomadic groups, adapting to different locations and seasons. Sharing and cooperating were necessary for survival, along with good nutrition, sleep, exercise and technology.

2.5 million years ago, humans were making tools out of stone. They found out how to harvest and set aside plants to be eaten later and how to keep meat. The priest, theologian, philosopher and social critic Ivan Illich (1973)[6] wrote that 'Tools are intrinsic to social relationships' and to our achieving what we need and want. When we use technology without coercion or external control and as much or as little as we want, tools become a natural part of our shared lives: 'Convivial tools are those which give each person who uses them the greatest opportunity to enrich the environment with the fruits of his [or her] vision'.

What stood out for the art historian Neil MacGregor (2010)[7] about the first two million years of human existence was a 'constant striving to do things better, to make tools that are not only more efficient but also more beautiful, to explore not just environments but ideas, to struggle towards something not yet experienced'.

Taking Control

When things become difficult or go wrong and when new opportunities crop up, we have to raise our game. It takes energy, time and the will to puzzle things out. This entails making many different kinds of connections—between us and between things.

The anthropologist and evolutionary psychologist Robin Dunbar (2016)[8] wrote about how 'an animal can survive in a given habitat only if it meets its energy and nutrient requirements and ensures cohesion of its social group... Brain size determines social group size as a response to environmental conditions, and group size and environmental conditions between them impose demands on time budgets that must be satisfied if a new evolutionary step change is to be possible'. Cohesion both costs and benefits us. If we don't come together and cooperate, we won't be able to meet the increasingly taxing and complex demands our choices make on us.

Humans learned to control an urge to dominate, not always or fully but enough sometimes to check and moderate aggression and megalomaniacal fantasies. Having this capacity to channel emotions 'unleashed the unique power of human cooperation'—socially, artistically, scientifically and commercially. Our genes, hormones, instincts and appetites give rise to responses and interventions that help us avoid and convert unpleasantness, correct mistakes, innovate and improve our lives. Unfortunately, they also expose our flaws. The professor of literature Brian Boyd (2009)[9] wrote that our 'selfish' genes might just as well have been called cooperative—for good and ill.

It is the combination of minds and cultures that makes the difference: 'Without the complex shared architecture of the mind, culture could not exist. Because of that shared design, there are many universals across cultures: there is a human nature'. It is in our nature to create technologies, stories, arts, sciences, customs and beliefs that shape what and who we are.

What examples of human cooperation do you think of as being most impressive or startling?

Rutger Bregman (2019)[10] wrote that 'most people, deep down, are pretty decent'. His book is full of examples. The emergency on the sinking Titanic in the northern Atlantic was one: there was no overwhelming panic; on the contrary, there was an orderly evacuation. Similarly, during and after Storm Katrina, New

Orleans in the USA wasn't 'overrun with self-interest and anarchy. Rather, the city was inundated with courage and charity'.

Voice and Mind

Thanks to the invention of radio-carbon technology in the 1950s, skeletons tell us when humans developed control of the tongue, larynx and breathing muscles. Anthropologists have explained that 530,000 years ago changes in our mouth and chest and the U-shaped bone in our throat enabled us to sing.

The psychiatrist, writer and former literary scholar Iain McGilchrist (2019)[11] described how humans could sing before they had words. Before we began talking, our singing brought us comfort and delight: we took our place in and were connected with nature. Musicality and the subtleties of semantics arise in our brain's right hemisphere: 'the aspects of speech that enable us truly to understand the meaning of an utterance at a higher level—including intonation, irony, metaphor, and the meaning of an utterance in context—are still served by the right hemisphere'. Intonation, like all the other non-verbal and phonic features of communication, make up a large part of our vocalising and responsiveness to voices.

Sound becomes meaning for us and meaning takes multiple phonological, lexical and semantic forms, all of which we interpret practically, socially, aesthetically and morally. Susie Orbach referred to how important being sung to is to our development. (See the 'Starting Out' section of chapter 1.)

Around 300,000 years ago, humans began to use fire for protection, for cooking, for warmth and to have light in the dark, be safe and sing together—all early forms of cooperation. Similarly, the rhythms of motion and physical work lent themselves to singing accompaniment.

Around 150,000 years ago, we began to talk to ourselves inside our heads. Inner, silent speech became a sign of our nervous system's recognising events—both outside and inside ourselves. This became a cognitive tool and the onset of making up our mind. As minds joined together, we found we could use our perceptions in new ways and for different purposes.

Sometimes there are two or more voices inside our head. Holding diverging and contrary views is sometimes entertaining or fruitful, sometimes difficult or painful. The social psychologist Leon Festinger (1956)[12] described how, often unconsciously, we look for ways to ease the discomfort of having conflicting feelings and thoughts. We reach for whatever wards off unsettling information; we abandon facts, and bury our head in the sand. But, if we're lucky and if we're going to survive, we tolerate and learn from ambiguity and complexity.

The professor of the history and philosophy of science Peter Godfrey-Smith (2017)[13] wrote, 'We can reflect on our inner states by forming inner questions, commentaries, and exhortations about them'. Consciousness is born of interactions between our body and brain and gives rise to articulation, hence to analysis, in many forms—coherent and incoherent; balanced and disturbed; informal and formal; lyrical, narrative and objective; imaginative, exploratory and declaratory.

The works of the neurologist, naturalist, historian of science and writer Oliver Sacks (2017)[14] asked why we notice what we notice. His answer was that 'Reflections, memories, associations, lie behind [our noticing]. For consciousness is always active and selective—charged with feelings and meanings uniquely our own, informing our choices and interfusing our perceptions. … [N]atural coalitions in different parts of the brain talk to one other in a continuous back-and-forth interaction'. Just one 'conscious visual percept may entail the parallel and mutually influencing activities of billions of nerve cells'. For something to reach consciousness, it 'must not only cross a threshold of intensity but also be held there for a certain time—roughly a hundred milliseconds. This is the duration of a "perceptual moment"'.

Becoming Powerful

What we know about what we're doing is limited, yet our minds have become forces as powerful as nature. We are capable of being persuaded and persuading others. We evolved to invent the practical, decorative, instructive, diverting, regulatory, supernatural, spiritual and systematic.

Languages of all kinds allow us to stand outside ourselves, asking new kinds of questions leading to new kinds of answers. So we recall, reflect, commemorate, wonder, conceive, debate, plan, act and judge. And what individuals became capable of, groups also found pleasure and power in.

Drawing, painting, miming and using objects to represent things are plastic means of communicating. Between 100,000 and 50,000 years ago, we began making representations in signs, pictures and sculptures. As described by Godfrey-Smith, our many kinds of language 'bring ideas together in an organised form'. This is how our brain 'creates a loop, intertwining the construction of thoughts and the reception of them'.

Relatively recently then, humans began to use sounds, shapes and symbols to make real, virtual, possible and previously inconceivable worlds. We developed what the historian Yuval Noah Harari (2011)[15] called fictive language: 'As far as we know, only *Sapiens* can talk about entire kinds of entities that have never been seen, touched or smelled'.

We make choices, and our choices bring us dangers and dilemmas as well as insights and benefits. Our evolution and heritage make us resourceful, complex and flawed. We are as capable of discord and destructiveness as we are of living together harmoniously and constructively.

The philosopher Toby Ord (2020)[16] wrote that 'Humanity lacks the maturity, coordination and foresight necessary to avoid making mistakes from which we could never recover. As the gap between our power and our wisdom grows, our future is subject to an ever-increasing level of risk'. His was, however, no counsel of despair. He focused on 'the scope of what we someday might be able to achieve. Living up to this potential will be another great challenge in itself'. We can look for clues in how healthy we are—physically, mentally and socially. We can choose to come together and seek what is good for everyone. This requires leadership and cooperation.

By the end of this book I will have highlighted some of the things Ord suggested we concentrate on: for example, recognising the limits of our understanding and our inevitable fallibility; valuing the range and richness of human capabilities; expressing and sharing our ideals for life on Earth. If we can do these things, we will come to understand better what we must do and how we can continue learning.

Adapting

What foragers knew seems to have been available to everyone. We can imagine they lived in close, homogenous groups, sharing their knowledge more straightforwardly and transparently than many of us do now.

Harari wrote that hunter-gatherers understood much more about their surroundings than we do about ours: 'Today, most people in industrial societies don't need to know much about the natural world in order to survive'. Our ignorance, though, might be a time bomb. Today, we tend to have our 'own tiny fields of expertise, but for the vast majority of life's necessities [we] rely blindly on the help of other experts, whose own knowledge is limited... The human collective knows far more today than did the ancient bands. But at the individual level, ancient foragers were the most knowledgeable and skilful people in history'.

The professor of behavioural and evolutionary biology Kevin Laland (2018)[17] proposed that some species evolved a 'cultural drive'—a feedback loop between social behaviours and genetics which has enabled accurate copying of one another's behaviours and selects for better cognitive skills and bigger brains. This process leads to 'enhanced social behaviours and technical skills and even diet—all of which results in bigger brains and ultimately greater efficiency in teaching and copying'.

As our ancestors learned to develop cultures and teach one another, we became more diverse and more able to be 'creatures of our own making'. Passing valid information accurately between us increases our understanding and influence: 'The size of a species' cultural repertoire and how long cultural traits persist in a population both increase exponentially with transmission fidelity. Above a certain threshold, culture begins to ratchet up in complexity and diversity... [O]nce a given threshold is surpassed, even modest amounts of novel invention and refinement lead rapidly to massive cultural change'. But when information is inaccurate, culture transmits potentially harmful bugs and errors.

Humans have lived for 95 percent of their existence as hunter-gatherers. Around 70,000 years ago, the population fell to about 10,000, probably as a result of an ice age caused by volcanic ash darkening the skies. Around the same time, *Homo sapiens* spread beyond Africa and brain-size grew to meet new demands.

Around 12,000 years ago, a first agricultural revolution began. Anatomically modern humans settled down and became farmers. Commerce, money, temples, schools, armies, kingdoms, empires and tax systems were established. Languages developed to accommodate new, specialised roles, enabling groups to deal with one another across previously inconceivable distances and barriers. Human experience of space and time changed radically, expanding and complicating our capabilities and susceptibilities.

Taking and Losing Control

Writing is graphic speaking. It appears to have developed independently in at least four civilisations: in Mesopotamia between 3400 and 3100 BCE; in Egypt around 3250 BCE; in China around 1200 BCE; and in lowland areas of Southern Mexico and Guatemala by 500 BCE. Cuneiform and script were used to measure and monitor social and cultural phenomena. Commemorations and curses were carved on pots, pillars and coffins. Deals, oaths and promises were signed to; contracts were drawn up, argued about, broken and kept to.

During this revolution, in Harari's words, we 'acquired unprecedented power'. But now 'we' no longer referred to all of us. Communication, and trade that came in its train, introduced new forms of cooperation and colonisation, along with misunderstanding and exploitation. Through the arts, humanities, economics, engineering, sciences and government, literacy brought unique benefits *and* blights.

Harari noted some of the downsides of changes that took place between approximately 10,000 and 2,000 BCE, depending on the region. The average peasant ended up working harder than her or his forebears had done and 'got a worse diet in return', along with slipped discs, arthritis and hernias. Harari asked, 'Why did people make such a fateful miscalculation?'

His answer was 'For the same reason that people throughout history have miscalculated. People were unable to fathom the full consequences of their decisions'.

Societies which delayed their transition to settled agricultural living have had virtually no incidence of the diseases the rest of us are now susceptible to. The neurologist Josh Turknett (2013)[18] wrote that hunter-gatherers didn't suffer from diabetes, obesity, heart disease, stroke, asthma, stomach ulcers, appendicitis, arthritis or gallstones. These are common in 'developed' societies, but are still absent in the indigenous peoples of West Africa, the Inuit in Canada and native Americans in the Southwest of the USA and northern Mexico. Outside 'primitive' societies, many of us get most of our calories in the form of carbohydrates—eating breads, pastas, biscuits, cakes, pancakes, waffles and breakfast cereals made from wheat, rye, barley, rice, maize and sugar. The diet of modern civilisations depends chiefly on sugar and grains—grasses of the monocot family—cultivated so that we can eat their fruit seeds.

Turknett asked 'Why didn't our hunter-gatherer ancestors eat grains?' His answer was 'Probably because they didn't want to die.' For newly settled farmers in 10,000 BCE and for their descendants ever since, grains and sugar seemed to be good options, in part because they're 'packed with energy, can be grown in large quantities on relatively small plots of land, and can be stored for long periods of time without spoiling'. The hunter-gatherers' diet of meats, vegetables and fruits was nutrient-rich. Our modern grain-based diet is both micro-nutrient-poor—missing essential vitamins and minerals—and macro-nutrient-poor—lacking carbohydrates, fats and proteins that give us energy and support tissue structure. Further, when our diet consists chiefly of processed grains and sugar, we're not so good at absorbing vital nutrients from other foods.

Striving and Strife

There are proteins in food that make our body attack itself. When certain white blood cells in our body detect what they interpret as threats, our immune system responds by producing antibodies. Unfortunately, some of our protective responses cause us disproportionate problems. Because our ancestral diet didn't include sugar and grains—still less, processed sugar and grains—we were, and many of us still are, unused to digesting them; and that has compromised our immune system.

Most of us in the 'developed' world are bound to know people who suffer chronically or have died from immune-system failings or auto-immune and inflammatory illnesses, such as, cancer, celiac disease, lupus, rheumatoid arthritis, multiple sclerosis, Crohn's disease, hypothyroidism, migraines and type 1 diabetes. And, as the geographer, historian, anthropologist, ornithologist and author Jared Diamond (1997)[19] concluded, overall, 'compared with hunter-gatherers, citizens of modern industrialised states enjoy better medical care, lower risk of death by homicide, and a longer life span, but receive much less social support from friendships and extended families'.

About 12,000 years ago, the self-sufficiency of group began to give way to dependence on patronage, regulation and virtual systems of social organisation, trading and statecraft. Not everyone had money. Not everyone could read and write. What people did was no longer determined by everyone or even most people in a tribe or area.

We began to affect one another anonymously and with profound and far-reaching consequences. Proportionally fewer minds controlled more and more aspects of many people's lives. Leadership provided by a minority of the population became a decisive factor in societies' health and fortunes.

There is an Olmec Stone Mask, in the British Museum, London. MacGregor (2010)[20] saw in its decorative design that the Olmec civilisation placed itself at the centre of what they understood to be their universe. Being at the centre or apex of things tends to symbolise majesty and power, hence advantage and dominance, until an external force, internal conflict or greater wisdom breaks the mould. Contemporary with Egyptian culture and the Chinese philosopher Confucius, the Olmec Empire flourished from around 1400 to 400 BCE in what is now Mexico, creating cities the size of ancient Rome, pyramids, palaces, ornate tombs, probably the first calendar, a written language and rubber-ball games.

Increasingly, time and energy became things we could use, exchange and barter with. The more things there are and the more of us there are, the more precarious our peaceful coexistence may be to build and maintain, and the more intelligent our routes to mutual understanding have to be.

The professor of psychology and neuroscience R. Brian Ferguson (2018)[21] traced the origin of wars to the same period: 'A close look at archaeological and other evidence suggests that collective killing resulted from cultural conditions that arose within the past 12,000 years... The preconditions that make war more likely include a shift to a more sedentary existence, a growing regional population, a concentration of valuable resources such as livestock, increasing social complexity and hierarchy, trade in high-value goods, and the establishment of group boundaries and collective identities'.

Feeling, Thinking and Acting

The political philosopher Hannah Arendt (1958) and (1964)[22] proposed that to know who we are we have to be 'people who are ourselves through our actions: not anonymous, not doing someone else's will'. She explored how speech is a form of action and makes political beings of us. She understood that we fulfil our potential as humans when we respect our interdependence: 'Humanity is never gained in solitude... To be human is to use reason and so be free: we begin something; we weave our thread in a network of relationships;

and what shall become of it we never know.' We continue to run up against what we can't predict, understand or control, and so we need all the information and insight we can access.

Our simplest feelings and thoughts favour yes/no questions and answers; things are on or off, hot or cold, half-full or half-empty. We are capable of much greater sophistication, but we never quite abandon simple oppositions. Robert Sapolsky (2018)[23] explained, 'It is impossible to conclude that a behaviour is caused by a gene, a hormone, a childhood trauma, because the second you invoke one type of explanation, you are *de facto* invoking them all'.

Our genes, hormones, infancy and ongoing shared and cultural experiences blend to give rise to what each of us and each of our groups feel, think and do. In society as in nature, rarely is there just one cause and just one effect. Rarely do we have just one problem which is amenable to a single or one-dimensional solution.

Chris Frith (2007)[24] observed that 'an ordinary, healthy brain does not always give a true picture of the world'. Nor can machines give us a true picture, because we programme them and our brain has to interpret what they present to us. Yet we tend to know more than we think we do. There are 'all sorts of things our brains know that never reach our conscious minds', including many things about our bodies.

What each of us and each of our groups end up doing comes from a mix of what we inherit, who we've become, how we live and what is happening amongst and around us. What we have in common includes that we are confrontational and cruel as well as kind and caring. Our biology and genes write a musical score for each of us and our group in a key that is our culture. Our lives depend on how we choose to interpret our score and on how other people, groups and leaders interpret their scores.

Michio Kaku (2021)[25] used a musical metaphor to explain life's fundamentals: 'the universe was not made of point particles but of tiny vibrating strings, with each note corresponding to a subatomic particle. If we had a microscope powerful enough, we could see that electrons, quarks, neutrinos, etc. are nothing but vibrations on the minuscule loops resembling rubber bands. If we pluck the rubber band enough times and in different ways, we eventually create all the known subatomic particles in the universe'.

Paying Attention

Excess carbon dioxide in the atmosphere dissolves in the oceans, changing the water's normal mild alkalinity. This, combined with increasing pollutants, new micro-organisms and reducing habitats, has inflicted accumulated stresses on a great many creatures, including bees. There was no single factor responsible for this. For quite some time, bee colonies coped by working harder and harder, but in recent years they have begun to fail.

Will what has happened to bees happen to us?

It could. Without pollinators like bees, crops and essential plants suffer, decline and disappear. The extinction of bees would be one more disaster for our world, in a long line of accidents and mistakes caused by our short-sightedness, carelessness and selfishness.

Are we going to be our own next victims?

Possibly, if we aren't more careful and resourceful.

Shankar Vedantam and Bill Mesler (2021)[26] wrote that 'psychological mechanisms involving self-deception and group-dynamics explain why so many of us reach for unfounded theories, and why so many of us are reluctant to discard them in the face of the facts'. Their book contains numerous examples of our seeing meaning in patterns that are not real: we are drawn to irrational explanations for things that exist only in our minds. Too easily we make rules, instructions and prohibitions out of what are better treated as no better than potentially illuminating but far from unchanging, universal patterns.

Rodents are chiefly moved by what they smell. Primates are chiefly moved by what they see. Smell and sight are involved in the human brain's limbic system and, as Sapolsky wrote, its function is central to 'emotions that fuel our best and worst behaviours'. Though we sometimes ignore or overrule our surprise or dismay, we've evolved to be able to notice and react when our brain picks up mismatches between what we intend or expect and what transpires. If we pay attention to what we didn't foresee, we're in a position to consider and test different ways of acting. We can choose to keep an eye on what we want to achieve, and so take care to plan and track what happens.

Unfortunately, what we learn can never be enough for us to know for sure what will happen next or over time. We can do no better or worse than to keep on learning as we look forwards and back. The greatest dangers we face—divisions in and between societies and the depleting and spoiling of our environment, for example—include the results of our being beguiled by false patterns, misleading reports and conspiracy theories. Most dangerous perhaps is when our leaders are prey to and purvey delusions and deceptions.

Sapolsky noted that there is a part of our brain responsible for controlling our impulsivity, postponing gratification, organising what we know, deciding priorities, making short-, medium- and long-term plans, starting and monitoring action—all of which feed and support our capacity to care about and for one another. We have some control over our behaviour and lives. Our brain can help us 'do the harder thing when it's the right thing to do', and so can give us all a better chance of living well together.

This fits with Capra's (2019) view that *mind* is not a thing but a cognitive *process*, and *brain* is the *structure* through which mind is achieved. The radical implication of this is that all living things—whether or not they have central nervous systems—are mindful insofar as they generate creative and responsive actions.

Balancing Body and Mind

Sapolsky explained that 'the brain is heavily influenced by genes. But from birth through young adulthood, the part of the brain that most defines you is less a product of the genes with which you started life than what life has thrown at you'—the frontal cortex. This is the last region of your brain to develop and the 'least constrained by genes and most sculpted by experience'. It helps you select priorities, goals and methods, including ways of monitoring progress and evaluating outcomes. You may improve how you set and pursue goals. Still, when you say you learn from mistakes, it doesn't mean that what you next predict or aim for will definitely come to pass.

The neuroscientist Antonio Damasio (2019)[27] wrote about how organisms tend towards homeostasis within and between the elements they're made of. Adjustments are made in the direction of, but falling short of, achieving permanent equilibrium, because total stasis brings entropy and death. Damasio's analysis was that, for humans, homeostasis finds mental expression in feelings: 'feelings tell the mind of the good or bad direction of the life process.' It is as if our bodies speak tacitly to us through our instincts, intuitions and insights which are 'catalysts for processes of questioning, understanding and problem solving'.

Homeostasis has a partner, allostasis, defined by the anatomist, physiologist and neuroscientist Peter Sterling and the epidemiologist Joseph Eyer (1988)[28] as servant systems that use change to keep essential processes stable. Allostasis is the action of a kind of thermostat. Whether we be awake, asleep, lying down, standing or exercising, this action registers and adjusts our physical state. It causes our blood pressure to rise and fall and other functions to adapt so that we might, for example, 'cope with noise, crowding, isolation, hunger, extremes of temperature, physical danger, psychosocial stress and microbial or parasitic infections'. Whether we're 'exposed to danger, an infection, a crowded and noisy neighbourhood, or having to give a speech in public, the body responds to the challenge by turning on an allostatic response, thus initiating a complex pathway for adaptation and coping, and then shutting off this response when the challenge has passed'.

If we experience high levels of stress hormones for prolonged periods, we tend to suffer 'allostatic load and overload, with resultant pathophysiological consequences'. Lisa Feldman Barrett (2018)[29] explained an aspect of this: we're designed to maintain a balanced 'body budget'. We experience as negative whatever puts too much stress on our physical and nervous systems. We're pained and drained when our body and mi can't rest and repair themselves. Our brain checks and predicts what our sensations mean, figuring out where to allocate attention and energy. When we notice and dwell on these sensations, we're making sense of what's happening to us.

Things may work well enough as long as our central nervous system is alive to present and potential conditions and challenges. Unfortunately, we all have a propensity in certain situations to choose selfish or short-term gratifications: we give ourselves a sugar rush, choose alcohol- or drug-induced distraction or oblivion, vent our feelings and take frustration out on other people.

Learning from Experience

Emotions aren't external or objective things. They are internal signals. They help you notice matches and mismatches between what you expect and what actually happens. These signals help you learn what distinguishes events that warrant excitement and events that warrant distress, events prompting boredom and events prompting anxiety, events registering inclination and events registering addiction.

Feelings and thoughts act as catalysts and vehicles for accurate, helpful choices, but also convey misperceptions, prejudices, biases, denials of evidence, illusions and delusions. For example, a person or situation in the present reminds you of past experience and brings past feelings to the surface—sometimes hurtfully, sometimes helpfully and sometimes both hurtfully and helpfully. In a psychoanalytic or therapeutic setting, this is called transference. Though we sometimes bring together helpful facts and ideas and then act with sounder than average prospects of success, echoes of previous discontents and fears also give rise to prejudice and grievance, thereby undermining our clarity and effectiveness. The same happens within groups.

In Barrett's analysis, anxiety, depression, heart disease, type 2 diabetes and Alzheimer's are metabolic illnesses that result from strained body budgets. Working too hard, not sleeping enough and eating poorly put us in chronic deficit. Our brain evolved for the purposes of regulating its immediate environment—our bodies. It determines how to invest its resources—automatically more often than consciously, sometimes erroneously or unhelpfully, but sometimes healthily. The same happens when our group's or community's resources are over-stretched.

No one is immune from seeing things awry. It takes effort and experience to review our feelings and responses, and test them against our reflective reasoning, against one another's impressions and perspectives and against external evidence. It takes effort and experience to avoid sterile and counterproductive mantras. It takes effort and experience to approach things from different angles, look at things in a new light, seek agreement, cooperate and organise.

Sapolsky noted that 'Many of our best moments of morality and compassion have roots far deeper and older than being the mere products of human civilisation'. We can see from archaeology, ancient artefacts, cave paintings and burial sites that humans felt pity and respect and appreciated beauty, long before there were civilisations. But when we found ways to make some of us richer and more powerful than others, some of us were corrupted and felt entitled, while others of us came to feel worthless or helpless or both. Feeling worthless or helpless can turn to resentment and grievance, and sometimes then to outcry and retaliation.

To survive the ill-effects of our actions, we have to realise that our flaws, as well as our talents and virtues, are in our ways of feeling and thinking. This challenges us to urgent and long-term work—as individuals, groups and societies and, if we can manage it, as a species.

The social psychologist Daniel Gilbert (2006)[30] noted that 'For most of recorded history, people lived where they were born, did what their parents had done and associated with those who were doing the same... But the agricultural, industrial and technological revolutions changed all that, and the resulting explosion of personal liberty has created a bewildering array of opinions, alternatives, choices and decisions that our ancestors never faced'.

The journalist, author and public speaker Malcolm Gladwell (2008)[31] wrote that it takes in the order of 10,000 hours to lay down traces in our central nervous system, brain and musculature to become proficient in competitive and advanced fields of activity. He drew on work by K. Anders Ericsson, Michael J. Prietula and Edward T. Cokely (2007) who studied data gathered by more than 100 scientists. They concluded that reaching elite levels of performance is associated with our exerting ourselves beyond our customary abilities and comfort levels. This applies to surgeons, chess players, artists, athletes and other experts who practise hard for many years, continually analysing their mistakes, adjusting their techniques, striving to improve and develop their 'inner coach'.

Looking Ahead

Our evolution has equipped us to learn lessons that turn out to be reliable, but doesn't stop us being mistaken or deceived in all sorts of ways about all manner of things. It isn't just that diverse and new information can make it difficult to discriminate between fact and non-fact; it is also that some people have an interest in issuing and passing on misinformation and disinformation.

The philosopher A. C. Grayling (2021)[32] wrote about how human knowledge expanded as a result of the scientific revolution of the 16th and 17th centuries. Now, few of us have either an overview or any kind of grasp of crucial areas of science and technology that have profound influences on our health and prospects. What is more, 'specialism, necessary for genuine advances in knowledge to be made, places us in silos'. Fragmentations and ultra-sophistications in our feeling and thinking continue to make it more and more difficult to take real account of 'social, political, legal, moral and humanitarian considerations'. We will have to learn better how to pool what we know between us and work together for everyone's benefit.

How we heat, cool and ventilate buildings, how we reduce our dependence on plastics and how we share the world's food and fuel resources are cases in point. It has become vital to find ways to keep in view how much is knowable but known only by distant specialists. We must help one another realise how the range and infinite number of shifting environmental, biological, social and psychological variables interact to produce the situations we find ourselves in. Compassion and acceptance of kindness grow out of identification with one another and our predicaments, and we identify with one another more readily through our imaginations than through our reasoning. Unfortunately, sometimes, some of us have no mind to share.

It is rational and pragmatic to welcome diverse and divergent contributions and then work together. We are well advised to think of our knowledge as 'our best and most rigorously supported belief'. As Grayling put it: 'if we are all paddling in the boat of enquiry together in an ocean of ignorance, our perspective changes—for the better'.

Preparing

We come to feel at one with others and shape our lives to our mutual benefit when we:

Appreciate our differences
Build on what we have in common
Explore how to make the most of our joint capacities and opportunities.

These are ways of coming to workable agreements about what to do. It takes serious, individual and collective effort: feeling, imagining, experimenting, observing and reasoning.

When in 2019 I asked the educationalist Fiona Carnie to comment on some of my writing, she replied that 'What you have written resonates closely with an international learning summit I attended last month. It started from a question about how we can put the holistic well-being of people and our planet at the heart of education. The organisers' aim is to come up with some kind of plan that can be used in different countries, with different systems. We split down into 10 groups to explore the question from different perspectives and to agree next steps. 100 people were there from right across the globe and the idea now is that people go back and develop the work further in their own countries and settings.

'The whole thing is very ambitious and is funded by an entrepreneur who is committed to finding ways to increase holistic well-being. Whilst there is a lot of fine-tuning to do, I think the process is similar to what you are envisaging in terms of a community-led approach to addressing the challenges we face. It is becoming clearer and clearer that top-down models on their own often fall short because of the failure to engage folk. It is fascinating how, through the current crisis (in relation to Covid-19), people are finding the importance of building community connections.'

That is one example and a microcosm of how we can approach the threats and risks we face. We must look beyond the immediate and selfish; we must set aside entrenched animosities and intransigent ideologies.

The theoretical physicist Albert Einstein, working with Leopold Infeld, (1938)[33] wrote that a new concept 'allows us to regain our old concepts from a higher level. ... [C]reating a new theory is not like destroying an old barn and erecting a skyscraper in its place. It is rather like climbing a mountain, gathering new and wider views, discovering unexpected connections between our starting point and its rich environment. ... [T]he point from which we started out still exists and can be seen, although it appears smaller and forms a tiny part of our broad view gained by the mastery of the obstacles on our adventurous way up'.

New Possibilities

There is now an exponential acceleration in changes affecting our lives. We are, for example, evolving genetics and artificial intelligence (AI) to a point where 'our biology is yet another form of information technology'. That's the prediction made by the technology futurist and geopolitical expert Jamie Metzl (2019)[34]. Our genetic code is 'increasingly understandable, readable, writable, and hackable': 'in very short order, most of us will have our genomes sequenced as part of our electronic health records our doctors and their artificial intelligence algorithms will use when deciding how best to treat us'. We're moving 'very quickly from a paradigm of precision medicine to one of increasingly predictive medicine, health, and life that will transform the ways we think about human potential, parenting, and fate'. Choices about our lives are taking on new dimensions and introducing previously impossible consequences.

Karl Deisseroth (2021)[35] and his co-workers have forged connections between psychiatry and new technologies, particularly in optogenetics, using light to turn specific brain cells on and off. Applications are being researched relating to depression, psychosis, schizophrenia, autism, narcolepsy, Parkinson's disease, anxiety, addiction and sociopathy. And treatments are being applied, sometimes managing symptoms, sometimes achieving cures for a range of conditions and psychological and behavioural disorders. Extraordinary developments are in prospect and underway.

New methods have shown that it's possible in an instant to control violence in mice. This prompts moral and policy questions about their application in humans. As psychiatry and the capacity to control behaviour via the brain's circuitry develop, 'we might be wise to begin awkward conversations for which we feel unready'.

As Deisseroth explained, not everything we do is because we want or choose to do it: our brain spontaneously produces sensations and impressions, not so much because it's helping us do something we're concerned with, but because a few of its cells come together to produce signals, sometimes unbidden. Signals produce sensations. Sensations produce internal representations and actual behaviours. Via micro-bioengineering 'something resembling a specific sensation' can be induced. In other words, we can be made to feel something is happening and so act on it, whether or not we feel we're making choices. It's possible in experiments, with as few as two to 20 cells, to make an animal see things that aren't there.

When our sensations are 'delivered' by medical interventions, are they any less our own?

Are we ready for this?

How can we be partners with machines and retain oversight and control?

Summing Up

Symbiosis is 'a ubiquitous feature of life'—a kind of interdependence whereby one organism provides or becomes what another organism needs but can't make or do for itself.

There are many reasons why we see meaning in patterns that aren't really there, absorb theories that have no basis in fact and are misled by artificial rules.

We humans learned to control an urge to dominate, not always or fully, but enough sometimes to check and moderate aggression and fantasies of megalomania.

Our emotions are a sign of our efforts to understand what we experience and help us decide what to do.

---

[1] See Peter Godfrey-Smith's (2017) *Other Minds: The Octopus and the Evolution of Intelligent Life*, published in London, UK, by William Collins.

[2] See Merlin Sheldrake's (2020) *Entangled Life: How Fungi Make Our Worlds, Change Our Minds, and Shape Our Futures*, pp 18 and 117, published in London, UK, by Bodley Head/Penguin Random House.

[3] Charles Darwin (1859) popularised the term 'natural selection' in *On the Origin of Species*, published in London, UK, by John Murray.

[4] See Fritjof Capra's and Pier Luigi Luisi's (2014, 2016) *A Systems View of Life: A Unifying Vision*, published in New York, NY, by Cambridge University Press.

[5] See Fritjof Capra's talk (2019) *Mind, Matter, and Life*, courtesy of Science and Nonduality: https://youtube/ TFERd65UCh8; and *The Systems View of Life* at capracourse.net. Capra and Luisi belong to an organisation whose mission is to foster a new generation of world leaders in this critical period of worldwide political, moral and environmental instability: see more at http://www. cortonafriends.org/.

[6] See Ivan Illich's (1973) *Tools for Conviviality*, published in London, UK, by Marion Boyars, pp 29-32.

[7] See Neil MacGregor's (2010) *The History of the World in 100 Objects*, published in London, UK, by Allen Lane/Penguin Books, pp 25 and 30.

[8] This is a cornerstone of Robin Dunbar's (2016) *Human Evolution: Our Brains and Behaviour*, published in New York, NY, by Oxford University Press, pp 22, 24, 56, 84 and 276.

[9] See Brian Boyd's (2009, 2010) *On the Origin of Stories: Evolution, Cognition, and Fiction*, published in London, UK, by Harvard University Press, pp 23, 26 and 28. He appreciated the contribution made by the biologist Richard Dawkins' (1976, 2016) *The Selfish Gene*, published in Oxford, UK, by Oxford University Press.

[10] See Rutger Bregman (2019), pp 2 and 5.

[11] See Iain McGilchrist's (2019) *Ways of Attending: How Our Divided Brain Constructs the World*, published in London, UK, by Routledge, p 10ff.

[12] See Leon Festinger's (1956) *When Prophecies Fail*, published in Minneapolis, MN, by the University of Minnesota Press; also his (1957) *A Theory of Cognitive Dissonance*, published in Redwood City, CA, by Stanford University Press.

[13] See Peter Godfrey-Smith (2017).

[14] See Oliver Sacks' (2017) *The River of Consciousness*, published in New York, NY, by Alfred A. Knopf and in London, UK, by Picador, pp 179 and 182-183; and his many studies relating to questions of identity and diverse neurological conditions, e.g. (1985) *The Man Who Mistook his Wife for a Hat and Other Clinical Tales*, published in London, UK, by Gerald Duckworth, and (2007) *Musicophilia: Tales of Music and the Brain* published in New York, NY, by Alfred A. Knopf. Also his (2015) autobiography *On the Move: A Life*, published in New York, NY, by Alfred A. Knopf.

[15] See Yuval Noah Harari's (2011) *Sapiens: A Brief History of Humankind*, published in London, UK, by Random House Penguin, pp x and 27.

[16] See Toby Ord's (2020) *The Precipice: Existential Risk and the Future of Humanity*, published in New York, NY, by Hachette Books, pp 3-4 and 240.

[17] See Kevin Laland's (2018) 'How we became a different kind of animal: An evolved uniqueness', pp 29-31. Also his (2017) *Darwin's Unfinished Symphony: How Culture Made the Human Mind*. This relates to Michael Tomasello's work referred to in the 'Becoming Inclusive' section of chapter 3.

[18] See Josh Turknett's (2013) *The Migraine Miracle: A Sugar-Free, Ancestral Diet to Reduce Inflammation and Relieve Your Headaches for Good*, published in Oakland, CA, by New Harbinger Publications, pp 68, 71-73, 76 and 99.

[19] See Jared Diamond's (1997) Pulitzer Prize winning *Guns, Germs and Steel: A Short History of Everybody for the Last 13,000 Years*, published in New York, NY, by W. W. Norton, p 11.

[20] See Neil MacGregor (2010), p 183.

[21] See Brian Ferguson's (2018) 'War may not be in our nature after all: Why we fight', published in *Scientific American*, 319, 3, pp 71-73.

[22] See Hannah Arendt (1958) *The Human Condition*, published in Chicago, Il, by the University of Chicago Press, pp 3, 52-53, 55, 58, 180 and 203; and hear the interview (1964) between Arendt and journalist Günter Gaus; go to https:// aeon.co/videos/whats-essential-is-i-must-understand-a-rare-candid-interview-with-hannah-arendt.

[23] See Robert Sapolsky (2018), pp 5-6, 8, 25 and 45. He wrote about the cultural, moral complexity of violence that 'we don't hate violence. We hate and fear the wrong kind of violence, violence in the wrong context… When it's the "right" kind of violence, we love it', p 3. For detail about the frontal cortex, see p 173. For the effects of our mating patterns and for emotional capacities we had before civilisations developed, see pp 673-674.

[24] See Chris Frith (2007), pp 60, 105, 126-127, 134, 136, 138, 145-146 and 152-155.

[25] See Michio Kaku (2021), p 3.

[26] See Shankar Vedantam and Bill Mesler (2021), pp 65-66, 197-202.

[27] See Antonio Damasio's (2019) *The Strange Order of Things: Life, Feeling, and the Making of Cultures*, published in London, UK, by Penguin Random House, p 25; also pp 5-7, 12-13, 45 and 113.

[28] See Peter Sterling's and Joseph Eyer's (1988) *Allostasis: A new paradigm to explain arousal pathology*, published in Hoboken, NJ, by John Wiley & Sons.

[29] See Lisa Barrett (2018), p 82ff.

[30] See Daniel Gilbert's (2006) *Stumbling on happiness*, published in London, UK, by Harper Press, pp 235 and 238.

[31] See the journalist, author and public speaker Malcolm Gladwell's (2008) *Outliers: The Story of Success*, published in New York, NY, by Little, Brown and Company.

[32] See A. C. Grayling's (2021) *The Frontiers of Knowledge: What We Now Know about Science, History and the Mind*, published in London, UK, by Viking/Penguin Random House, pp 336-338.

[33] See the physicists Albert Einstein's and Leopold Infeld's (1938) *The Evolution of Physics*, published in Cambridge, UK, by Cambridge University Press, pp 211-212, quoted by Oliver Sacks (2017).

[34] See Jamie Metzl's (2019) *Hacking Darwin: Genetic Engineering and the Future of Humanity*, published in Naperville, IL, by Sourcebooks Inc., p xx-xxi.

[35] See Karl Deisseroth (2021), pp 207-212 and 216-219.

3 Us and Them

People we hear from in this chapter include Henri Tajfel and John Turner; Hannah Arendt; Patricia Churchland; Carl Rogers; and Maximilien Ringelmann.

How do we become united and inclusive?

Our Biology

We're not usually aware that proteins and hormones shape how we feel and behave. Nor do we generally realise that how we feel and act reflects how our tribe or community feels and acts. We identify with people we see are like us. Robert Sapolsky (2018)[1] reported research on an aspect of this.

When a face is flashed on a screen for less than a tenth of a second, we're unlikely to know we've seen it, but we've a better than average chance of correctly guessing the race of the person whose face we glimpse: 'Our brains are incredibly attuned to skin colour'. We may say we judge someone by the content of their character rather than by the colour of their skin, but 'our brains sure as hell note the colour, real fast.'

When we're shown a video of someone's hand being poked with a needle, in most cases our hands tense in sympathy. Whatever shade of Black, Brown, Red, Yellow or White we are, we identify more quickly with another individual's pain if she or he is of the same race as us. When we're shown a picture of a face and in the same moment receive a small electric shock, our amygdala links the face with the alarm we feel, and fear-conditioning happens more quickly for other-race faces than for same-race faces. More than that, we judge other-race faces that show no marked emotion to be angrier than same-race faces that look expressionless. We are alike in that we register who is like 'us' and who is not.

Whoever we are, our brains are 'prepared to associate something bad with Them'.

Because difference can signal danger, our amygdala's rapid responding must have brought us evolutionary advantages. Alarm registers a need to act—probably urgently. It isn't fool-proof and 'we are less rational and autonomous decision-makers than we like to think'. The information our radar picks up can't always be complete or reliable, but it is quick and that may be the difference between life and death. Wariness is potentially useful, but sometimes out of proportion or mistaken. Our responses can be counter-productive and become entrenched, especially when we have contact only or predominantly with like-minded people.

Channelling Energy

Some people—in sport, for example—channel their aggression and even fear, in order to achieve outstanding things. The competitive swimmer Adam Peaty (2021)[2] has spoken about how in the pool he generates a kind of focused fury—to be better than he was yesterday. The same seems to apply to entrepreneurs, explorers, inventors, scientists, artists, entertainers and any one of us.

Women and men produce testosterone in their adrenal glands and gonads. But having high or low testosterone levels doesn't make us more or less prone to aggressive behaviour. Testosterone levels rise when we feel our self-esteem is challenged. As Sapolsky put it, 'testosterone amplifies and exacerbates tendencies we already have… it prompts whatever behaviours are needed to maintain status'. It seems that it's our biochemical sensitivity more than our personality that makes us prone to aggression. And our readiness to attack or defend changes according to our ongoing experience. The more often we're aggressive, the less testosterone it takes to become riled again—whatever our ethnicity, social position or wealth.

Sapolsky observed about us all that 'We implicitly divide the world into Us and Them, and prefer the former'. Differences between can be inconsequential, or they may prompt offensive attitudes and behaviours. We trust our group, and that easily comes to mean we mistrust certain others or even all others. The appeal and pay-off are that we gain simplicity and certainty, however misguidedly, along with expectations or promises of protection, identity and entitlement.

Our identification with individuals and groups extends beyond race, skin colour and physical features. We align ourselves with and distinguish ourselves from others according to language, dialect and accent; hairstyle, skin-markings, piercings, ornamentation and clothing; apparent abilities; choice of weapons; preference for certain brands; education; occupation; class; caste; sexual orientation; gender; neighbourhood; nationality; taste in food and music; religious and other kinds of beliefs; affiliation with sporting teams…

What have been your experiences of how people identify *with* or *against* others?

The art critic Laura Cumming (2016)[3] gave an example of the artist Diego Velázquez (baptised in 1599, died in 1660): 'if the art of Velázquez teaches us anything at all it is the depth and complexity of our fellow human beings. Respect for the servants and the dwarves, the jesters and the bodyguards, the old woman frying eggs and the young boy with his melon, for the princess and the palace weavers, for the seller of water and the seller of books; that is what his art transmits. To respect these portraits is to respect these people. … All men are born equal to him. … What Velázquez emphasises is the dignity of all people'.

Social equality may be a natural impulse or an attitude we learn. For some of us, like Velázquez, it seems to be an aesthetic concept before or in the same moment as it becomes ethical or philosophical and then a guide to how we behave.

Making Others 'Other'

Do you believe that someone who isn't like you probably doesn't understand you?

Much of the time, many of us identify with some people, and not with others; we make 'in-groups' and 'out-groups'. The experimental social psychologist Henri Tajfel (1970)[4] explored why it's common to feel some other people are different from *and* worse than us. He asked, 'Can discrimination be traced to an origin such as social conflict or a history of hostility?' The answer was 'Not necessarily': 'Apparently, the mere fact of division into groups is enough to trigger discriminatory behaviour.'

With his colleague John Turner, Tajfel (1979) developed a theory that just being divided into groups triggers negative prejudice. His experiments showed that we take our identity from groups we feel we belong to or decide we had better belong to. Group identity makes us feel good about ourselves, which easily leads us to feel our group matters more than others.

When we're asked about why we behave as we do and why other people behave as they do, most of us say that how we behave is prompted by things outside ourselves including things beyond our control, but that other people behave according to their character and choices. In other words, we feel we respond to objective factors while other people are guided by subjective factors. Psychologists called this a 'fundamental attribution error'. The professor of cognitive, linguistic, and psychological sciences Bertram Malle (2004)[5] explained that how we frame our own and other people's motivations and intentions colours our attitudes and initiatives and so helps determine how we lead our lives.

Feeling we have to be against others seems to have had an evolutionary function, protecting and strengthening us. It seems often to be associated with fearing we'll lose what we have, and so we compensate by looking down on or dominating others. As far as we can tell, this tendency runs through all human history. Consequences range from apparently inconsequential, potentially offensive, stereotyping 'jokes' and labelling of groups or types, to forced segregation and outright violence.

How we're treated informs how we treat others—up to the point when we realise it's time to rethink how we treat people. Personal interactions in the home, in the wider community, amongst friends and peers, at school and at work make a culture which moulds us, but can also prompt us to find different, more reliable and enriching ways of feeling, thinking and behaving. It seems that, whether we are wealthy, privileged, powerful, poor, disadvantaged or disenfranchised, we tend to discriminate against those who are different from us, unless or until we learn and choose to feel, think and act differently.

Drawing Together

We learn to communicate and cooperate when we accept we can't do it all on our own. A first step is to understand that we are no better than anyone else and that in the long-term we don't gain by discriminating against or dominating other people.

When we share our difficulties and disappointments, celebrate our progress and help one another plan next steps and new ventures, we begin to make a positive difference. It is humbling to recognise that our lives are intertwined; and humility helps us be courageous enough to pursue our mutual interests. And when things go well, our interactions give stimulation and support in processes—sometimes called proximal processes[6]—that enable us to think and act beyond what we've so far been capable of.

An example of this was Donald Winnicott's (1971)[7] developing a practice of literally 'taking the child's side'. He would leave a piece of paper with a quickly drawn squiggle on it, together with pencils and more sheets of paper, on a low table in his consultation room. As a child came in, she or he had something to pick up and do—continuing the drawing or making her or his own. Winnicott developed diagnostic and therapeutic techniques like this, based on his view that play, discovery and creative communication occur in a shared 'area of experiencing'—a space between us—where contributions from each of us can be exchanged, overlap and merge.

Winnicott wrote that 'What happens in the game and in the whole interview depends on the use made of the child's experience, including the [psychological] material that presents itself… It is almost as if the child, through the drawings, is alongside me, and to some extent taking part in describing the case'. Child and therapist talk to one another about what has happened, what is happening and what might happen. Their joint experience helps them share and develop understandings which ring true or look useful.

As a teacher, I came to feel that things went well when it seemed that my students were one point of a triangle and I was another, the third point being what we shared an interest in and focused on. This is a different dynamic from one which would have me possessing knowledge or skill to hand over or impose.

We are helped to grow—physically, emotionally and intellectually—when we're guided and supported by those who want us to thrive: we grow with the help of someone by our side. Whatever our backgrounds and circumstances, we are shown how to grow by people and experiences that nurture our confidence, resilience and perseverance. Neither money nor social status guarantees these advantages[8].

Regardless of whether we come from a family in a high or low socio-economic group, those of us who have little protection against the risks we face tend to be relatively unsuccessful at school and vulnerable at home and in the community. Neither money nor social status guarantees well-being or satisfying progress. Those of us who have socio-economic advantages can be as neglected or harmed as any who are materially less well-off. And those of us, whom socio-economic measures might classify as disadvantaged, can be as valued and supported as any who have material advantages.

Numbers Make a Difference

Robin Dunbar (1992)[9] showed that, much of the time, most of us have social connections with around 5 to 150 people. Depending in part on how well our long-term memory works, it seems we can keep up stable relationships with no more than between 100 and 250 people. Introverts might have 100 and extroverts 250 people in their largest circle. Our brain's neocortex can't be relied on to deal with more than those numbers if we are to keep up meaningful relationships. These are 'Dunbar's numbers'.

Human groups larger than between 100 and 250 depend on transparent protocols and explicit standards if they're to have rational integrity and be at all coherent. Above 250, we move beyond the interpersonal into public and/or virtual realms. And, in our industrialised, urban, suburban, global lives, many of us have an ever-expanding range of technologically assisted contacts with exponentially many more people than those we feel we know.

Around 150 members of the International Association of Trichologists, for example, attend their annual conference. Their concern is to study and treat people's hair and scalp. Over the course of two days, they share practice and promote collegiality, research and development. The gathering invigorates and evolves the group's identity, enabling its influence to spread to professionals and patients beyond the conference and beyond the association. Similarly, the Swedish tax authority may have been aware of the part group-size plays when it decided in 2007 to limit each of its offices to 150 staff members.

Mutual understanding and cooperation grow out of our seeing ourselves and others as belonging to a circle that is wider than the few people we are closest to. We help ourselves by recognising the signals and triggers of anxiety and antagonism, by developing strategies to calm ourselves and by considering facts relating to our essential and shared interests. Counteracting instincts and cultural traits is a serious challenge. Rushing to judgement and following the tide of prejudiced opinion stop us checking evidence. Seeing differences between us and others is no reason to deprive anyone of a welcome, rights or privileges.

We can choose to see that our humanity transcends our individual and group differences. The challenge is for as many of us as possible to find, express and fulfil our true and better selves by pursuing what is good for us all.

Resisting 'Othering'

In the early 1990s, I revisited the school in Frankfurt am Main, Germany, where more than 20 years before I had spent a year as an assistant teacher. The new head teacher kindly gave me an hour of his time. He told me that the school had evolved since I'd been there. Boys now attended as well as girls. A significant proportion of the students' homeland was Yugoslavia, and some went there regularly for long weekends and holidays to join their fathers, brothers and uncles fighting a civil war. The school's main purpose had become learning and teaching about conflict-resolution.

Developing understanding of our differences is essential to supporting and sustaining lives as complex as ours. It lays a foundation for peace-making and reconciliation. These tasks fall to wise and generous people who choose vocations and occupations in international cooperation, government and education and in many spheres of scientific, clinical, therapeutic, charity and security work. But success depends on a significant majority of us learning to value our humanity and help construct a just society.

Our best guide to being fair is that we should treat other people as we'd like them to treat us. When we want for others what we want for ourselves, we begin to tackle dehumanising discrimination. When we stop seeing others as human, we open the way to abuse and hatred. We see differences between us more readily than we see similarities. But discriminating doesn't have to mean oppressing or destroying others; it can help us decide where friendships may be forged and help be given. From the 1970s onwards in the UK for example,

Economic Priority Areas and Education Action Zones have received exceptional resources to compensate for disadvantage—a case of positive discrimination.

'Othering'[10] means denying a person's or group's humanity. We use it to justify our baser instincts and meaner impulses. It prompts 'them' to do the same to us, and so perpetuates cycles of animosity, fear and brutality. It discriminates and disenfranchises by denigrating or condemning others' race, ethnicity, religion, gender, sexuality, caste, class or any other distinctive characteristic. It condones victimisation, accepts segregation and apartheid, feeds xenophobia and stokes genocide.

If we don't promote our shared humanity and act against othering, we prevent our respective identities and diversity from playing their part in enriching all our lives. If we're determined and work together, we can stop automatically mistrusting all or certain others. We can extend our allegiances beyond group, tribal and societal distinctions and boundaries.

There are many examples of how different faiths, traditions and languages, have lived peaceably and creatively alongside one another. Between the eighth and fifteenth centuries Muslim, Christian and Jewish peoples lived in productive, rewarding *convivencia*. Neil MacGregor (2010)[11] saw enriching multiculturalism as being embodied by a Hebrew brass astrolabe, probably made in what is now Spain around the mid-fourteenth century, now displayed in the British Museum.

Getting Over Our Differences

It took over 200,000 years of human history for this planet's human population to reach 1 billion. It took only 200 years more to reach 7 billion. Today, our interactions are more numerous and complex than they've ever been. Often we can't see who we're communicating with or being influenced by; often we can't verify their character, status or intent. This is exploited by telephone, email and Internet scammers and propagandists.

Adam Phillips (2013)[12] wrote that we do well to 'protect our pleasure in each other's company'. Other people are vital to our health, economy and development: they 'are only a problem for us if we have to give up on too much of ourselves in order to be with them', or if we're coerced or deceived into submitting to their manipulation or what they dictate. The strength of our relationships seems to correlate with two things: first, our aspirations and intentions for ourselves and others; second, the mutual satisfaction and reciprocal advantage we derive from our interactions.

Do you think we are now more susceptible to tribal divisions and manipulation than we've ever been?

When I understand what is on your mind, sooner or later I realise how we differ. When you understand what is on my mind, you may realise how we differ. To understand one another is to have some insight into and empathise to some extent with one another's situations, experiences and intentions.

Appreciating each other's situations, experiences and intentions is sometimes called having a 'theory of mind' or 'mentalising'. Dunbar (2016)[13] explained that there's a 'recursive hierarchy of mental states known as the orders of intentionality'. The first order is what each of us knows or assumes about 'what I feel, think, believe and intend'. The second order is what each of us knows or assumes other people feel, think, believe and intend. The third order refers to knowing what we know or assume other people know about what yet further others feel, think, believe and intend. Fourth, fifth and so on orders refer to what others feel, think, believe and intend, at greater and greater removes. The more distant and disconnected we are from one another, the more challenging it is to construct, organise and retain our perceptions of one another's wants, wishes and ideas.

This book is about how those who lead and those who are led might grow to appreciate differing interests, purposes and choices, then arbitrate and resolve disagreements and prepare joint enterprises.

Becoming Inclusive

The professor of psychology and neuroscience Michael Tomasello (2018)[14] showed that joint and collective intentionality evolved alongside individual intentionality. About 400,000 years ago, our direct human ancestor—*Homo heidelbergensis*—began looking for better food sources: 'Individuals chosen for the hunt were selected because they understood implicitly the need to cooperate and not hog the resulting spoils. A "second-person morality" emerged in which it was understood that a "me" had to be subordinated to a "we"'.

About 150,000 years ago, as the size of human groups grew, the smaller bands that made up each tribe developed their own cultures: 'norms, conventions and institutions grew up to define the group's goals and establish divisions of labour that set roles for each of its members—a collective intentionality that distinguished a tribe'. Each tribe member internalised regulation as an 'objective morality' and 'everyone knew immediately the difference between right and wrong'.

Drawing on neuroscientists' discoveries from the 1990s onward, the analytic philosopher Patricia Churchland (2020)[15] surveyed current understanding of this. She explained that our behaviour has costs and benefits in terms of energy, effort, reward and penalty. When we behave selfishly, there's usually a cost to other people: they give something up. When we behave altruistically, there's usually a cost to us: we give something up. Then we sense that if we don't help one another, we'll be the poorer. Altruism benefits everyone and tends to make us happier as well as healthier. This is a credo in some people's ethics and politics, but seems to be anathema to others.

Tomasello's view was that 'The challenge of the contemporary world stems from an understanding that humans' biological adaptations for cooperation and morality are geared mainly towards small group life or cultural groups that are internally homogeneous—out-groups not being part of the moral community. Since the rise of agriculture, human societies have consisted of individuals from diverse, ethnic and religious lines. As a consequence, it becomes less clear who constitutes a "we" and who is in the out-group'. Sometimes we can't help trying to resolve ambiguity and ambivalence by making false or unhelpful assumptions, distinctions and agglomerations. Our challenge is to learn to do otherwise.

Compromising

In the industrialised West at least, more often than not, many of us seem to frame our experience in personal rather than collective or public terms. Yet, we do value social events and gatherings. Think of how we are drawn to congregating, in arenas, stadia, cinemas, theatres, concert halls, leisure centres, places of celebration and worship, museums, galleries, archaeological and historical attractions and sites of natural beauty and scientific interest… When getting together is restricted, as in the time of pandemic restrictions, we suffer a sense of loss and are disorientated.

Critical mass is necessary for shared and benevolent intentions to produce complex, beneficial, social change. Enough of us have to see the point and be engaged if we're to enjoy what is good for us all. One familiar and potentially useful strategy is for representatives of groups, communities, regions and jurisdictions to meet and work together on everyone's behalf. Sadly, sometimes long-standing antipathies and grievances mean such efforts never get out of the starting blocks. Sometimes such efforts are blocked by vested interests, or get bogged down in arcane arguing or are hamstrung by red tape. Sometimes they succeed.

We need to understand more about what makes the difference. Following the killing of the truck driver and bouncer George Floyd in May 2020, the Chief of Petersburg Police in Minneapolis, USA, threw down his helmet and baton and stood with protesters who were angry about their unequal justice system.

Spirituality, socio-cultural sensibility and politics can be compatible and complementary, but compromise is likely to be necessary whatever path we choose.

Has compromising ever been a bad experience for you?

How have you benefited by compromising?

Phillips (2013)[16] wrote that 'There is a real sense in which education begins as education in compromise. Children have to learn to wait, to share and to bear frustration, which means they have to learn to compromise'. To compromise is to take on board that we need one another: 'Every child has to find a way of being sociable without betraying themselves'.

Without compromise, agreements can be shallow or hollow and consensus can be misleading and short-lived. This is critical when we consider what we must do to understand and act on what is good for us all. Compromise, like respect and trust, is a mark of equality. When we feel we are equal and part of a whole, we understand we belong, we participate in, contribute to and care about everyone's well-being. When our leaders are committed to discriminatory, unilateral decision-making and dominance, our chances of achieving those things are slim.

When we are conscious of depending on one another, we appreciate being well led—for everyone's sake rather than to privilege a few or dominate others. We lose faith in social order when we're more dissatisfied with the quality of our lives than other identifiable groups are with theirs. And some of us are dissatisfied on behalf of others whose lives we feel are unjustly neglected or made worse by society. Poverty is more than not being able to meet essential needs and/or having them met. We can be materially rich but otherwise unhappy; we can be materially poor but happy, though the feeling can wear off.

The Importance of Equality

Research has shown that being unequal and powerless undermines and hurts us. Being equal and empowered helps us grow and be well. The economists Johan Graafland and Bjorn Lous (2019)[17] found that 'life satisfaction inequality may be an essential factor in the relationship between income inequality and trust'. Their analysis of data from 25 OECD countries in the period 1990–2014 was that 'If life satisfaction inequality is high, distrust is generated among the least happy. This will increase polarisation and the risk of rebellion, thereby also affecting trust among the happier people'. Their results implied that 'policy options for increasing trust are not limited to countering income inequality, but can also include policy measures that directly reduce inequality of life satisfaction'. Being too powerful, like being too confident or too trusting or too respectful, is not good for anyone.

A benefit of equality is that we don't have to rely on ourselves alone. Inequality pushes us toward depending unilaterally on others for our essential needs, consolation or empowerment. In their *Letter to a Teacher*, the children of the School of Barbiana in Tuscany, Italy, (1973) gave an analogy of the tanner who isn't allowed to reject any of the animal hides he or she is given to work on. These students must have watched and listened to their parents, and realised that a teacher should not reject, hold back or sell short any in her or his care. More recently in some countries this became the slogan 'No one left behind.'

The Royal Society in the UK has the motto: *Nullius in verba* (take nobody's word for anything)—a shortening of one of the poet Horace's[18] sayings, which expresses determination both to stand against the domination of authority and verify statements by referring to facts validated by experiment. The ability to take nobody's word for anything comes from seeing you are everyone's equal. To be equal, we must be sceptical and ask questions; to be sceptical and ask questions, we must be equal.

Understanding and Being Understood

To communicate well you have to appreciate who you're talking to; you have to want to say what you mean; and you have to adjust what you say according to how it's being received. The more accurately you express what you mean, the more likely it is you'll be understood and the more fulfilling your interactions and relationships are likely to be. The more equal you feel you are to people around you, the more open and straightforward you can be.

What you say and do, what you mean and how you are understood are three different things. The philosopher J. L. Austin (1955)[19] distinguished between these dimensions in verbal communication. There's the intention you have, which is what you wish to achieve by speaking—'illocution'. There's the surface literal meaning of what you express—'locution'. And there's the meaning your listeners take from what you say—'perlocution'. Illocution, locution and perlocution can be perfectly aligned, but they may overlap, diverge and/or contradict one another.

The psychologist Carl Rogers (1961)[20] offered the following way of checking. You make a statement.; I have to tell you what I understand you to be saying, and you have to be satisfied with my version of what you've said before I can go on to what I want to say. And so on, to and fro, moving our mutual understanding forwards through attentive dialogue and feedback.

What are the benefits of checking understanding?

If there are downsides of checking understanding, what are they?

This gets us close to the heart of trust (discussed in chapter 8 and crucial in chapter 13's 'Meeting, Focusing' section). It became an attitude and a way of behaving in my work as a teacher and consultant. It sometimes affects how I engage in everyday conversation. I become boring or baffling or both because it isn't common practice to keep checking what we mean.

Working alongside other teachers, I helped develop ways of finding out what students felt and thought about how they were taught[21]. As a consultant I found ways to agree with teachers, school leaders and governors what they wanted to aim for. If the people I was working with weren't going to make and circulate their notes, I'd send my notes promptly after an event or phase of activity for them to approve or amend. As soon as the record was thought to represent what had been said and approved, we could all use it however we chose.

Uniting

In Rogers' view, communication is like a good life: 'a process, not a state of being ... a direction not a destination'. Whether or not we like it, our lives intersect and our interests merge and diverge. We have to learn how to negotiate and arbitrate our differences.

We achieve a good measure of social integrity and contentment when we're with people in conditions that allow each of us to feel we can be true to ourselves, meet our needs and pursue our goals. This is quite different from signalling or sending messages: transmission is incomplete communication. It is through trusting our communications that we keep learning to help one another and be helped.

The better we appreciate how we depend on one another, the more likely we are—as individuals and as groups—to regard and treat one another with respect, communicate openly and want to cooperate. In good faith, we can make efforts to be clear about what we mean, check what our listeners understand we're saying and address mismatches between the two. And we can check we understand what others say, then address mismatches between what they mean and what we hear. All of this takes honesty, good will, time and effort.

We can afford to be open when we have reason to believe that we and those we're dealing with will act in good faith. It's unlikely to be in our interest to trust those we see are acting in bad faith. If some show no sign of aligning themselves to others' sincere and plausible causes, we'd be foolish to accommodate them without question or in the vague hope they'll change their mind and behaviour. If and when they show signs of wanting genuine cooperation, it's pragmatic for us to try working together.

We have to acknowledge that, because none of us knows everything, we must help one another find answers to our questions. We do this by being open about what we mean and what we want. When we're discussing and deciding things that have profound and far-reaching consequences, we do well to pay careful attention to our respective intentions, commitments and expectations. In personal, social and collective relationships, we take confidence from knowing what each of us values and seeks. We're much the poorer without that confidence.

Teamwork

Our chances of achieving our goals increase when other people confirm we're managing to say what we mean and are pleased to know we understand what they mean. If we underestimate the challenges, we're unprepared for the effort that's required and the ups and downs of shared endeavour. Successful communication and cooperation are no mean achievements. They are a necessary foundation for survival, satisfying relationships and well-being.

What have been your experiences of team efforts—successful and otherwise?

What factors do you think made those experiences what they turned out to be?

The agricultural engineer Maximilien Ringelmann (born 1861, died 1931) gave his name to an effect he discovered in how teams and groups of colleagues and co-workers behave: as our number grows, we tend to become less efficient and less effective as our number grows. This goes against an assumption that by working as a bigger team we are likely to be more successful. And it may be why less richly resourced military forces, for example, may prevail over an ostensibly more powerful aggressor.

According to Ringelmann (1913)[22], groups fail to reach their full potential for two main reasons: they have to work hard both to stay motivated and coordinate their efforts. As group size grows, individuals tend to struggle to see what they're contributing and struggle to feel motivated.

Research up to the present day has replicated and confirmed Ringelmann's findings:

> When each of us feels our task is both worthwhile and challenging, it is much more likely we'll all play our full part to the best of our abilities
>
> We tend to work as hard as we can when each of us feels we bring something specific to the collective effort, and when each of us knows our individual efforts are noticed
>
> When everyone knows what we're aiming for and understands how well we're doing, we strengthen our commitment to the group and are better prepared to work harder and smarter.

Many of us spend much of our time experiencing something else. Effective coordination depends on everyone's focusing on what the groups is aiming for, working in tune with everyone else and making the maximum effort.

Fellow Feeling

It's difficult to develop communication and cooperation when fellow-feeling is absent. In a governmental news conference, journalists who have little sense of common cause with politicians in power, treat the podium as a pillory and use questions to expose what they expect is incompetence or deceit. Managers who don't listen to their workforce and workers who don't talk to their managers remain suspicious of each other and fail to find common cause. Some of us behave as though we're convinced there can only ever be division and conflict—unless a would-be all-powerful or righteous force takes charge.

At its richest and most dependable, 'we' implies a reciprocal relationship or set of relationships. As long as, in good faith, I have well-meaning hopes and fears for you and you have well-meaning hopes and fears for me, we can negotiate, plan and act together and on one another's behalf. As long as, in good faith, we have well-meaning hopes and fears for other people and they have well-meaning hopes and fears for us, we and they may negotiate, plan and act together and negotiate on one another's behalf. We can't all be secure if the whole we might be part of depends on there being 'others' whom we denigrate or oppress.

Without shared interest and fellowship, individuals and groups fall back on doing things separately from and/or against each other[23]. To flourish we need a real sense of sharing something that transcends what is individual or 'private' and so becomes common or 'public', and everyone has opportunities to participate and contribute. Being at one with our true or better self mirrors being at one with others, and *vice versa*. What is individual and personal need not be selfish or anti-social. What is social and common need not be mediocre or alienating.

The philosopher and sociologist Jürgen Habermas (1962)[24] offered this definition: 'We call events and occasions "public" when they are open to all, in contrast to closed or exclusive affairs'. Our experiences of child, health and social care, charity and aid, security and defence, business and employment depend on evident trust born of everyone's mutual, reciprocal and symbiotic contributions. These are the lifeblood of relationships in companionship, friendship, partnership, community, therapy, education, democracy and regional, national and international enterprises. These relationships endure and grow stronger in difficult times, if we're determined to have humanity and rationality guide and support us.

For you and your people not to become 'them' to me, and for me and my people not to become 'them' to you, each of us has to value what the other brings to our interaction. When groups develop in healthy ways, individuals appreciate one another as part of 'us'. Reciprocal relationships are characterised by their lack of condescension and exploitation, by everyone's having the same access to information and by everyone's testing and trusting the integrity of their intentions and agreements. Unhealthy and inauthentic bonds prevent us from acting autonomously and cooperatively. When we are secure in ourselves and united, we have confidence to grow and achieve good things. Then, each of us feels we have things to offer as well as things to gain. Then, humanity is capable of the extraordinary.

Summing Up

Group identity makes us feel good about ourselves which, sadly, sometimes carries a message that our group has more value than others.

We're better placed to understand and respect one another, if we don't see ourselves as being above or central to everything.

If any given interaction or relationship is going to work, the parties really have to want it to work and so be prepared to compromise.

When we are secure in ourselves and united, we have confidence to grow and achieve good things without giving up too much.

---

[1] See Robert Sapolsky (2018), pp 31, 84-88, 98, 105-106, 135, 172 and 673.

[2] See Adam Peaty's (2021) *The Gladiator Mindset: Push Your Limits. Overcome Challenges. Achieve Your Goals*, published in London, UK, by Quercus Publishing.

[3] See Laura Cumming's (2016, 2017) *The Vanishing Man: In Pursuit of Velazquez*, published in London, UK, by Penguin Random House, pp 264-265.

[4] Henri Tajfel's and John Turner's developed what came to be called Minimal Group Theory in their (1979) 'The social identity theory of intergroup behaviour', published by W. G. Austin's and S. Worchel (eds.) *Psychology of Intergroup Relations*, then as a 2nd edition, in Chicago, Il, by Nelson-Hall. It built on Tajfel's (1970) experiment carried out in Bristol, UK.

[5] See Bertram Malle's (2004) *How the Mind Explains Behaviour: Folk Explanations, Meaning, and Social Interaction*, published in Cambridge, MA, by MIT Press. The expression 'fundamental attribution error' was coined by the social psychologist Lee

Ross (1977) in his essay 'The intuitive psychologist and his shortcomings: Distortions in the attribution process', published in *Advances in Experimental Social Psychology*, Volume 10, pp 173–220. Both Ross and Malle built on the social psychologists Edward Jones' and Victor Harris' (1967) 'The attribution of attitudes', published in the *Journal of Experimental Social Psychology*, 3, 1, pp 1–24.

[6] See the psychologist (born 1896, died 1934) Lev Vygotsky's (1978) *Mind in Society: The Development of Higher Psychological Processes*, published in Cambridge, MA, by Harvard University Press. His concept of 'the zone of proximal development' is a social principle, applicable to all cognitive processes. It helped inspire David Wood's, Jerome Bruner's and Lee Ross' (1976) research.

[7] See Donald Winnicott's (1971) *Playing and Reality*, published in London, UK, by Tavistock/Routledge. This connects with Alice Miller's (1979) work, referred to in footnote 3, chapter 1.

[8] See the professor of child development and education Iram Siraj's and professor of education Aziza Mayo's (2014) *Social Class and Educational Inequality: The impact of parents and schools*, published in Cambridge, UK, by Cambridge University Press.

[9] See Robin Dunbar (1992) 'Neocortex size as a constraint on group size in primates'. The number 150 includes past school or neighbourhood friends, ex-colleagues and so on, with whom we would want to connect again. Lapsed and stop-start relationships are not counted. About intro- and extroverts, see the writer Susan Cain's (2012) *Quiet: The Power of Introverts in a World that Can't Stop Talking*, published in London, UK, by Penguin Books.

[10] See the entry on 'otheringJennette' in the historian Alan Bullock's and the writer, editor and filmmaker Stephen Trombley's (1977) *The New Fontana Dictionary of Modern Thought*, published in London, UK, by Fontana, p 620. See also Dunbar's (2016) *Human Evolution: Our Brains and Behavior*, published in New York, NY, by Oxford University Press, p 271, in which he wrote about identity as a shorthand for trust sufficient to get things done.

[11] See Neil MacGregor (2010), pp 399-403.

[12] See Adam Phillips (2013), p 376.

[13] See Robin Dunbar (2016), pp 42, 174, 195, 211, 268 and 293.

[14] See Michael Tomasello's (2018) 'How we learned to put our fate in one another's hands: The origins of morality', published in *Scientific American*, 319, 3, pp 64-67, pp 66-67. Also his (2016) *A Natural History of Human Morality*, published in Cambridge, MA, by Harvard University Press.

[15] See Patricia Churchland's (2020) lecture *Good Natured: Mammalian genes and the origin of morality*, given as The Royal Institute of Philosophy Annual Lecture 2020; go to https://www.youtube.com/watch?v=TOy3AVLGEs8. Also her (2019) *Conscience:*

The Origin of Moral Intuition, published in London, UK, by W. W. Norton and Company.

[16] See Adam Phillips (2013), p 367.

[17]. See Johan Graafland's and Bjorn Lous' (2019) 'Income Inequality, Life Satisfaction Inequality and Trust: A Cross Country Panel Analysis', published in *Happiness Studies*, 20, 6, pp1717-1737. In keeping with this, see also the social epidemiologist Richard Wilkinson's and epidemiologist Kate Pickett's (2009, 2010) *The Spirit Level: Why Equality is Better for Everyone*, published in London, UK, by Penguin Books.

[18]. See Horace (1793) *The Works of Horace, Vol. II*, published in London, printed for R. Baldwin. The full saying was *Nullius addictus iurare in verba magistri*: not having to swear allegiance in words to a master.

[19]. See J. L. Austin's (1955, 1962) *How to Do Things with Words: The William James Lectures delivered at Harvard University*, delivered at Harvard University, edited by J. O. Urmson and M. Sbisà, and published in Oxford, UK by Clarendon Press.

[20]. See Carl Rogers' (1961) *On Becoming a Person: A Therapist's View of Psychotherapy*, published in New York, NY, by Houghton Mifflin Books, p 187.

[21]. See my chapter 'English at Comberton Village College' in the book *Outcomes of Education* (1980), edited by the author, journalist, educationist and emeritus professor in the philosophy of social institutions Tyrrell Burgess and the writer and inspector of schools Elizabeth Adams, published in London, UK, by Macmillan. Also my *Out in the Open: A secondary English curriculum* (1986), published in Cambridge, UK, by Cambridge University Press.

[22] See Maximilien Ringelmann's (1913) 'Recherches sur les moteurs animés: Travail de l'homme' [Research on animate sources of power: The work of man], published by *Annales de l'Institut National Agronomique, 2nd series*, 12, pp 1-40: available on-line in French at: http://gallica.bnf.fr/ark:/12148/bpt6k54409695.image.f14.lang EN. The Ringelmann effect has been explored by many researchers including, for example, S. H. Czyż, A. Szmajke, A. Kruger and M. Kübler (2016) in 'Participation in Team Sports Can Eliminate the Effect of Social Loafing', published by *Perceptual and Motor Skills*, 123, 3, pp 754–768. Go to doi:10.1177/0031512516664938. There is an echo here too of Dunbar's numbers (see the 'Resisting Othering' section of chapter 3).

[23]. See Adam Phillips (2013), p 376.

[24]. See Jürgen Habermas' (1989) *The Structural Transformation of the Public Sphere: An Inquiry into a Category of Bourgeois Society*, published in Cambridge, MA, by The MIT Press, and translated (1962) by Thomas Burger from the German *Strukturwandel der Öffentlichkeit: Untersuchungen zu einer Kategorie der bürgerlichen Gesellschaft*, published in Berlin, Germany, by Suhrkamp Verlag, Taschenbuch-Wissenschaft, p 1. For analysis of some of the ways in which there are interfaces between personal and

public experiences, see works by the sociologist and social psychologist Erving Goffman, for example: (1959) *The Presentation of Self in Everyday Life*, published in Edinburgh, Scotland, by the University of Edinburgh Social Sciences Research Centre; (1961) Asylums: *Essays on the social situation of mental patients and other inmates*, published in New York, NY, by Anchor Books; and (1963) *Stigma: Notes on the Management of Spoiled Identity*, published in Upper Saddle River, NJ, by Prentice-Hall.

4 Learning

In this chapter the people we hear from include Matthew Syed, M. L. 'Jane' Johnson Abercrombie and Daniel Kahneman.

How keen are we to learn new things?

Responding to Your World

Brothers Kwame, aged 14, and Oteng, aged 12, came to stay with us for 10 days on a Ghana-UK school exchange. Kwame was the more confident. I asked him, 'What do you want to do while you're with us?'

'Learn to swim,' he said.

After school the next day, we went to the pool. In the water, he asked, 'What do I do?' I showed him how to lean forward, let his legs and feet come up behind him, and pull and push himself forward with a breaststroke and frog-kick. He mimicked my movements, rapidly and energetically. I held my arm as a safety net under the water. After several minutes' vigorous effort, he stood, breathing deeply, his face calm and concentrated. 'Pull longer and slower,' I said. He repeated the sequence a dozen more times, each time making further and further progress and having less and less need for support. Then he tried on his own. He swam to the far side of the pool and looked back at me, beaming. I applauded. He had learned to swim in 10 minutes.

What enables you to go beyond what you've so far been capable of?

Adam Phillips (2013)[1] wrote 'To have the courage of one's preferences is to have the courage of one's feelings. Every wish is an experiment in consequences'. The journalist, broadcaster and table tennis player Matthew Syed (2019)[2] quoted research carried out by the psychology professor Angela Bahns into how much we experiment. She compared the demographic diversity of two

Kansas colleges in the USA—one large, one small. The University of Kansas (UoK) had 30,000 students and Bethel College (BC) had 105.

You might think that UoK students would have many more opportunities to meet people from different backgrounds than BC students. But Bahns discovered that UoK students' social networks were narrower than BC students', 'not just in terms of attitudes and beliefs, but also politics, moral convictions and prejudices'. The bigger the group you find yourself in, the more you tend to consolidate connections with people you feel are like you, rather than welcoming or seeking opportunities to explore differences.

If you don't counteract this tendency to stay with what you know, you expect things will continue to be as you guess they've always been or should be. You enact self-fulfilling prophecies and so miss opportunities and challenges. To expect something is not the same as *thinking* something. Much of what you do comes from routines, habits, assumptions and prejudices.

If what you expect or predict turns out to be correct, things may go well. If you're wrong, and if you survive, you have an opportunity to learn. You don't help yourself learn and grow by avoiding contact with people and ideas you're unfamiliar with. Sticking to what you think you know is one of the reasons you get into difficulties; another reason (referred to in the 'Adapting' section of chapter 2) is that you do things without understanding possible consequences. We learn by having varied and novel experiences and by reflecting on them.

How Your Brain Works

Most of our predictions are spontaneous. Speed of response has given us an evolutionary benefit, prompting us to escape danger, go for the obvious advantage, overcome hesitancy, avoid difficulty and preserve energy.

In Chris Frith's (2007) words, 'Perception is a loop' which starts with our beliefs. What we believe tells us what to expect, until we remind ourselves, or we're forced to accept, that the unexpected does happen. Our brain predicts what messages our senses will pick up and compares the predictions with signals being received: 'Usually only a few cycles of the loop are sufficient, which might take the brain only 100 milliseconds.'

It's tempting to think our mental models and muscle maps are permanent or at least durable blueprints. But our brain's models and maps are not like photo albums, video-clips, soundtracks, data bytes or parts of programmes to be stored, downloaded, retrieved, played and replayed without loss of fidelity or alteration. It is true that, through repetition, our brain trains our body to perform more or less consistent actions, reducing effort and deliberation to virtually nil, using what we call muscle memory; but every iteration of the loop is live and leaves its own trace. Far from being smooth, consistent and reliable, these are unstable processes and subject to change every time they're activated.

We aren't machines or computers. We don't have to repeat our errors, though of course we sometimes do. We don't have to walk M. C. Escher's (1960)[3] Möbius-strip-like stairway forever. It sometimes feels or looks as though that is exactly what we're doing.

The experimental psychologist Frederic Bartlett (1932)[4] foresaw Frith's loops when he explored the role of memory in perception and performance. He explained that, as you move to hit a ball, you merge the sense you have of your intent with your awareness of your posture. He noted that how you position yourself is 'a result of a whole series of earlier movements, in which the last movement before the stroke has a predominant function'. As you begin the action, you don't 'produce something absolutely new'. Nor do you ever 'merely repeat something old'. Producing a shot such as you've never produced before is likely to involve an element of chance as well as imagination and then applied understanding: it's a game.

We conjure up what we perceive. *Everything* we project, predict and recall is *adjusted*, at least a little. Our perceptions are consolidated, refined and revised, often incrementally, less often radically. Every day, hardly thinking about it, we confirm and check what we 'see'; we note, ignore and deny impressions.

We never know anything for sure and we can never be confident about everything. But, for as long as we're free to express our autonomous feelings and think for ourselves and together, we can learn and help one another learn. The pay-off is that we can keep refining our understanding and so be better placed to prepare, keep track, achieve much of what we hope for and avoid much of what we fear. This may be the single most persuasive reason to be optimistic that we can improve our quality of life and save ourselves and our planet.

Seeing Things Differently

On a week's holiday in Florence, Italy, one morning I walked out of the city and climbed the hill towards Fiesole. After about an hour's walking, I came across a bar and someone sitting outside, glass of beer in hand. I joined him. We gazed over the valley. 'Just look at all those greens,' he said.

An exclamation can be the start of questioning and observation. I began to look. Every cluster and line of trees and every patch and strip of every field was a unique green. He was an artist and prompted me to see in technicolour.

We improve our prospects of living well when we learn to see things differently. We see things differently when we alternate immersing ourselves in activity with standing back to observe and ask questions. If we don't do these things, we reduce our chances of solving everyday puzzles and tasks, let alone the global problems we now face.

What experiences have you had that helped you to see things differently?

Being observant and thinking critically help us; so too does receiving feedback and feedforward. We may not often consider feedforward and not realise we're doing it when we envisage what we're about to do and how it might pan out. More deliberately, we can call on researchers, advisers, practitioners and professionals to give us advance warning and advice.

Once our activity is underway, checking the feedforward we've created or been given can remind us of what to watch out for. This is what sports people are doing when they visualise their performance; when scientists carry out preliminary explorations and experiments; when designers, inventors, technologists and manufacturers trial prototypes; when artists make sketches; when sculptors make maquettes; when musicians and actors rehearse …

In a similar vein, the psychologist and economist Daniel Kahneman (2011)[5] recommended we hold 'pre-mortems', particularly when quality of life is at stake: 'Before starting on a project, ask everyone to imagine that a year from now it has failed. Ask them to write a brief history of that disaster. What you learn from that pre-mortem should hopefully help you avoid having to hold a post-mortem.' This is an example of using experience and imagination to treat time as a sliding vantage point from which to cast forward and back, and so gain a fuller picture of possible outcomes. And what applies to us as individuals applies equally when we learn and work as a group.

Learning from our peers is one of the most obvious and effective ways we have of acquiring understanding and skills. We often do this when we study, work and play alongside one another. M. L. 'Jane' Johnson Abercrombie (1960)[6] researched how to enable students of medicine, architecture and education to broaden, deepen and sharpen their judgement-making. She came to understand how valuable it is to use one another as an audience and as a source of alternatives to our initial impressions and ideas.

In one experiment, her objective was for medical students to read of radiology plates. Johnson Abercrombie saw that her students weren't able to understand an x-ray as if it spoke to them. Nor did it help them to be told what to see. Images need to be interpreted, just as texts do; and interpretation is something individuals have constructively and creatively to do for themselves, albeit sometimes guided and supported by others. Just as we co-construct our emotions[7], so do we influence one another as we notice, observe and reflect. Her insight was that 'How to tell students what to look for without telling them what to see is the dilemma of teaching'. That was something my Post-Graduate Certificate in Education at The North-East London Polytechnic course did exceedingly well.

Learning Together

Johnson Abercrombie was interested in how to help her students tease out key elements in what they were looking at, discriminate between facts and opinions and resist baseless or muddled conclusions. The strategy she found, called free or associative discussion, involved the students comparing and contrasting what they said they saw. They were prompted to rearrange and reassess what they already knew rather than receive 'new packets of facts'. The method was remarkably successful, and can be adapted to any context or occasion when we try to help one another improve how we interpret things. We need to do this when we confront social and international problems.

Focused and challenging discussions bring a more effective range of factors into play than can be achieved by lecturing and instructing. Johnson Abercrombie's interventions pointed her students toward one another's ways of looking, listening, judging and deciding. Dialogue helped them consider their assumptions and approaches. They grew to tolerate and make use of ambiguities, uncertainties, diverse and contradictory views. They learned to think beyond questions that are framed as questions with yes/no answers. We are much more likely to succeed in tackling problems and pursuing our aspirations if we avoid the limitations of binary and linear thinking. Large-scale, complex challenges demand we engage with one another's ways of seeing[7].

What tasks have you engaged in that made important differences to your life? What helped you?

Tasks that are too easy or too difficult often don't help you learn. Tasks that are 'just right' are satisfying because you discover—with or without help—that you do well when you feel you're exerting yourself and growing[8]. Your autonomous skills expand rapidly when you have a strong enough sense of pleasure and benefit gained by *your* problem-solving and skill-building. If you don't feel motivated, you can't be bothered. And if you don't take the risk of trying something different, you don't have half the joy and success that you might have.

The psychologist Jerome Bruner (1972)[9] explained that 'What distinguishes man as a species is not only [a] capacity for learning, but for teaching as well'. Our most natural learning and teaching occur when we engage with one another in thinking about what we're doing in situations and activities we're interested in.

Have you been able to pass on to someone else or other people something useful or important that you've learned?

If it went well, what helped make it a good experience?

Much hinges on how keen we are to share-what we learn. We are helped by anyone who guides and prompts us to approach things from different angles and look at things in a new light. This highlights the notion of vantage points and viewpoints. The historian E. H. Carr (1961)[10] wrote about this when he explained how he saw the study of history. He likened understanding events in the past to surveying a hill—coming at it from as many different terrestrial and aerial angles as possible. Understanding becomes a process of bringing things together in order to see more clearly rather than arriving at a finite, supposedly objective, 'correct' view.

That is why seeking agreement plays an important role in efforts to survive threats and disasters and learn to live better lives: there is no single right perspective, no one way to guaranteed success. This is something that informs what many effective leaders and chairs of meetings and organisations do. By their example and methods, they help us pause, stand back, look around and take different points of view. We can't avoid meeting ambiguities, anomalies, contradictions and complexities in our experiences. Situations we encounter and events we become involved in can't help but have upsides and downsides, positive potentials as well as risks.

Learning to Learn

Our unconscious contributes tacitly to what we do[11]. Deliberate, self-conscious thinking also has a contribution to make.

Kahneman (2011) wrote about how we benefit from two potentially complementary ways we have of thinking. System 1 Thinking works 'with little or no effort and no sense of voluntary control'. To save time and effort, it relies on our making assumptions and using routines. It is busy generating actions at the expense of preparatory or analytical thinking. System 2 Thinking is more deliberate, slower, more effortful, logical and conscious. It enables us to think about what we going to do, what we're doing and what we've done, and therefore requires special kinds of attentiveness. It looks beyond the familiar and habitual, questions assumptions and brings to the fore factors and processes that guide and check our actions.

System 1 gets things done that probably wouldn't get done if we left our decision-making to System 2. System 2's planning and reflection cost time and effort. Often, we sense there's a good enough chance of achieving the results we're looking for by acting spontaneously or routinely and avoiding being overly procedural, abstract or self-conscious. Having to be analytical sometimes makes us uncomfortable, resentful even. But when we face life-changing decisions or when the unexpected or unintended happens, System 2 encourages us not to take things for granted and be critically aware and deliberate.

Some of us are more disposed than the rest of us to step back and think about what's said, what's apparent, what's not obvious and what's left unsaid. We can ask natural observers amongst us to comment from time to time on how well we're focusing and listening. They can give us feedback and help us learn about *how* we go about things. They might be our group's specialist System 2 thinkers—most helpful when the scale and complexity of what we're doing escalate.

The psychologist and pioneer of organisational and applied psychology Kurt Lewin[12] developed a way of doing this in the workplace. Called 'action research', it is a way of consulting research and advice and relating it critically to practical and experimental realities. In Lewin's words, it is 'a spiral of steps, each of which is composed of a circle of planning, action and fact-finding'. I was influenced and encouraged in action research by educationists such as John Elliott, Bridget Somekh and Jack Whitehead.

Neither forethought nor afterthought guarantees anything, but in many circumstances, cycles of planning, practice, analysis and experimentation make it likelier we'll perform to the best of our abilities. The more complex the task and the more of us that are involved, the more carefully and sophisticatedly we need to cooperate and the more we all benefit.

Summing Up

'Every wish is an experiment in consequences.'

Everything we project, predict and recall is *adjusted*, at least a little.

For as long as we're free to express our autonomous feelings and think for ourselves and together, we can learn and help one another learn by practising seeing things differently.

We do well when we learn to follow 'a circle of planning, action and fact-finding'.

---

[1] See Adam Phillips (2013), p 196.
[2] See Matthew Syed (2019), *Rebel Ideas: The Power of Diverse Thinking*, published in London, UK, by John Murray, pp 179-181; and about the Internet, see p 183.
[3] See M. C. Escher's (1960) lithograph Klimmen en dalen (Ascending and Descending): the strip is an impossible object, it was created by Oscar Reutersvärd and made popular in the late 1950s by the psychiatrist, medical geneticist, paediatrician, mathematician and chess theorist Lionel Penrose and his son, the mathematician, mathematical physicist, philosopher of science and Nobel Laureate in Physics Roger Penrose.
[4] See Frederic Bartlett's (1932) *Remembering: A Study in Experimental and Social Psychology,* published in Cambridge, UK, by Cambridge University Press.
[5] See Daniel Kahneman's (2011) *Thinking, fast and slow*, published in London, UK, by Penguin.

[6] See M. L. 'Jane' Johnson Abercrombie's (1960) *The Anatomy of Judgement: An investigation into the processes of perception and reasoning*, published in London, UK, by Hutchinson, pp 28-29, 33 and 63.

[7] See Lisa Feldman Barrett (2018), pp xii, 289 and 293. See also Barrett (2021) talking on the Jordan Harbinger Show, *How to Fix Your Brain Biases That Hold You Back*. Go to https://www.youtube.com/watch?v=EybxFWtLlAw.

[8] See the psychologist Lev Vygotsky's (1978) *Mind in Society: The Development of Higher Psychological Processes*, published in Cambridge, MA, by Harvard University Press.

[9] See Jerome Bruner's (1972) 'Nature and uses of immaturity', published in *American Psychology*, 27, pp 1-22, and in P. K. Smith's and A. D. Pellegrini's (2000) *Psychology in Education: Major Themes, Vol. 2*, published in London, UK, by RoutledgeFalmer, p 52ff.

[10] See the historian, diplomat, journalist and international relations theorist E. H. Carr's (1961) *What Is History?* published in Cambridge, UK, by Cambridge University Press.

[11] See Adam Phillips (2013), pp 65-66.

[12] Kurt Lewin coined the term action research in 1944. See his (1946) 'Action research and minority problems', published in the *Journal of Sociological Issues*, 2(4), pp 34–46. Also the teacher researcher and educator Clem Adelman's (1993) article 'Kurt Lewin and the Origins of Action Research', published in *Educational Action Research*, 1, 1, pp 7-24.

5 Trying to Think

In this chapter the people we hear from include Iain McGilchrist and Albert Bandura, along with others whom we have met before.

How can we learn to think?

Learning by Teaching

Do you sometimes think intuitively and act spontaneously?

Do you sometimes pause to reflect and take time to observe?

When do you need to think fast and when do you need to think slow?

A specific exercise helped me help students and then teachers think about learning and teaching by thinking about becoming involved and becoming an observer. Participants work in threes. One has to teach another person something she or he knows about or knows how to do. The third person has to observe what happens. These are the instructions:

When you are being the teacher, you have to help a partner to do or understand something.

When you are being the learner, you have to pay attention and try to learn what you are being taught.

When you are being the observer, you have to look out for what the teacher does that helps the learner, and for what the learner does that helps her or him learn.

At the end of the episode, the observer has to sum up for the other two what she or he noticed about what helps the teaching and learning go well. Finally, all three discuss these questions and then present their answers to everyone else:

What makes a good observer?
What makes a good teacher?
What makes a good learner?

Given time, each member of the trio takes each of the roles.

This kind of teaching and learning helps us understand more about how to solve all sorts of problems. It can help us succeed in many endeavours.

Learning at School and at Work

What have been your best experiences of learning how to study or do a job?

The professor of developmental psychology Margaret Donaldson (1978)[1] explained that, to do well in school, we have to be more disciplined and more deliberately transparent in our thinking than we're probably used to: 'the normal child comes to school with well-established skills as a thinker. But [his or her] thinking is directed outwards on to the real, meaningful, shifting, distracting world. What is going to be required for success in our educational system is that [she or he] should learn to turn language and thought in upon themselves. [She or he] must become able to direct [his or her] own thought process in a thoughtful manner... [Her or his] conceptual system must expand in the direction of increasing ability to represent itself'.

Success hinges on whether or not we're inclined to 'play the game', with all its mannerisms, tropes and conventions. Learners have to meet their educators at least half way; and they're helped if their educators meet them half way. It can be extremely helpful to think about how we think and how we can learn more effectively.

The linguist William Labov (1972)[2] found intellectual power in what might appear to be merely casual forms of expression. He showed there were parallels between some New York teenagers' discourse and Aristotle's rhetorical methods, and illustrated how demotic speech can be as articulate and disciplined as any elevated language. His detailed account of young Black speakers' forensic skill in critical analysis and argument supported his contention that 'There is no reason to believe that any nonstandard vernacular is in itself an obstacle to learning'. We all can use our familiar language to think about thinking and learn about learning. And we benefit especially when we learn from peers.

Labov wanted every learner to have the chance and encouragement to find their true and better self within conventional systems, particularly those that give them access to advantageous and otherwise privileged forms of culture. Education systems tend to prescribe how students should show they know what they're meant to have been taught. Educators' role then has to be to help learners develop their comprehension and expression via their first language and dialects in order to become competent in the required 'standard'. They need to be helped to achieve what's asked of them to enter further and higher education and employment, if these are their goals.

The purpose of education in particular and of government in general, we might say, is to enable as many people as possible to be full and equal members of their society. Learning and working together are both the goal and the means of living well. Healthy engagement with society entails being open to one another's imaginations and discoveries. Because we and the situations we face change, doing well depends on our evolving and growing. Today's challenges are most likely to be met when as many of us as possible are involved in efforts to:

> Find out who and what can help us
> Question anything and anyone, however obvious, awkward or unlikely the issue may seem
> Continue to learn through what we do.

Doing well isn't a fixed or final state; it comes from learning to learn. We learn to learn when we:

> Are helped by experienced people who share and inform our concerns
> Try to be clear about our priorities
> Pay attention to diverse information and evidence
> Celebrate progress
> Update our success criteria as part of adapting to events.

Learning informally from each other is at least as powerful as being taught formally. It is a feature of outstanding coaches, mentors, tutors, advisers, carers, medics, therapists, entrepreneurs, executives, managers and leaders that they empower and enable us to learn for ourselves and with one another. Learning and working together provide us with support and stimulation—practically as well as cognitively and emotionally.

Becoming Aware

It's easy to have the impression that we're mostly conscious of what we're doing and in control. If we think at all about our unconscious, we might say it's an irrelevant, sometimes meddlesome intruder on our general awareness of what we need to be aware of. But it's more likely to be the other way round: to grab our attention, consciousness has to finds its way through our everyday state of semi- and unconsciousness. Many of us only think about our unconscious when we wonder why we feel bothered or unaccountably below par.

Matthew Syed (2019) summarised a study of 100 businesspeople who said they wanted to meet new people and were invited to an after-work event for that purpose. Electronic name-tags meant researchers could track and time encounters, without hearing exactly what was said. Who did the guests end up talking to? Answer: most spoke to people they already knew. Even though they said they were interested in meeting new people, most didn't.

Syed noted that 'For all its promise of diversity and interconnection, the Internet has become characterised by a new species of in-groups, not by the logic of kin or nomadic tribe, but by [our own] ideological fine-tuning'. And our responses are channelled by algorithmic filters according to what we click on using digital devices. We tend to seek out, *and we're fed*, what we're familiar with and that confirms how we already feel and think. Dealing with what is unfamiliar is metabolically expensive, that is, costly to our resources and energies. (This is what Lisa Feldman Barrett's (2018) work has shown, referred to in the 'Starting Out' section of chapter 1.) FMRI scans show that, when we're exposed to information we've not met before, we tend to have a negative emotional response. We have many different ways of dealing with this and sometimes respond with anger or aggression. As far as we can tell, this applies to all humans, whatever our ethnicity, culture, class, caste or status.

Intentions and Purposes

It helps sometimes to stand back from your moment-to-moment living to notice what you wish for, before you do something about it. Articulating goals can be helpful. While you're pursuing a goal, you may avoid wasting your energies on random, distracting or futile efforts.

When what happens confirms our expectations, it seems we've guessed 'correctly' and that may make us feel we're wiser than we are. Guessing wrongly points to shortcomings in our memories, predictions, simulations and routines. It's telling that so many outstanding coaches emphasise how we grow through our mistakes and failures.

Predicting wrongly doesn't have to shatter our confidence. Errors and disappointments may shake up a faulty memory or model, and we may try new ones and learn how they work out. Yet we never quite eradicate our old thinking; it sits in the background of what we're currently capable of and what we do next.

What we mean to do and then what we do arise from our interactions with the environment and express our needs, impulses, drives, whims, wishes, fantasies, fears, revulsions, values and commitments. Without intentions and efforts which we make for ourselves, we are passengers or robots. Our aims limit us, but also motivate and guide us. Our purposes and goals contain the success criteria for whatever we do. If we didn't have implicit and/or explicit directions and considerations, we'd have nothing to tell us whether to be satisfied or disappointed by what we actually make or let happen.

Think of a time when you were sure about what you were aiming for. How did things turn out? What contributed to success and/or failure?

What we aim for affects and is affected by how we speak and listen to one another and by how we work together. Motivation, communication and cooperation are interconnected: the more confident we are about why we're aiming for something, and the better we communicate and cooperate with whoever is involved, the more successful we are likely to be. The better we react, adapt and learn, the more likely we are to develop our skills and understanding. We do this as groups as well as individuals. Our culture and civilisation are the mind we share.

Adam Phillips (2013)[3] wrote about this in terms of having 'ambitions—and therefore fantasies (conscious and unconscious)—of what it would be to succeed or fail'. For these to exist, you need an initial 'object of desire, an ideal, a state of the world' you want to bring about. Or you need to envisage yourself in a state 'sufficiently separate' from yourself and aspire to achieve it. So you need to have perceived yourself as lacking and/or wanting something. You also need to believe you have time 'as a promising medium' to do things in. It helps to know you will probably have to 'suffer the pains and pleasures of anticipation and deferral' and compromise. Finally, you need to believe strongly enough that you really can achieve what you want or at least something close to it. Grounded confidence feeds your commitment and directs the energy required to make the effort and overcome limitations and obstacles.

When you fail to achieve what you aim for, you have choices. You can ignore or deny mismatches between what you wanted or expected to happen and what actually happened. Or you can rethink and consider alternatives. When you pay attention to what you expect and then notice what actually happens, you get better at guessing and predicting, and then better at following up doubts, asking questions and revising your methods.

Getting Involved, Standing Back

My thinking about expectations, planning and reflecting crystallised in my work with students, teachers and teacher educators. In one project, I found that asking variations on three questions led to illuminating conversations between students, between students and their teachers, and between students, teachers and outsiders who fund, oversee and influence the work:

What are you trying to do?
What are you getting better at?
What are you going to do next?

These questions apply to many contexts and concerns, at home, at work and at play. They apply to everyone involved in working together to increase our chances of living better. If we don't answer these questions in relation to the opportunities, risks and threats we face, we have little prospect of making a better future.

To survive and succeed in our most significant endeavours we need both to focus minutely *and* take account of the widest and most pertinent fields of information. Iain McGilchrist (2010)[4] wrote that, 'By standing back from the animal immediacy of our experience we are able to be more empathic with others, who we come to see, for the first time, as being like ourselves.' The way our frontal lobes evolved allows us to go beyond raw sensation and perception and 'learn to take another's perspective and to control our own immediate needs and desires'. There is currently a consensus about the fact that the left and right sides of our brain together contribute to how we feel and think about things, but there's no agreement about *how* this cooperation takes place within the brain.

McGilchrist argued that our left-brain hemisphere majors on seeing the world explicitly and abstractly, as compartmentalised, fragmented and static, whereas the right side sees things as '*present* to us in all their embodied particularity, with all their changeability and impermanence, and their interconnectedness, as part of a whole which is forever in flux. In this world we, too, feel connected to what we experience, part of that whole'. He saw the hemispheric combination as making 'betweenness'—an enriched kind of connectedness which allows for exchange and cooperation between different elements and processes in the vast, complex, sentient networks that we comprise both as individuals and as groups and communities.

Whether or not our two-sided brain works in the way that McGilchrist proposed, scholars now agree that we are enabled by various means both to become involved in events and situations *and* to pause, look around and consider. The philosopher, literary critic and university administrator Stuart Hampshire (1989)[5] explained the vital part that is played in the growth of individuals' and societies' self-awareness and autonomy when we alternate standing back with becoming immersed: 'We could not ever be observers unless we were sometimes active experimenters, and we could not ever be experimenters unless we were sometimes observers. To observe is to learn what obstructions, instructions and constructions there are in the environment; and to experiment is to act with a view to perceiving what happens when we act in a certain way'. Led by the deputy head teacher Moira Bearwish, this was a major feature of a year-long film-making project I assisted in a first school.

The students worked hard on alternating busy engagement with carefully considered analysis and preparation. Professionals from all of the specialist fields of film-making tutored and guided small groups of pupils in every aspect of film-making so that those few could pass on what they learned to the rest of their classmates. Every single one of them became actively involved in making and enacting specific decisions. Each year-group devised job descriptions, advertised, interviewed and appointed one another to specific jobs. Between them, they devised their own story-outlines and plots, wrote scripts, cast actors and procured and made props and costumes. Together, they put on make-up, directed, acted in, shot, edited and advertised their films, which were premiered on a summer's evening in a large marquee at the local secondary school to an audience of families, friends and invited guests. This went further than individuals' developing personal self-efficacy. Teams, classes, year-groups and the whole school developed their collective effectiveness, contributing to a constructive, shared, inclusive, celebratory culture.

Teaching by Example

Have you been an originator?

Have you worked alongside people who come up with new ideas and ways of doing things?

Have you learned important things by learning about, witnessing, testing or adapting how originators or proficient practitioners do things?

We become motivated by sharing and enriching our own and one another's experience and expertise. One of the most significant things leaders of all kinds can do is to enable us to learn from one another. This capitalises on our powerful tendency to emulate peers' attitudes and behaviours[6]. This is not top-down 'transfer of good practice', but 'joint practice development' between more and less confident, more and less experienced peers[7]. Our motivation is best driven by our learning and working together on focuses we choose. The hallmarks of this are constructive relationships and mutual trust.

Too many attempts to make organisations more effective and efficient take place at a remove from where the main work actually gets done. Peer observation and coaching take everyone's attention to where the vital action is played out. Individuals, teams and groups tend to have more frequent and more cumulatively influential contact with one another than they have with their trainers, coaches, teachers, mentors, doctors, advisers, managers, leaders, directors, investors, stewards, trustees and governors.

When we learn voluntarily from one another, it's not a matter of supposed experts handing over their understanding or skill to junior or 'weaker' colleagues, as though there were standard or sacrosanct solutions to our problems. Voluntary, peer teaching and learning:

> challenge our habits and customs
> encourage us to experiment
> ask and help us to be patient and painstaking
> are not a one-off or quick fix.

In these ways we're helped to make clear:

> what we're aiming for
> how we will know how successful we are
> what we need to do better.

Crucial are the exploring and revising of success criteria. This asks for, and in turn informs, creative and critical thinking. It is empirical, intuitive and pragmatic. The better the balance is between our taking the role of observer or coach and our taking the role of being observed or being coached, the healthier and richer our lives generally are likely to be.

The intention in peer observation and coaching is to enable us to work to the best of our ability and continue learning. There are other occasions when observations may have to record judgements about the quality of our performance according to prescribed, in-house, external or standards, as well as occasions when non-voluntary coaching and observation are provided because our has been work judged to be below what's expected. In those instances, the advantages of equality and mutuality can't apply because we don't freely enter into the experience. That is not to say that being observed and judged can't be made respectful and caring, but that learning from obligatory inspection by others has specific challenges which can't promise to provide the potential benefits of being observed by and observing peers.

What matters most about feedback is what we do with the encouraging, prompting and guiding we're offered. And when we choose to engage in activities we're more likely to relax into them and learn from them.

Self-Efficacy

We can't be sure how we'll affect other people and our world, but we can pay attention to *why* we do what we do, *how* we do it and *what* we achieve. The psychologist Albert Bandura (1997)[8] saw that we influence our chances of success by controlling things we're in a position to control. He gave the name self-efficacy to those kinds of attentiveness. And the clearer we become about what we intend and how we'll set about it, the more confident our commitment becomes and the better we prepare, plan, monitor and improve our efforts.

Daniel Kahneman (2011)[9] spelt this out with the following illustration. If it matters that you hire the person best suited to a job, focus your attention on what you understand the essential skills and qualities to be. Select up to six key traits that are needed for success in the role—including, for example, technical proficiency, engaging personality and reliability. As far as possible, choose discrete, distinctive traits and be ready to assess them by asking a few factual questions about each of them. Make a list of the questions and decide how you'll score them, say, on a 1 to 4 scale. To avoid halo effects, collect the information for each trait one at a time and score each one before you move on to the next one.

Do you know if that is how you were chosen for any of the positions you've been appointed to?

If it's your responsibility to hire people, how close is your method to Kahneman's recommendation?

The quality of life you experience depends on your agreeing what you need and want with everyone concerned, and then on agreeing what to do about it. One of your most valuable freedoms is to decide for yourself and with others what counts as success. This enables you to understand what you want to aim for and how to improve your efforts in the light of experience.

Have you had experience of doing your very best because you owned your goals and efforts, and had no need to rely on authorities in the background or 'above' you to direct and judge you?

Having a sense of self-efficacy dispels any impression you might have that you can't change your fate and helps you realise you can learn and grow. How well you do is not a matter of sheer luck or the fulfilling of prophecy. What *you do* is crucial to your success and affects how well other people do.

Learning for Everyone's Sake

The professor of biographical studies Richard Holmes (2009)[10] wrote about how human invention has transformed ways of thinking and practical living. A first scientific revolution was led by the philosopher, mathematician and scientist René Descartes (born 1596, died 1650), the philosopher and physician John Locke (born 1632, died 1704), the scientist and architect Robert Hooke (born 1635, died 1703) and the mathematician, physicist, astronomer and theologian Sir Isaac Newton (born 1642, died 1727), among others.

A second revolution 'swept through Britain at the end of the 18th century', giving birth to sciences which weren't recorded exclusively in Latin but were available to interested citizens in their vernacular and so stimulated debates, experiments and enterprises. There were numerous innovations, including the voltaic battery, the electrical generator, the scalpel and the air pump.

It seemed there was an 'ideal of a pure, "disinterested" science, independent of political ideology and even religious doctrine', and it took root with people committed to social progress via science and commerce. Major contributors included the botanist and naturalist Sir Joseph Banks (born 1743, died 1820), the chemist and inventor Sir Humphry Davy (born 1778, died 1829), the civil and mechanical engineer George Stevenson (born 1781, died 1848), and the mathematician, astronomer, chemist, inventor and experimental photographer John Herschel (born 1792, died 1871).

Furthermore, progress is enhanced by inter-disciplinary working. The professor of vaccinology Sarah Gilbert (2020)[11] came from that scientific tradition and emphasised how key discoveries are often made at the boundaries of disciplines and where they overlap. In her view, success depends on working with others who prepare carefully, have sufficient resources and are determined to monitor systematically and critically evaluate outcomes.

In science and in clinical provision, 'breakthroughs are rare'. The technologies and processes for the Covid-19 vaccine which her team worked on are the fruit of many decades prior to the crisis that started in 2019. A key has been 'doing things in parallel and being flexible', so that a vaccine could, for example, be adapted and modified very rapidly. Gilbert learned long ago that it's *not* possible to predict or simulate events and outcomes with certainty, so her team has explicit, well-practised processes that allow them to respond to developments quickly and inventively. She described her team as 'developing different cargoes for a vehicle' that has been built, trialled and modified by repeated and continuing experience.

This is a model that can serve any enterprise and help us meet any challenge: significant change comes about incrementally, and many elements have to be lined up. Competition and friendly rivalry play their part. And we can't expect decisions or solutions to last forever or even very long at all.

Karl Deisseroth (2021)[12] wrote that 'scientific truth—a force that can rescue us from weaknesses of our own construction—arises from free expression and pure discovery'. As we face problems that threaten our survival, science brings a tough reliability to the solutions—perhaps more comprehensively than technology, humanitarianism or spirituality—but still imperfectly. Science is not the only means we have to meet the challenge expressed by Deisseroth, but it seems indispensable because few other methods are as dependable: 'We need to be what we might be, so we can discover who we are'.

Expert Learning

Echoing Gilbert's and Deisseroth's approaches to research, the professor of social psychology Clifford Stott (2019)[13] explained his interest in political dissent which led him to analyse riots. In recent decades in a number of places, conventional policing of crowds has tended to prioritise identifying and dealing with key trouble-makers or hooligans. Stott's and his colleagues' methods have emphasised the importance of understanding crowd behaviours. Far from being 'formless, random and chaotic', crowds work in 'structured, normative patterns that reflect ideas and beliefs'. This is not to accept, excuse or condone public violence, whether it's committed by crowds, law-enforcers or security forces. This furthers our understanding of how people behave *en masse*.

Typically, crowd members start with a sense of their need and/or right to express their enthusiasms and/or voice opposition; and the police take what they believe are legitimate measures to disperse or contain mass gatherings when they see or anticipate disorder and threats to people and/or property. Most individuals in a crowd believe they have a justifiable impulse and right to defend themselves against insult or injury.

If the police treat the crowd as 'other'—one-dimensional, amorphous, anonymous—the effect is to 'create a unity between peaceful and violent groups in the crowd'. What starts as a situation in which only a minority is ready to be violent becomes a dangerous conflict. Realising that alternative approaches were needed, Stott and his colleagues have worked successfully alongside police forces to experiment, for example, with officials acting as civilians in the crowd. The aim has been to get away from a construct of them-*versus*-us and 'align peaceful citizens with police against violence and rioting'. The approach was first used successfully in the 2002 football World Cup finals and continues to be learned about.

Successfully implemented, those strategies enable willing crowd members to regulate their behaviour and influence others in the public interest. This concept can be traced to the foundation in 1829 of London's Metropolitan Police Service by the commissioners for the Home Secretary of the day, Sir Robert Peel. It was decided that policing should rely on communities' consent: 'The police are the public and the public are the police; the police being only members of the public who are paid to give full time attention to duties which are incumbent on every citizen in the interests of community welfare and existence'. The Metropolitan Police[14] set out to embody nine principles which express commitment to protection, assistance, support, guidance and governance of the people, by the people and for the people.

Stott saw it as his job to 'produce knowledge, but also to navigate it into the world around' him. The question he addressed was 'How can we respond deliberately, constructively and preventively to problems of public unrest?' And 'we' includes members of the public and crowd members as well as local government officials, police, emergency services and volunteers. Dialogue becomes crucial for everyone involved and everyone affected. This response pays attention to the reality of communities' histories, an appreciation of the immediate context, careful preparations and diligent study of ongoing events, for example using live social media.

Summing Up

Learning and working together are both the goal and the means of living well.

Our purposes and goals contain the success criteria for whatever we do.

To survive and succeed in our endeavours we need both to focus minutely *and* take account of the widest and most pertinent fields of information.

We can pay attention to *why* we do what we do, *how* we do it and *what* we achieve, without ever being sure how we'll affect other people and our world.

---

[1] See Margaret Donaldson's (1978) *Children's Minds*, published in London, UK, by Fontana/Collins, pp 89-90.

[2] See William Labov's (1972) *Language in the Inner City: Studies in the Black English Vernacular*, the fifth chapter 'The Logic of Nonstandard English', published in Philadelphia, PA, by University of Pennsylvania Press.

[3] See Adam Phillips (2013), pp 66-67.

[4] See Iain McGilchrist's (2010) *The Master and His Emissary: The Divided Brain and the Making of the Western World*, pp 22-31.

[5] See Stuart Hampshire's (1989) *Thought and Action*, published in London, UK, by Chatto & Windus, p 53.

[6] See Sarah-Jayne Blakemore (2019), referred to in chapter 1. Blakemore showed that during adolescence many young people's introspective ability increases, and levels out in adulthood, pp 27-29.

[7] See Michael Fielding's (2005) report, written with colleagues at Sussex University, *Factors Influencing the Transfer of Good Practice*, published by the University of Sussex & Demos and as the UK Department for Education and Science's Research Report RR615.

[8] See Albert Bandura's (1997) *Self-Efficacy: The Exercise of Control*, published in New York, NY, by W.H. Freeman and Co.

[9] See Daniel Kahneman (2011), p 232.

[10] See Richard Holmes (2009), pp xiv-xv and xviii-xix.

[11] Sarah Gilbert (15 Sept 2020) spoke to Jim Al-Khalili on BBC Radio 4's programme *The Life Scientific* about her work developing a vaccine for Covid-19. Her interest in practical interdisciplinarity is shared and advocated by Clifford Stott, as well as Edward Wilson and Ankhi Mukherjee, and by others in different periods of history, such as Jan Amos Komenský or Comenius (born 1592, died 1670).

[12] See Karl Deisseroth (2021), pp 209-210.

[13] Clifford Stott (16 June 2019) spoke to Jim Al-Khalili on BBC Radio 4's programme *The Life Scientific* about his work. Some of the issues he discussed are taken up here in chapter 10's section 'Standing Out From the Crowd'.

[14] See, on the UK Government's website *Definition of Policing by Consent*: https://www.gov.uk/government/publications/policing-by-consent/definition-of-policing-by-consent, retrieved 5.5.21.

6 Helping One Another Learn

In this chapter we hear from Michael Polanyi, Maryanne Wolf, Sugata Mitra and others whom we've met in previous chapters.

> How can fruitful teaching be a part of our most frequent and important activities?

Swapping Roles

Daniel Kahneman (2011)[1] explained that 'following our intuitions is more natural, and somehow more pleasant, than acting against them', but our developing instinctive expertise depends on the speed and quality of our feedback. To be well and do well, we have to generate our own feedback by being self-critical, considering feedback we're given and committing to acting on it when we've made sense of it.

The design teacher, maker and facilitator Ian Malthouse and I planned a conference for about 20 school leaders. As we waited for colleagues to arrive, I suspected both of us were nervous about what we'd planned. I took a cue from Ian. We greeted each of the delegates, looking them in the eye and saying we hoped they'd find our programme of activities useful. At the mid-morning coffee break, the two of us compared notes. Both of us felt things were going exceptionally well. When people who don't know one another well come together, it's common for many to feel tense and hold fast to what's familiar. Perhaps the personal greeting on arrival tipped a balance in our favour and helped them accept the unusual programme we'd devised for them.

At the centre of the room, we'd placed six chairs round a block of tables, surrounded by a circle of 20 or so more chairs. We invited the school leaders to sit in the big circle, Ian and I amongst them roughly opposite one another.

Though we had often invited students to take part in and contribute to training events for teachers and school leaders, we hadn't previously started by making the focal point students' speaking to everyone—without interruption.

On time, as arranged, six 13- to 14-year-old students arrived from a class in a local school. They occupied the tables and chairs centre-stage. Ian and I introduced ourselves and thanked everyone for coming to play a part in our learning about learning. We asked everyone to introduce themselves by saying their name and the school they represented. We explained that we adults were going to listen to the students up to the break, after which the adults would be able to ask questions and discuss with the students. The students would return to school at lunchtime. In the afternoon we'd work on the implications we took from the morning.

Each student had brought a bag containing their folders, books, equipment and artefacts and used them to illustrate how they felt they were doing in their studies. They also spoke about how they might be helped to do even better. The school leaders weren't going to have an opportunity to speak until after the first break. They had to be patient; and they were. The day was an unqualified success, as the activities and evaluations afterwards testified. Listening carefully to the people we're meant to be leading, serving or helping can give us the most valuable feedback we're likely ever to receive.

How do you think the students felt?

How do you think the school leaders felt?

How can we help one another listen to the people we need to listen to if we're to succeed?

Being Inspired to Inspire

Asked by colleagues about how he rewarded his students, the primary school deputy head teacher Basil Lodge in Portsmouth, UK, said, 'I give them something harder to do'. We learn very little of value without there being a level of challenge. (Remember Michio Kaku's observation in the 'Being Yourself, Helping Others' section of chapter 1.)

The primary and secondary school teacher, advisory teacher and consultant Norman Schamroth in Leicestershire, Devon and Dorset helped learners use drama conventions to explore 'What if ...?' Different vantage points offer moments of reflection, prediction and improvised enactment: trying out possible scenarios and consequences, freezing action in tableaux and taking it forwards and backwards in time. He described his intuitive decision-making as a process of immediately envisaging 'branching options' and then deciding on the most promising way forward, whenever possible involving participants in identifying and choosing between options. (This resonates with Gary Klein's work, referred to in the 'Analysis and Intuition' section of chapter 12.)

The teacher, researcher and head teacher Michael Armstrong (2019)[2] wrote that teaching at its best 'seeks to sustain learners' critical engagement with thought in all its forms'. Highly effective teaching helps learners pursue what they're curious about and interested in.

My teacher and the university fellow in German Ray Ockenden said to me about his one-to-one tutorials, 'When students read their essay to me, they can become their own critic'. He extended and enriched that idea when he introduced seminars as a way of enabling us to appreciate and critique one another's ideas and questions. It was a new experience for us to benefit from so many teachers in the room.

For learning to be shared across the whole group, there needs to be a feeling that everyone has something to gain. Accordingly, the teacher is conscious of wanting to keep everyone together while respecting their different needs, interests and abilities. A suitable image is that you are leading a group on a hill-climb. To sustain cohesion, the group should go no faster than its slowest member. You don't want the fittest and strongest to be frustrated waiting for those at the back. You don't want the slowest to drop out. You want them all to reach the top, if that is feasible, or reach the highest point they can. On a visit to the mathematics department at Twynham School, Christchurch, UK, I observed a lesson that illustrated that idea.

A class of 11- and 12-year-old students, representing a wide range of abilities and needs, was working in small groups on a particular problem. There was a sense in the room that they were all getting somewhere. Ten minutes or so before the end of the lesson their teacher, Ann Miller, asked a group to present their findings, and they did. Their fellow pupils appreciated what they had done. A second group was asked to step up. And so on. Ann had sequenced the group presentations to show a progression in the complexity of ideas. By the end everyone was up to speed with alternative working methods, the last of which was the most elegant. Everyone had played their part and constructed their own learning path.

All of those are examples of teaching that helps learners take charge. Those are principles and practices that apply equally to whenever we try to work together on tasks that benefit us all.

Self-Reliance, Cooperation

When we're expected to be knowledgeable or expert, the temptation is to say too much and to listen too little. As managers, leaders, coaches, mentors, tutors and chairpersons—especially when we want to engage everyone and help us all learn—we do well sometimes to hold back some of what we know. That doesn't mean being obscure or sly. It takes attentiveness and humility to do it.

Adam Phillips (1995)[3] wrote that 'By not answering the patient's questions, the analyst allows the patient both to repeat the answers of the past, and to recover the answering voices in himself ... only the patient has the answers'. This is a way of using a 'transitional space' between us to meet and negotiate next steps (referred to in chapter 1 relating to child development and to drama in education[4]). It allows us to stand apart from our immediate needs and concerns and look *together* from *unfamiliar* viewpoints. Being prepared to meet on shared, neutral or new ground is a valuable part of mutual confidence-building and essential to mediation, reconciliation and reparation.

Helping one another learn involves our recognising what each of us does well. It doesn't help to stay fixed on what hasn't gone well. It's better to highlight and build on successes, strengths and motivations. Then, we see how trust becomes warranted and grows, and we're ready to learn more and practise more. This isn't as easy as it may sound. If we're used to being under-estimated, corrected and criticised, we have to dismantle habits of seeing faults and failures in ourselves or others before we see anything else. We learn better by understanding what we want help with. And we learn to teach by helping others get the help they need.

It does no good to drip-feed or shower vague or empty positivity on those we want to help, teach, coach or lead, not least because it probably won't chime with what they feel is true. Self-esteem doesn't come from soft soap. It doesn't help to over-protect those we're keen to support or guide. On the contrary, effective help steers us towards tolerable, enjoyable ways to take up worthwhile challenges. Most of us sense when encouragement is bland or clichéd. The daughter of a friend of mine, Ellie, bewailed her lack of progress in art at school.

She summed it up by saying, 'I'm useless.' One of her parents said, 'You're not useless, darling.' Ellie groaned, 'But Luke is crap, and I'm crapper than him!'

Outstanding teachers, coaches and leaders prompt us to identify how well our methods fulfil our intentions and then be ready to amend them. Instead of being given a direct answer, we can be asked 'How will you find that out?' Instead of being given a fact as an answer, we can be shown how one example illustrates a pattern and be encouraged to 'Find more examples'. When we think 'I've got it', we can be asked 'How else can you tackle it?' or 'Can you do it as well as that again, or even better?'

We can be helped to be less certain, less insistent and more curious, hence keener to be thoughtful. We can learn to dig deeper than polarising questions ask us to. We can learn to appreciate diversity and complexity.

Virtual Learning

Recently, my wife and I went to the London consulate of a European country. We had an appointment relating to our requests for visas. We waited on the street in line until we were invited in.

Before we were allowed to step up to the glazed counter, we were told to put our piles of documents on a ledge, and an assistant began to look at them. Straightaway, she found our general medical practitioner's certificates to be stamped and signed but deficient: they lacked a Hague Apostille which, in our case, was the imprint of the UK's Foreign, Commonwealth and Development Office, authenticating the certificates. Neither the consulate's website nor the lawyer we consulted in the country we wanted to visit had indicated that our medical certificates required authentication. We were told we'd have to make fresh requests. There was no explanation or expression of regret. This was our feedback: 'You've failed.' We weren't invited to give feedback. It was a Kafkaesque experience[5].

A useful starting point for an improved service would be to ask, 'How can we help petitioners understand the process and feel they are being treated reasonably and fairly?' Using virtual-reality media could offer officials ways of exploring and developing their methods. But I'm not sure how interested the consulate would be in such things. I'm not sure whether they really want us to visit their country. In all the months we spent preparing our requests, we weren't given any sign that we'd be welcome. But, if you show you have invested £500,000 in the country, you don't need a visa.

The computer scientist, visual artist, computer philosophy writer, technologist, futurist, composer of contemporary classical music and co-inventor of virtual reality (VR) Jaron Lanier wrote (2017) and spoke (2021)[6] about how influenced we are by our artificial, imagined and virtual-reality experiences. VR creates the immersive impression of person-to-person presence and interactive, lived experience. It can be populated by 'avatars'—representing characters or embodied roles that communicate, walk and 'teleport' to any location. Used in training, business consulting and therapy, avatars have been found to be at least as plausible and beneficial as their real-life human counterparts.

In 'classic' immersive virtual reality, people don goggles and headphones and are transported to three-dimensional, sound-rich, even odoriferous worlds. They have the experience of being in the same room. Sharing the same space makes settings and experiences relatively easy for users, or 'travellers', to engage in and learn from. Even when the bounds of space are stretched to make the illusion of 'metaverse' settings, as in Linden Labs' *Second Life*[7], you have the same opportunity and invitation to make sense and use of where you are and who you're with. There is considerable scope for VR to enhance learning, training and assessment in every field and context of human endeavour.

Changing Attitudes and Behaviours

Lanier said, 'I have always found the very most valuable moment in virtual reality to be the moment when you take off your headset and your senses are refreshed and you perceive physicality afresh as if you were a new-born baby. With a little more experience you really notice how incredibly strange and delicate and peculiar and impossible the real world is.' He was confident that VR has the capability and potential to 'lead to a new level of communication between people: for instance, with simulations that embody feelings and sensibilities. There have also been experiments in filtering virtual worlds so that one gets a sense of what it's like to be dyslexic, colour-blind or face blind.'

Flat-screen avatar technology is now being used in a variety of ways. A potential manager or leader, for example, is placed in a virtual world with an avatar 'employee.' She or he is told she or he must get the employee to accomplish the task of putting a puzzle together to form a box. At some point the avatar sabotages the exercise, scattering the pieces. Attention can then be paid to finding ways to work with employees when they make mistakes—homing in on motivation, perseverance, lateral thinking and decision-making. The journalist, editor and member of the University of South California's Centre for Health Journalism Tori DeAngelis (March 2012)[8] wrote encouragingly about this. With her colleagues over the last 30 years, she has helped companies develop effective leaders and productive teams and contributed to psychologists' learning to use innovative media for the therapies, training and education they offer.

Relatively mundane purposes can also be well served by these technologies. A Microsoft gaming program called *Kinect* is now enabling users to create avatars that mirror their own looks, facial expressions and gestures. These technologies will keep growing. We all have a responsibility to take them in directions that contribute to understanding one another and working together better.

Advantages of these media and methods include that you can log on anywhere, making sessions flexible in location, duration, pace, focus and intended outcomes. There is evidence that you are likely to continue with virtual counselling longer than you would with conventional training or therapies. In an ongoing study of teenagers with substance-abuse problems, Dick Dillon—of the not-for-profit behavioural health-care company Preferred Family Healthcare, funded by the Missouri Foundation for Health—has discovered that young people who receive treatment in a secure, *Second Life*-type environment are twice as likely to stay in treatment than those in traditional programmes. Patients enter scenes resembling those that fuel and trigger their addiction—bars, gambling venues, family settings ... The fact that the experience is felt to be real provokes the emotions that replicate those that clients suffer from, and so allows them to freeze-frame, brainstorm alternative responses and experiment with 'refusal skills'. Other examples are in treating people with phobias, post-traumatic stress disorders, explosive anger, social anxiety and autism. The applications are countless.

As Lanier (2017)[9] wrote: 'Our fate rests on human traits that haven't yet been defined in scientific terms, such as common sense, kindness, rational thought and ingenuity. While the AI fantasy is that we'll be able to automate wisdom any minute, can we all at least agree that these qualities can for now only be *harnessed* by our systems? That they can't be *generated* as yet by our systems?'

Using New Technologies

The professor of education Maryanne Wolf (2018)[10] used a range of studies to explain how young learners can be helped to make healthy use of digital technology. She showed that children's interacting with digital devices tends to short-circuit 'the more time-demanding cognitive processes nurtured by print-based mediums ... such as critical thinking, personal reflection, imagination, and empathy'. In particular, they are seduced by the frequent changes of image and are prone to attention-flitting and task-switching. These conditioned responses disturb the kinds of slowing down, becoming immersed, being patient, focusing and monitoring that are characteristic of reflective, appreciative and evaluative reading, listening, feeling, thinking, discussion and experiment.

We humans have an evolutionary and involuntary reflex to notice whatever strikes us as new. An advantage of our 'novelty-bias' is that it prompts us to respond to diversity and changes in ourselves and in our environment. The more we play with what we imagine and see as new, the better we may solve problems and gain by opportunities and challenges. But there are downsides. The delight of a surprise overrules our prefrontal cortex which 'wants to stay on task and gain the rewards of sustained effort and attention'. Children with diagnosed attentional issues 'appeared less able to focus their attention on one task because they could not stop paying attention to all the other tasks'. Many adults have the same problem.

Memory too can be adversely affected: 'At the heart of both deep reading and cognitive development is the profoundly human capacity that allows children to use what they know as a basis for comparing and understanding new information to build ever more conceptually rich background knowledge'. The restlessness induced when we use a digital screen affects our learning, 'habituating us to ever faster and shorter units of thought and perception'. As a result, 'the convergence of more information and less time to process it may well pose the greatest threat to [our] development of attention and memory'.

We do well not to let children's or our own use of digital screens undermine the critical and reflective processes that are 'embodied in a fully elaborated reading brain'. Reading print and reading screens don't have to be at odds with one another. Each has its own value; at best, they're complementary.

Learning to Take Charge

The professor of educational technology Sugata Mitra's (2007)[11] *Hole in the Wall* project showed positive advantages in children's using digital technologies *for their own purposes*. Given stimuli and resources, learners created self-organised learning environments (SOLEs). Children and young people discovered a computer rather like an automated teller machine or hole-in-the-wall cash-dispenser in a patch of an area they frequented at Kalkaji, Delhi, India. They were able to use it at no cost, whenever and however they chose. Mitra's aim was to prove that children can learn computing by teaching themselves and one another. And they did.

Mitra's (2013)[12] *Build a School in the Cloud* project highlighted ways in which children and young people benefit from the company of grown-ups who don't necessarily know a great deal about what their tutees are doing, but who are appreciative and inquisitive. Each student has someone who is her or his personal Internet tutor, urging them forwards, saying 'Wow! How did you do that?' In this Minimally Invasive Education (MIE), learners benefited from roles models and moral support. Mitra showed how 'admiration rather than discipline drives the learning spiral', calling it 'the method of the grandmother'.

A benefit of screen-time is that it can provide the multiple reiterations that slow-developing readers need to develop their fluency, thereby diminishing the negativity they may experience with dyslexia or difficulties with controlling their attention. As Wolf (2018)[13] wrote, we should look for ways to help learners be selective when they use search engines, 'so as to see biases and attempts to influence opinion and/or consumption, and to recognise the potential for false, unsubstantiated information'. We should look for ways to help them know that, when we play some computer games, data about us is harvested and used to enable criminals and conspirators to send us false information, designed to divert us toward specific purchases, unfounded suspicions or political views.

How can we raise awareness that our use of digital devices carries risks of deception, manipulation and misinformation?

Toby Ord (2020)[14] warned, 'We need to learn how to align the goals of increasingly intelligent and autonomous machines with human interests, and we need to do so before those machines become more powerful than we are'. The professor of computer science Pedro Domingos (2018)[15] argued that technology is 'an extension of human capabilities. Machines do not have free will, only goals that we give them. It is the misuse of technology by people that we should be worried about, not a robot takeover'. He was optimistic that we can and will see technology from an ethical as well as a practical standpoint. He predicted we won't allow computers to run our lives or decide our future, and it's likelier that AI will bring about a 'proliferation of "digital doubles"—virtual models of ourselves that will interact with each other in countless simulations to help us make faster, more informed choices in our daily lives'.

Summing Up

We have to generate our own feedback by being self-critical *and* consider feedback we're given—then follow it up.

Highly effective teaching helps us pursue what we're curious about and interested in.

For learning to be shared across the whole group, there needs to be a feeling that everyone can has something to gain.

We can be helped to be less certain, less insistent and more curious.

---

[1] See Daniel Kahneman (2011), p 194ff.

[2] See Patrick Yarker's (2019) 'Another Way of Looking: Michael Armstrong's Writing for Forum', published in the journal *Forum for Comprehensive Education*. Go to doi: 10.15730/forum.2019.61.3. 453.

[3] See Adam Phillips' (1995) *Terrors and Experts*, published in London, UK, by Faber & Faber, pp xiv and 3.

[4] See Betty Jane Wagner's (1976) *Dorothy Heathcote: Drama as a Learning Medium*, published in Washington D. C., USA, by the National Education Association, available via https://files.eric.ed.gov/ fulltext/ED130362.pdf.

[5] See the parable contained in Franz Kafka's (1925) novel *Der Prozess* (The Trial), translated by Willa and Edwin Muir and published in London, UK, by Vintage Classics, also published in short story collections as *Vor dem Gesetz* (Before the Law).

[6] See Jaron Lanier's (2017) *Dawn of the New Everything: A Journey through Virtual Reality*, published in London, UK, by Random House Penguin, and (2021) *Virtual Reality, Social Media & the Future of Humans and AI*, available as Lex Fridman's Podcast #218 at website https://lexfridman.com/podcast.

[7] Second Life is an online platform that gives free access to avatars who pass through cyberspaces consisting of restaurants, college campuses, business settings, fantasylands...

[8] See Tori DeAngelis' (March 2012) *A second life for practice?* published by the American Psychological Association: https://www.apa.org/monitor/2012/03/avatars#.

[9] See Jaron Lanier (2017), p 336.

[10] See Maryanne Wolf's (2017, 2018) *Reader, Come Home: The Reading Brain in a Digital World*, published in New York, NY, by Harper. Also her (2017) *Proust and the Squid: The story and science of the reading brain*, published in New York, NY, by Harper Perennial, p 8.

[11] See Sugata Mitra's (2007) TED Talk *Hole in the Wall*.

[12] See Sugata Mitra's (2013) TED Talk *Build a School in the Cloud*.

[13] See Maryanne Wolf (2018), p 177.

[14] See Toby Ord (2020), p 29.

[15] See Pedro Domingos' (2018) 'AI will serve our species, not control it: Our digital doubles', published in *Scientific American*, 319, 3, pp 82-85. Also his (2015) *The Master Algorithm*, published in New York, NY, by Basic Books.

7 Knowing and Not Knowing

In this chapter we hear from Cailin O'Connor and James Owen Weatherall; John Keats; and David Wood, Jerome Bruner and Gail Ross, among others.

How do we make up our mind without then closing it?

Facts, Truths and Otherwise

Our first ways of knowing are via our senses: a bird is singing; I've got a headache; those people are angry ... We also come to know things because of what's commonly agreed or accepted as custom or law. Our most reliable knowledge leads us to understanding and is open to being modified: north is there; plants need particular nutrients; thousands of homes will be washed away when oceans rise by a certain number of centimetres ...

It is by sharing processes of trial and error that we develop expertise that includes learning to be respectful and compassionate as well as precise and critical[1]. Dependable facts and truths tend to be arrived at by intuition in the first instance, but then to be strengthened over time by hypothesis, deduction, systematic observation, experimental testing and rational argument[2].

Unlike beliefs, facts and truths are open to scrutiny and evaluation. The virtue of facts and truths is that they are tested and either verified or found wanting. They are communicated by diligent enquirers who show us how they've made their investigations and arrived at their conclusions. We have access to their date-stamped processes and statements—in universities, public record offices, museums, archives, libraries and online. This knowledge is a cultural good which helps us solve problems and live better, not because it has hallowed status but because we can all use it in relation to our needs and interests.

It takes time and effort to think carefully and afresh, but it only takes a blink of an eye to adopt a belief or swap one for another. The more we realise that we are helped by people whose statements are open to challenge and verification, the better placed we are to act in our own and all our interests.

We have to accept that no one knows everything, or anything, completely. We do well to be empathic and curious and work together, just as long as we don't ignore signs of imminent danger or potential threat.

We manage a good proportion of what we attempt without becoming self-conscious and by assuming we're working with facts and truths. We get the job done because our instincts and latent knowledge come up with enough of the goods and our taken-for-granted methods more or less pay off. If we put too much pressure on tacit skills and try to spell them out, they may freeze or evaporate. Much of the time, it's enough that we 'just know', which amounts to believing. The proof of the pudding is usually in the eating. To solve difficult problems we don't have to know or understand all the available, relevant facts, truths, patterns, principles, rules and laws.

It's possible to know and still not understand. Much depends on how open or closed we are to rethinking our objectives, methods and conclusions.

Learning by Playing and 'Playing the Game'

Playing tends to make activities enjoyable. And in many playful situations, if you feel you're not doing well enough, you have the luxury of trying again and/or seeking help. You can see that success depends on how well you interpret and apply conventions and possibilities. Learning comes with noticing what works and what doesn't.

Playing depends on your being humble. You are bound to accept the game's framework, or stop playing. Part of being humble is knowing you can't always win. Trusting the game is crucial to competing. Scientists, artists and academics can be as motivated as anyone in sport, business or politics to earn respect or be first to achieve something. If you couldn't lose, playing would be pointless.

A game only breaks down when people who are playing or watching say it's not being played properly. An example is when authorities or fellow players intervene to stop those who are cheating or bullying and behaving as though they were 'bigger than the game'. But some of us are so concerned to win, we rig the game or make up our own rules. Some of us are so upset by losing, we convince ourselves and try to convince others that we've been unfairly treated. Respect for the 'game' and diligent practice enable you to apply what you're learning in different situations. This includes looking for attributes and aptitudes that will help you in any challenge or enterprise—patience, precision, visualising and memorising, for example. But skill sets and knacks aren't panaceas. In recipe form they interrupt the flow of what you're doing and have to be engaged in when you're preparing, rehearsing or having time out to review progress.

Whether or not you're playing an actual game or 'playing the game', you come to know what to do and how to do it by picking up tips and snippets. 'Playing the game' helps you learn important things, not least because you're able to join in with what other people are doing and follow their example without having to call attention to yourself. And for many purposes you're good enough at playing the 'games' of speaking, computing, experimenting and much more besides. Much of the time, you don't think about rules but rely on what you trust everyone like you knows[3].

This has risks as well as benefits. Just as hearsay and prejudice may mislead and let you down, what you absorb through your culture sometimes brings you difficulties. The ideas and ways of thinking you inherit can be as much of a problem as they are a benefit[4]. For good and ill, your experience combines what you're unconsciously, involuntarily and incidentally aware of with what you choose to concentrate on, investigate and try out. If this weren't the case, we probably wouldn't have survived as a species. Our actions are neither wholly autonomic nor wholly autonomous.

The physical chemist, economist and philosopher Michael Polanyi (1958)[5] wrote about how most of us adopt largely unspoken rules: 'To learn by example is to submit to authority'—authority that allows us and wants us to play. If we take advantage of it, our learning includes 'a fund of personal knowledge via our traditions and systems, Common Law being the most important'. This is how we come to believe more than we can prove and to know more than we can say. Having tacit wisdom, though, doesn't mean we can't benefit from trying to deduce or explain patterns and principles.

You don't always know you're 'playing the game'; and you can be content enough doing what others are doing. This can happen when you're swayed by leaders, manipulators and adherents of networks who don't pass on information that conflicts with their beliefs or their wanting you to do what they want you to do.

Have there been occasions when you and others have gained by 'playing the game'—that is, by doing what was expected or required?

Have you chosen not to 'play the game'? Were you alone or did others also break with convention? What were your reasons? How did it go?

Being Open and Critical

On the one hand, everyone has a right to be heard. On the other hand, no one has a right to be listened to when what they say dismisses propositions that are transparently arrived at and designed to help us be healthy. We should not prevent anyone from expressing herself or himself, but we can choose not to listen to those who deal in wilful ignorance, paranoia, misinformation or criminal deception. We might also try to avoid having them as leaders, mentors, advisers, coaches, tutors or doctors.

When a person says she or he is giving a factual account of what she or he understands to be true, we should pay attention, unless we have contrary evidence, or see errors in her or his reasoning or have to accept she or he is being dishonest. What someone has said or done in the past shouldn't lead us to believe she or he isn't being factual or truthful now.

Politicians' onerous responsibility is to do their conscientious best on everyone's behalf, and we should remember they know and behave no better than many of us. There will always be those who find it expedient not to be accurate or truthful. When people act in bad faith, they damage public processes and civic life. In Shankar Vedantam's and Bill Mesler's[6] view the only people who 'have no need of lies' are 'happy, well-adjusted people whose lives are marked by good health, professional success and material comfort'.

The chemical manufacturing corporation DuPont can't have set out to poison people and animals, but it hid the facts and then lied. DuPont delayed and hindered efforts to get at the facts which included that using perfluorooctanoic acid (PFOA) to make Teflon has unforeseen and catastrophic side-effects. Teflon's key property of being non-stick relies on an agent that neither air, soil and water, nor human beings and animals, can break down. It causes cancers and birth defects[7]. So do oil pollution and toxic waste dumped between 1964 and 1992 in the Amazon River, but lawyers for Chevron and Texaco succeeded in defending their clients until in 2018 an international tribunal in The Hague found in favour of the tens of thousands of affected people.

Substantiated facts and truths give us the best chance of living well and positively influencing our future. Sadly, some of us see it as being in our interest not to be accurate and truthful. Sooner or later we cause harm when we're driven by mere tradition or convention, narrow-mindedness, selfishness, arrogance, greed, fear, delusion, anxiety, hysteria, narcissism, paranoia, mania, psychopathy, prejudice, dogma or ideology.

Criticality is a remedy against unwarranted conviction and unreliable knowledge: being critical, we understand that contexts of time, place and culture determine how valid and useful a claim or assertion is likely to be. When we're critical, we consider a range of diverse views and factors; we question what is taken for granted; we examine evidence and reasons for interpretations and conclusions. Instead of accepting unquestioning confidence, mystery or helplessness, we search further and check.

Making Up Your Mind

When you say you've made up your mind, it usually means you've come to trust something or someone. A kind of empathy or compassion is at the core of constructive thinking and fruitful decision-making.

You have implicit trust in many kinds of information which may come from your experience, your instinct, your eyes, your ears, a video-clip, text, report, book or film, a friend, a neighbour, a leader, an organisation, a brand name, reputation or the word on the street. Sometimes it doesn't matter to you where if comes from; you trust it because of what it tells you: its value to you is in its usefulness. Unfortunately, sometimes you choose to empathise with people and accept ideas that turn out not to be trustworthy. And sometimes you choose not to trust people and ideas that turn out to be vital to your health and long-term well-being.

Finding you trust a source, but not what it tells you, confirms what you might already know: that no one is always right. Trusting information but not its source challenges some of your prejudices, allegiances and assumptions about who or what is to be believed. Hard though it is sometimes to accept, you should know that facts and truths are bound to be part of cycles of knowing and not knowing. It is an awkward fact and truth that you can rely most on facts or truths that have been tested, applied and amended. (There's more about trust in chapter 7.)

For you and me to *know* the same reliable facts and truths, we need to have access to the same accurate sources or information, or for you to believe me or for me to believe you. But how can you and I arrive at the same *understanding*?

When we think we're talking about the same thing, we may still be seeing things differently. It's as if you're using drone cameras and binoculars and I'm using a divining rod and a microscope. We'll probably grow further apart, unless we recognise that our experiences, outlooks and approaches differ. It's useful to try taking one another's stance and way of looking. And this is the case for groups as much as it is for individuals.

To arrive at the same understanding, we may take the same or similar paths, arrive at the same or similar vantage points, make the same or compatible observations and experiments and come to similar insights and conclusions. Or each of us may take careful account of what the other understands by putting or imagining ourselves in one another's shoes. Or we may combine the two processes.

We are affected by the majority around us and/or by figures who are respected in our group or community and charismatic leaders. Increasing numbers of us are part of cultural trends that emerge from images, videos, fragments of text, information-feeds and social media. We're influenced by individuals and groups whose inadvertent, calculated or sociopathic power to influence opinions and understanding is magnified by the Internet. Conspiracy theories grow out of our choosing to believe and spread false, groundless, casual, fervent or malicious ideas designed to distract us or foment conflict.

Each of us can know about other people's thoughts, beliefs and intentions by noticing what they say and do. The closer we are to one another the better are our opportunities to check what we mean, but the more difficult it may be to question or doubt one another. At further and further removes from us, we find it increasingly difficult to grasp, retain and handle what other people mean[8].

We show that we have the same understanding when each of us accurately represents what the other knows *to the other's satisfaction*. All of this depends on each of us speaking in good faith. When we can't understand one another, it's possible that at least one of us is acting in bad faith. Then different rules have to apply—or the interaction has to break off until integrity is established or restored.

Opinions and Beliefs

Some information fails to appeal to us because our mental wavelength is too narrowly tuned. Some information arouses vehement convictions in us and/or triggers primitive defensive-aggressive responses. I have found that I am most dogmatic about things I know least about. Sometimes, we want so much to be on the 'right' side that we can't process information and ideas that deviate from what we believe or feel we ought to believe or feel. Sometimes we can't explain why we make the choices we make. When that is the case, we do well to pause, think and find out more.

Much of what we say is of little or no consequence. When we say sincerely that's 'a good meal' or 'a good person' or 'a good way of doing things', we express private, circumstantial truths, and other people may agree or disagree. But sometimes opinions lead to significant actions. We should know that opinions, like beliefs, are neither factual nor true and can't always be relied on.

If an opinion has important implications, it helps us to know what went into the forming of it. The doctor, playwright and short-story writer Anton Chekhov (1886)[9] wrote that 'There are a great many opinions in this world, and a good half of them are professed by people who have never been in trouble.' Remember Michio Kaku's (2021) observation (referred to in the 'Be Yourself, Helping Others' section of chapter 1), that we have to struggle to achieve anything meaningful and worthwhile. It's easier to accept a conspiracy theory that suits our prejudices and suspicions than it is to recognise our weaknesses and the complexities of our lives. We tend to be more comfortable criticising others than making our own suggestions.

Some leaders, experts, broadcasters and teachers assert opinions and beliefs as though they were truths. Some of us want everyone to have the same opinions and so do what we can to enforce would-be universal truths. Some of us really don't care what we believe or what anyone else believes, just as long as we are free to do as we please or we gain power and hold onto it. That is the case with narcissists and sociopathic leaders.

When we don't care what is or isn't accurate and true, public discourse falls apart, or becomes tyrannical and later falls apart. Ordinarily in a free society, we're entitled to have opinions and beliefs, but none of us has a right to have them listened to. The opinions and beliefs each of us holds affect us all because they help determine our actions, and what each of us does affects others. It's foolish to rely simply on what someone says or retweets; but some of us do. We also trust shortcuts, previously trusted sources, old habits and taken-for-granted, spur-of-the-moment judgements.

We live in and amidst networks of individuals who affect what we believe and the choices we make. The philosopher of biology and behavioural sciences and evolutionary game theorist Cailin O'Connor and the physicist, mathematician and philosopher James Weatherall (2019b)[10] asked, 'How do we come to believe something, and then act on it?' They proposed that what we end up doing is determined by a combination of what we need to decide and who or what we choose to believe and follow. Sadly, we sometimes rely on little more than casual adherence to things proposed by people we mistakenly choose to trust or sources we haven't thought to doubt.

At the time of my writing this, many of us have come to think or believe that Covid-19 vaccination is sufficiently safe and effective for us to accept and benefit from it. Others feel or believe it isn't, and a greater proportion of them become infected and go to hospital than those who trust the science.

If you are vaccinated and notice that nothing bad happens to you, you may conclude that vaccination is mostly safe and protective. Anti-vaxxers seem to trust what they learn through their community or preferred sources. They ignore or distrust medical research, accredited authorities and others who report the facts of their experience and research.

The more often you repeat your opinion and hear others repeat it, the stronger your conviction tends to grow. As a result, 'anti-vaxxers do not learn from the very people who are collecting the best evidence on the subject'; and 'where individuals do not trust evidence from those who hold very different beliefs, communities polarise and those with poor beliefs fail to learn better ones'. Blind suspicion, gullibility and tribal opposition harm us. They corrode trust, social order and public health.

Can you think of situations in which you are well advised *not* think for yourself?

Can you think of situations in which you are well advised *not* to take careful account of a range of views, including the most reputable?

Game Changing

If we only ever acted on what we've been told or what we've read, we'd have no mind of our own. But we humans can't help imagining, inferring, predicting, simulating and innovating. We have evolved to produce 'multiple models of reality' for ourselves. These cognitive moves encompass what is *no-longer*—in an infant's language 'all gone', hence irretrievable except in our minds; what is *not-yet*—expected, conceived or aimed for; and what is *not-really*—imagined or explored.

Brian Boyd (2010)[11] wrote that, to make the most of what we interpret and expect, our minds 'mine the present for clues [we] can refine with help from the past—the evolutionary past of the species, the cultural past of the population, and the experiential past of the individual—to anticipate the immediate future and guide action'. We connect the dots between the facts, myths, beliefs, opinions and rumours we've had access to. We make mistakes but, as Daniel Kahneman (2011)[12] noted, 'it's easier to recognise other people's mistakes than our own'.

We're likelier to adopt new ideas and new ways of doing things if they contain seeds and signs of what we already know and are used to. Most of us are challenged by radical departures from comfortable, customary ways of thinking and acting. For a while at least, revelations and revolutions tend to be controversial and unsettling[13]. The more significant a breakthrough is, the likelier it is to meet resistance. 'Paradigm shifts'[14] open up previously unthought-of understandings and practices. Upheavals of attitude and approach may be gentle, but the more significant a breakthrough is, the likelier it is that vested interests will resist and fight back—in academia, in society at large and close to home. It seems there are always individuals or groups who have something to lose when new ways of thinking and doing things come to light.

Competing paradigms offer choices of methods and outcomes and demand to be judged by divergent criteria or novel standards. They suggest more or less irreconcilable accounts and treatments of the way things seem to be and how they might go on to be. They have to gain acceptance to become commonplace. Richard Holmes (2009)[15] wrote that 'Science is truly a relay race, with each discovery handed on to the next generation. Even as one door is closing, another door is already being thrown open'. Sometimes, intolerable change is sidestepped: a new paradigm is rejected and we go back to 'normality', putting aside or suppressing disputes and schisms. But, if divergent and contrary testimony and evidence build up and take hold, a crisis is reached.

Yet new ideas and practices rarely eradicate every trace of what they replace. And when old paradigms fail to withstand emerging ones, they collapse and are subsumed along with stubborn discrepancies, ill-fitting methods and anomalous conclusions. This is another case of cognitive dissonance (referred to in the 'Voice and Mind' section of chapter 2): we have ways of holding onto ambiguous, diverging, discrepant and contradictory ideas.

Making New Connections

Looking back, it is as though new ways of thinking and doing things were bound to be as we've now accepted they are. Paradigms shifted with Galileo Galilei's observational astronomy; Isaac Newton's classical mechanics; Charles Darwin's proposition that all species descended from common ancestors; Marie Curie's theory of radioactivity; Albert Einstein's theory of relativity; Sigmund Freud's method for treating psychopathology; Rosalind Franklin's understanding of deoxyribonucleic acid (DNA), ribonucleic acid (NRA) and viruses; and Vera Rubin's work on the existence of dark matter. If you deviate from an accepted norm, you may be thought misguided and even be treated as 'other'—deviant, subversive or wicked. But this is how science and everyday life proceed. We change our ideas and practices by questioning, bending, altering and displacing paradigms.

Outsiders and newcomers may have a head-start when it comes to reframing thinking and ways of working. Perhaps their advantage is that they understand and accept they see things differently. Over 65 percent of Nobel Prize winners from the USA in recent decades have been immigrants. Matthew Syed (2019)[16] noted how, when we stay within one perspective or on a single topic, we may 'become prisoners of our paradigms. Stepping outside the walls, however, permits a new vantage point'; and 'when ideas are shared, the possibilities do not add up, they multiply'.

The entrepreneur, chairman and CEO of Netflix Reed Hastings and the author and professor at the INSEAD business school in Paris, France, Erin Meyer (2020)[17] wrote that 'In most organisations people join the dots the way that everyone else does and has always done. This preserves the *status quo*. But one day someone comes along and connects the dots in a different way, which leads to an entirely different understanding of the world'.

Just in case we're tempted to think that ground-breaking and game-changing are all innovators and originators ever do, Adam Grant (2016)[18] reminded us that 'Originals are *not* that different from the rest of us. They feel fear and doubt. They procrastinate. They have bad ideas. And sometimes it's not despite those qualities but because of them that they succeed'. His advice was that we should 'know that being quick to start and slow to finish can boost creativity'. We 'need a lot of bad ideas in order to get a few good ones', and can motivate ourselves 'by doubting our ideas and embracing the fear of failing to try'.

Being original is a considerable achievement. Game-changers must admit to themselves at least that they may not know but will find out and be inventive. If we're going to live a better, more sustainable, more harmonious life, we have to have doubts, confront our ignorance, and look again and elsewhere. Perhaps game-changers' and originals' crucial characteristic is that they have a self-reflective observer's heightened sense of what they imagine and do. More than the rest of us, they attend to and experiment with their intentions, methods and effects.

Not Knowing

Do you know people who are excited or motivated by not knowing or not understanding?

Do you know people who seem unwilling to recognise or admit they don't know or understand?

Not knowing is so uncomfortable for many of us that we transmit more readily or more often than we receive information. We blot out incoming information and stick to familiar ideas and stories. And we are poorly served by leaders and professionals who deny they sometimes don't know or understand.

It may be that high-achievers, or those with most power to lose, are most inclined to feel they lose face if they own up to gaps and problems in their thinking. We'd all become healthier and better democrats if we could say in truth, 'I'm receiving you loud and clear. Now, what more do we need to find out about this?'

We can't know for sure how elements in natural, social and technological situations will vary, or how variables will interact. We face much more complex challenges than our hunter-gatherer ancestors dealt with—with so much more changing at previously unimaginable speeds. We need reassurance and guidance.

In our everyday lives, as in science and politics, there can be shame, fear or despair in saying we don't know. Sometimes we're angry when it turns out that our leaders and representatives don't always know what's accurate or right. We feel impatient with scientists who tell us they're still working to find answers.

The epidemiologist Margot Gage Witvliet (2021)[19] explained how crucial it is for clinicians to understand they have biases and irregularities in their judgement-making. Their errors are sometimes to the detriment of women and people of colour. Over the course of a year, a series of doctors failed to diagnose Witvliet's Covid-19, even denying what was printed on the test packaging—that it is possible to have 'false negative' results. It seems they didn't trust what their patient said, repeatedly putting her severe breathing difficulties down to anxiety and saying her oximeter scores were wrong. It wasn't until she insisted she had a drug test and it showed she was 'clean' that, in her words, doctors started treating her with compassion.

How could people trained in sciences not have understood that, like the rest of us, they have to recognise their limitations and be ready to learn?

We may know that nothing is absolutely certain except for death and taxes[20], but we tend to hold fast to a default belief that everything will be all right in the end. Daniel Kahneman's (2011)[21] view about dyed-in-the-wool optimists is that the main benefit of emphasising the positive is that it can help us be resilient in the face of setbacks. Accepting that sometimes we just don't know gives rise to insights and ingenuity we don't call on when we're fully content with what we believe or hope is true. Accepting our own and others' not knowing or understanding is among the best predictors of our being able to explore, experiment and create.

The poet John Keats[22] wrote about this in a letter to his brothers George and Tom in 1817. His notion of 'negative capability', taken up by many writers and thinkers, refers to what we may achieve when we're 'capable of being in uncertainties, mysteries, doubts, without any irritable reaching after fact and reason'. It helps us to recognise that all fact, truth and reason eventually turns out to be incomplete.

The psychoanalyst Wilfred Bion[23] (born 1897, died 1979) thought it critical that we spend time in the discomfort and confusion of not knowing and not understanding. He saw the analyst's role as helping the analysand to live with uncertainty, for a while at least and periodically. With an open and critical mind, we can get beyond customs, orthodoxies and ready-made answers and solutions. When we don't admit to not knowing, we ignore the limits of what we do know, and that can be dangerous. If we don't own our not knowing, we stop asking the questions that will help us solve mundane and vital problems, survive and flourish.

Welcoming Uncertainty

Oliver Burkeman (2012)[24] praised our willingness 'to pause and take a step back; to turn to face what others might flee from; and to realise that the shortest apparent route to a positive mood is rarely a sure path to a more profound kind of happiness'. We can remind ourselves that all things change, then 'flash forward to catastrophe' and prepare for the worst.

Mistakenly, we sometimes try to overcome our doubts by 'committing harder' to goals or projects. Sadly, that may bring about what we least wanted. When we're at our most determined, it's helpful to ask: How can we be sure? What have we got as a back-up or exit? How ready are we to deal with disappointment and failure? How might we prepare for what we should accept is no more likely than possible?

Good intentions don't guarantee happy outcomes. To live well and plan for a better future, we must sometimes be unsettled. Often, our habits, routines and customs are what got us where we wish we weren't. Feeling vulnerable can trigger a resourceful response and be part of working towards better founded, more worthwhile possibilities and satisfactions.

Welcoming uncertainty is a feature of the philosophical tradition called pragmatism. It recommends we treat all things human and natural on a case-by-case basis, paying attention both to what is particular *and* to what is regular and repeated[25]. We need to understand that we make progress by pooling what we know *and* what we want to know more about.

Has it been useful for you to put up with feeing uncertain? If so, what helped you?

As individuals and groups we tend not to calculate risks as rationally as theory would have it, and what we do sometimes endangers us. There are advantages in seeing potentially separate fields of study as symbiotic and then combining them. When we build networks and cooperate across boundaries of locality, background, expertise, role, status and allegiance, we give ourselves a better chance of solving all sorts of problems.

How effective we are is determined by how we use our collective wisdom. We become confident, capable and proficient, not by slavishly or dutifully following patterns or paradigms, but by trialling and improving them. To do well, we require much more than being told what to do or being rehearsed in tasks we haven't identified as important to us. This applies whether we're learning, working or playing.

In every field of human endeavour, we learn by connecting what we're incidentally, involuntarily and unconsciously aware of with what we choose to concentrate on and try out. We learn by testing the authority and usefulness of our own and others' insights and expertise. We are creative when we challenge rules and conventions—not because we want to find eternal or absolute facts and truths, but because we want to understand better, feel better and do better.

Being Humble and Courageous

Sensing and making sense come before words. Iain McGilchrist (2010)[26] wrote about how 'Most thinking, like most communication, goes on without language… Language is not essential to communication or to thinking—and may interrupt or interfere with both'.

Language's contribution is to firm up particular ways of seeing the world and hold them still, for a while at least. Language supports consistency, but also restricts what and how we think. Culture and society take a leap forward when we find new frameworks for action and interaction. We don't have to be given instructions, or even be told very much at all, to improve what we do. Neither rules nor targets tell us in this moment how to play this game. We have sometimes to be self-reliant and inventive.

So it must have been with Leonardo da Vinci's drawings, Michelangelo's sculptures, and Johannes Vermeer's use of perspective and light; William Shakespeare's comedies and tragedies; and Johann Sebastian Bach's cantatas, fugues and variations. Likewise with the chess master Eugène Rousseau's gambit; the gymnast Olga Korbut's balletic style, back tuck and flip; and the footballer Johann Cruyff's turn. But, for all their creativity, none of them would have said that they had no need of anyone else's experiences and ideas.

Humility starts with recognising that our horizons are limited. The more important an activity is to us and to others, the more important it is to take advice and risks. We can emulate one another's example, test, bend, blend and breach rules and conventions, and so find out how to do things differently or better. We're helped by anyone willing to share what they understand, what they fear and what they hope for.

Unfortunately, we are as capable of passing on to one another irrational, groundless fears and conspiracy theories as we are capable of passing on worthwhile ideas and beneficial practices. The very instincts and traits that make us want to fit in also lead us to join unhealthy, destructive causes and campaigns. Further, many of us don't easily absorb technical, mathematical and statistical information. Changing our world for the better requires us to interpret and respond to data in ways that were unimaginable only a generation ago. We're helped by effective leadership and organisation. As Boyd (2010)[27] noted, we're also vitally helped by those who offer and exemplify 'the idea that the sciences, the humanities and the arts should connect with one another, so that science, especially the life sciences, can inform the humanities and the arts, and vice versa'. No single expert, no one discipline, no one perspective or approach, has a monopoly on accuracy, truth or effectiveness.

Ankhi Mukherjee (2018)[28] spoke about the example of interdisciplinary cooperation in medical humanities which combine 'statistical, epidemiological data with narratives, with literary and cultural representations, with key studies, with photo archives …' In these ways, lives are viewed and documented as 'a problem *and* a possibility'.

It takes courage and faith in our interdependence to welcome uncertainty, to leave well-trodden paths and make discoveries with people who are not traditionally our colleagues or allies. This was celebrated and promoted by the biologist Edward Wilson (1998)[29] and historically by schools or movements such as the 'pragmatism' of the philosopher Charles Sanders Peirce, the lawyer Oliver Wendell Holmes, the philosopher and psychologist William James, the philosopher, psychologist and educational reformer John Dewey and earlier by figures such as the philosopher, pedagogue and theologian Jan Amos Komenský, known now as Comenius (born 1592, died 1670).

Rising to Challenges

Karl Deisseroth (2021)[30] highlighted this paradox: 'the drives that support survival, in the end also drive extinction. Evolution creates intelligence that is unsuited for the world that intelligence, in turn, creates'. Human intelligence gives rise to forms of communication and technology that have the power to influence our behaviour in harmful as well as beneficial ways: our intelligence can be both humane and inhumane.

Humane intelligence draws on and develops our capacity for compassion, humility, imagination, courage, alertness, adaptability, ingenuity, integrity and rigour. It fulfils our wanting to express our true and better selves and so thrives on our meeting difficulties with a desire to serve the common good.

Whoever we are and whatever stage we're at, we're helped when there's a degree of challenge in what we take on and when coaches, mentors, tutors, advisers and friends help us overcome obstacles—without robbing us of initiative or task-ownership. Often, such individuals lead by having us lead them. The psychologists David Wood, Jerome Bruner and Gail Ross (1976)[31] found that, in the company of this kind of tutor, three- to five-year-old children learn to solve problems requiring physical and cognitive skills beyond their present capabilities. Someone who is available to us and intervenes with the intention of enabling us to learn for ourselves knows better than simply to tell us what to do. To learn and then do well is to attend to what we intend, observe what actually happens and then be ready to try alternatives. We become confident and capable by learning from experience and wanting to improve how we do things.

To solve a problem, we have to feel it's worth our time and effort. Finding things hard doesn't have to dishearten or disable us. The most effective, enduring support and guidance give us confidence to try what we're not sure we can manage. Our most successful tutors, coaches, mentors, therapists and advisers offer us a kind of scaffolding to help us clamber upwards. They get alongside us, play or work with us, respect and value our autonomy. They are interested in our learning to apply what we find out and so continue exploring and experimenting. The research by Lev Vygotsky (1978) and by Jerome Bruner's team showed that, with skilful and empathic support, our own interest-guided actions allow and prompt us to extend our skills and understanding *more quickly and more effectively* than we otherwise would.

Far from leaving us to learn for ourselves, this provision shrewdly moderates things we can't handle on our own, thereby enabling us to complete elements of tasks that we can manage. When we have a strong enough sense of what our problem-solving might do for us, we develop our skills and understanding on the spot and with a better chance of retaining gains we're making. Then we're glad to face challenges and try to match means to ends: 'it's this matching (and our correcting ourselves when mismatches arise) that is at the heart of problem solving'.

Efforts to promote learning are undermined when would-be friends, coaches, mentors, experts, therapists, managers or leaders behave as though 'telling, even detailed telling, is the most appropriate route to improvement'[32]. It takes experience and wisdom to realise this and avoid perpetuating that myth. One-way instruction doesn't help us connect what we know with what we're actually doing; nor does it allow our latent and incipient abilities to emerge. It's a truism, often tough to live by, that, whatever help we get, we have to learn by deciding things for ourselves. 'For ourselves' does not mean 'on our own'. This applies as much to getting through a tricky day as it does to finding ways to survive and thrive as communities and a species.

Being Helped to Learn

Fear, anxiety and wanting too much to please others can stop us trusting, but also make us trust too readily[33]. Adam Phillips (1990)[34] gave an illuminating account of methods used by Donald Winnicott to help children externalise and consider their anxieties, fears, hopes, wishes and intentions. It became his best-known diagnostic and therapeutic way of working.

First, the analyst quickly draws a twisted or wriggly line on a piece of paper, and leaves it with a collection of pencils for the child to discover when she or he comes into the consultation room. It's an invitation to the child to add elements to the drawing. The analyst may then draw some more, and the analyst and child may continue drawing and talking about it and about the feelings and thoughts that occur to them. They may comment to one another about its possible meanings. If the child chooses not to take up the invitation or wants to stop, the analyst accepts it and another tack is taken.

Winnicott's (1941)[35] view was that there's space between us to use in play, in problem-solving talk and interaction, where we can explore aspects of our own and one another's lives, and try out ideas for possible futures. By being together in this space we get 'outside ourselves'—a prerequisite for creative engagement with our world. It is how drama works as a medium for teaching and learning[36], allowing us to picture, simulate, enact and rehearse potential consequences of different actions, and so be better prepared to respond practically and morally to opportunities and challenges in 'the real world'.

It is an instinct and a habit of ours to explain what we come to understand by reaching for analogies, fables and parables. All stories—spoken, heard, written, read, improvised, enacted and witnessed—are versions of and metaphors for things. Iain McGilchrist (2010)[37] saw it like this: 'Metaphoric thinking is fundamental to our understanding of the world, because it is the *only* way in which understanding can reach outside the system of signs to life itself... Everything has to be expressed in terms of something else, and those something elses eventually have to come back to the body'. And this is as true of mathematics and the sciences as it is of the arts, humanities and technologies.

The mathematics teacher and education researcher Maulfry Worthington (2008)[38] has shown that, given the opportunity and careful guidance, young children use scribbles, drawings, writing, iconic marks and symbols—some spontaneously invented and others borrowed from conventions—to express or represent what they work out, for example, in terms of quantities, sizes and distances. It's difficult for them to derive deep understanding of written numbers and measurements if all they do is follow prescribed methods or copy examples: 'Using their own graphics to support their mathematical thinking builds on what they already know and can do and helps their development towards the standard, abstract written language of mathematics'. This recalls William Labov's advising that we engage with one another's ways of speaking and thinking, rather than imposing our own (referred to in chapter 5's 'Learning at School and at Work' section).

Worthington's is an example of the most effective kinds of leadership, coaching, mentoring and therapy that help us pursue our intentions by learning for ourselves—with and from others. We keep learning by being helped to play, tell stories, share ideas, experiment, invent, cooperate and find our own sense and paths.

Summing up

We do well to be empathic and curious and work with others, just as long as we don't ignore signs of imminent danger or potential threat.

Healthy trust and sound understanding sponsor uncertainty, surprise and spontaneity which are sources of genuine confidence.

We become confident, and capable by learning from experience and wanting to improve how we do things.

We learn best and most naturally by playing, telling stories, sharing ideas, experimenting, inventing, and cooperating, all the while finding our own sense and paths.

---

[1] See the philosopher, academic and social commentator Karl Popper's (1962) *Conjectures and Refutations: The Growth of Scientific Knowledge*, published in London, UK, by Routledge.

[2] See the work of the philosopher Charles Sanders Peirce (1992) in *The Essential Peirce*, edited by N. Houser, C. Kloesel and the Peirce Edition Project, published in Bloomington, IN, by Indiana University Press. For a useful introduction, see the social and political theorist and philosopher W. B. Gallie's (1952) book *Peirce and Pragmatism*, published in Harmondsworth, UK, by Penguin.

[3] See the philosopher and teacher David Egan's (2019) *The Pursuit of an Authentic Philosophy: Wittgenstein, Heidegger, and the Everyday*, published in Oxford, UK, by Oxford University Press, concerning Ludwig Wittgenstein's (1953) metaphor of game-playing. See also the biographer and philosopher Ray Monk's (1991) *Ludwig Wittgenstein: The Duty of Genius*, published in London, UK, by Vintage, 1991, and his article (15 September 2021) 'Ludwig Wittgenstein: a mind on fire' in the New Statesman, and at https://www.newstatesman.com/culture/ books/2021/09/ludwig-wittgenstein-a-mind-on-fire. According to Monk, Wittgenstein thought that 'Philosophers want to impose a single form on a multitude of phenomena; they want to … find the "essence" of a concept', but what philosophers should do is 'accept the irreducible variety of language. Instead of trying to identify its formal structure, they should look at how it is interwoven in our *practices*.'

[4] See Karl Popper's (1945) *The Open Society and Its Enemies*, published in London, UK, by Routledge & Kegan Paul, Routledge Classics, p 510: 'almost all the problems as well as the (non-authoritative) sources of our thought are rooted in traditions'.

[5] See Michael Polanyi (1958) (referred to in chapter 5 and later in this chapter), pp vii-viii, 3, 15-17, 27-28 and 53-54. This connects with Iain McGilchrist's (2010) picture of the expert having knowledge that the faithful servant can take on and convey to others.

[6] See Shankar Vedantam and Bill Mesler (2021), p 22.

[7] See the film (2019) *Dark Waters*, directed by Todd Haynes and written by Mario Correa and Matthew Michael Carnahan. Also the film (2000) *Erin Brockovich*, directed by Steven Soderbergh and written by Susannah Grant.

[8] See the concept of intentionality, explained by Robin Dunbar (2016) and mentioned here in the 'Becoming Inclusive' section of chapter 3.

[9] See Anton Chekhov's (1886) short story *At the Mill* in *The Short Stories of Anton Chekhov: A Comprehensive Collection*, published in New York, NY: Random House (The Modern Library).

[10] See Cailin O'Connor's and James Weatherall's (2019b) 'Why We Trust Lies: The most effective misinformation starts with seeds of truth', published in *Scientific American*, 321, 3, pp 48-55. The article reflected their (2019a) *The Misinformation Age: How False Beliefs Spread*, published in New Haven, CT, by the Yale University Press.

[11] See Brian Boyd (2010), p 134.

[12] See Daniel Kahneman (2011), p 28.

[13] See Karl Popper (1945), p 510.

[14] See the philosopher of science Thomas Kuhn's (1962) *The Structure of Scientific Revolutions*, published in Chicago, IL, by the University of Chicago Press, pp 24-25.

[15] See Richard Holmes (2009), p 468.

[16] See Matthew Syed (2019), pp 134, 50 and 269ff. The phenomenon of our 'being different' is a topic explored in Erving Goffman (1963), referred to in chapter 3's footnote 24.

[17] See Reed Hastings' and Erin Meyer's (2020) *No Rules Rules: Netflix and the Culture of Reinvention*, published in London, UK, by WH Allen/Ebury Publishing/Penguin Random House, p 24.

[18] See Adam Grant's (2016) TED Talk *The Surprising Habits of Original Thinkers*. Also his (2021) *Think Again: The Power of Knowing What You Don't Know*, published in London, UK, by Penguin Random House.

[19] See Margot Gage Witvliet's (19 May 2021) TEDx Talk *I've had Covid-19 for a year. Here's what I've learned*. Like Witvliet, the adventurer, writer and speaker Gail Muller documented her experience of not being properly diagnosed: see her (2021) memoir *Unlost: A journey of self-discovery and the healing power of the wild outdoors*, published by Thread.

[20] In 1789, the year of the French Revolution, the writer, political philosopher, scientist, inventor, statesman and diplomat Benjamin Franklin wrote in a letter to a friend 'Nothing is certain except death and taxes'.

[21] See Daniel Kahneman (2011), p 263.

[22] See *Life, Letters, and Literary Remains of John Keats* (1848), edited by Richard Monckton Milnes and published in 2013 by Cambridge University Press. The letter referring to negative capability was written on 22 December 1818.

[23] In their book *The Clinical Thinking of Wilfred Bion*, published in London, UK, by Routledge, the psychoanalysts Joan and Neville Symington (1996) wrote about Bion's use of John Keats' concept.

[24] See Oliver Burkeman (2012), pp 208 and 210.

[25] In his *The Metaphysical Club: A Story of Ideas in America*, published in New York, NY, by Farrar, Straus and Giroux, Louis Menand (2002) gave a Pulitzer-Prize-winning account of pragmatism, mentioned chapter 9's 'Wanting' section.

[26] See Iain McGilchrist (2010), pp 107 and 110. These ideas of his are close to those of the late teacher educator and mathematician Bill Brookes who, from 1985 to 1990, supervised my PhD studies at Southampton University.

[27] See Brian Boyd (2010), pp 334-335.

[28] See Ankhi Mukherjee (2018).

[29] See Edward Wilson's (1998, 1999) *Consilience: The Unity of Knowledge* published in New York, NY, by Vintage.

[30] See Karl Deisseroth (2021), p 211.

[31] See David Wood's, Jerome Bruner's and Lee Ross' (1976) 'The Role of Tutoring in Problem Solving', published in the *Journal of Child Psychiatry and Psychology*, 17, pp 89-100, and available via https://dx.doi.org/10.1111/j.1469-7610.1976.tb00381.x. They coined the term 'scaffolding' as a metaphor for an approach to tutoring that enables learners to develop their skills and understanding rapidly without robbing them of task-ownership and initiative. Their work built on Jerome Bruner's (1973) article 'Organisation of early skilled action', published in *Child Development*, 44, pp 92-96.

[32] See the researcher in assessment of learning in higher education Royce Sadler's (1989) 'Formative assessment and the design of instructional systems', published in *Instructional Science*, 18, pp 119-44.

[33] See Adam Phillips (1995), p 59.

[34] Adam Phillips' (1988) *Winnicott* gave an illuminating account of Donald Winnicott's methods.

[35] See Donald Winnicott's (1941) 'The observation of infants in a set situation', published in *International Journal of Psycho-Analysis*, 22, 229-249. Also his (1965, 2018) *The Maturational Processes and the Facilitating Environment: Studies in the*

Theory of Emotional Development, published in Abingdon, UK, by Routledge. His approach has much in common with Fred Rogers' (born 1928, died 2003) whose pre-school television series ran from 1968 to 2001 and is the subject of the 2019 Sony Pictures film *A Beautiful Day In the Neighbourhood*, directed by Marielle Heller, written by Micah Fitzerman-Blue and Noah Harpster, and inspired by the 1998 article 'Can You Say ... Hero?' by Tom Junod, published in *Esquire* magazine.

[36] See Betty Jane Wagner (1976), referred to here in the 'Self-Reliance, Cooperation' section of chapter 6.

[37] See Iain McGilchrist (2010), pp 115, 116 and 118.

[38] See Maulfry Worthington's (2008a) *Children's Mathematical Graphics: Overview*, available via http://www.childrens-mathematics.org/overview.pdf, and (2008b) *Effective modelling for early written mathematics,* available via www.childrens-mathematics.net/pedagogy_modelling.pdf.

8 Trusting

In this chapter we hear from Atul Gawande, among others previously referred to.

> Why is trust important and how does it work?

What It Means to Trust

When we trust, we accept or understand something and so feel reassured and connected. Some of us trust science. Others of us trust fate, divine power, group identity, mythology, ideology… Deciding what and whom to trust is one of the most important things we do.

Trust helps us frame and pursue intentions. Our intentions may not always be benign and constructive. When our intentions are aligned with how we truly feel about ourselves, we can act in good faith, and other people have good reason to trust and respect us. When other people's intentions are aligned with how they truly feel about themselves, they can act in good faith and we have good reason to understand and trust and respect them.

Trust between people is rooted in mutual understanding. When we lack trust or respect, we're thrown back on ourselves as unconnected individuals or groups. Trust and respect are tested, verified or found wanting according to how we treat one another. We can't expect to be trusted or respected if we betray the assurances we give or the confidence that others place in us.

For many reasons, we can't safely trust one another always to mean well and do the right thing. If we didn't become uncertain, we couldn't find or regain confidence. If promises couldn't be broken and trust couldn't be doubted and betrayed, there'd be no risk, regret, forgiveness, reconciliation or reparation.

Recovering from lost confidence and broken promises can lead us to revive and strengthen kindness and mutual respect.

Sadly, we can be mistaken, for example, when we're feeling low, when we're biased by collective euphoria or ideology, when we're beguiled or deceived, or at 2 o'clock in the morning. Whether we're family or friends, neighbours or strangers, workers or managers, traders, renters or owners, borrowers or lenders, artists, scientists, business people, public servants or citizens, sometimes we choose to trust someone or something that we'd do better not to trust.

Living with Uncertainty

Trust is an emotion you bestow or accept and then, when it's reciprocated, you co-construct. It is accompanied by a surge of the hormone oxytocin[1]. Your brain's limbic system has a bearing on this. Your 'default state is to trust' and so to join others in beliefs and actions. Opposing this, the amygdala injects 'vigilance and distrust' into your decision-making and puts a brake on instinctive and mutual openness[2]. At any given moment it might be right to trust, or it might be right to hesitate and check. Either way, the chances of things turning out well are stronger when, as part of your developing and testing trust and cooperation, you consider evidence for the pros and cons of your options. You have work to do to find even temporary certainty.

Adam Phillips (2021)[3] saw that being converted to a belief gives you what 'you need to know to get the life you want, the life you want being the life in which you change according to your wishes'. But, if the life you wish for is a life that enables you to know everything you need and are permitted to know, you might accept conversion to totalitarianism. When all you have to do is be and do what you're told to be and do,-you give up your freedom and right to decide what and whom to trust. Then, you can't learn for yourself and this prevents you from being the person you might be.

If you let go the fantasy of always being certain, you realise that you're changing—sometimes beneficially, sometimes not. Other people show you they change. Another way of expressing this is that cultures are provisional, like fashions and trends, but on a larger scale: they offer answers and prospects which can be no better than valid in certain contexts. There are no guarantees in what we do.

As Phillips put it, 'Everyone is in pursuit of the good but no one can agree about what the good is'. So, the best we can do is compare our ways of feeling and thinking, and experiment with ideas and practices: we must keep searching, questioning and challenging one another. These are remedies against passivity, laziness, mistrust, paranoia and sleepwalking onto quicksand or over a precipice. To live well, we have to find ways to 'become more able and willing to consider and discuss and create the kind of change we would like, the kind of change that we realise we need in order to get the lives we want'. Looking back on our difficult experiences can help us 'resist the temptation to get back to normal', because we may 'see more clearly what normality has involved us in'. We should know that what is normal doesn't always serve us well.

A healthy culture conveys the idea that none of us knows anything for certain or for ever, but we help ourselves by being confident enough to say what we feel and think *and* by finding out what other people feel and think. We must expect to face social, technological, ethical and political problems to which there are no single, right, tried and tested, universal or final solutions.

However much we trust a source of information, we do well to test and try to improve what it proposes. We do well to develop intelligence that's accessible to everyone. We do well also to avoid authority based on mere status or brute power[4]. This gives us a good chance that we'll promote intelligence that is humane in its aims and methods. Given positive and constructive intentions, the pragmatic, safest option is to safeguard ourselves, to question and try to improve the information we have, to rely on ourselves collectively and keep working to promote, extend and deepen trust, respect and understanding between us.

Spontaneous and Tacit cooperation

In Eastern Europe particularly, but elsewhere too, when the music stops at the end of a concert or entertainment and everyone begins to applaud, the clapping has no pattern. Then soon, the audience seems to develop a single mind. The science writer Philip Ball (2005)[5] described it like this.

Clapping becomes spontaneously synchronised for a while, and then reverts to being unsynchronised. It goes on oscillating between the two, until something else happens, such as an encore, or it's time to go home. Synchronised applause is quieter than unsynchronised applause, and, because happy concert-goers want to make more noise, they intermittently abandon their rhythmic unison and revert to a free-for-all. It seems to be a collective instinct. No one knows quite when or how synchronisation will break out or break up. The vigour-volume fluctuation resolves tensions felt between the appeal of acting in unison and wanting more individual expression.

This points to how unconscious decision-making can be shared, and to how vital cohesion can be and how it depends on individual autonomy. Coordinated action depends on individuals' wanting to unite—without diluting or abandoning their unique identities. Chanting is another example and shows how similar crowd and ritualistic or religious behaviours are.

Spontaneously synchronised applause is a case of instinctive cooperation. It depends on trust which expresses and supports alternating structural stasis and dynamic responsiveness. (This is a feature of homeostasis and allostasis, mentioned in the 'Balancing Body and Mind' section of chapter 2. It is also a feature of affirmative sociability, explored in the 'Working with Nature' section of chapter 11.) Dancing, musical performance, military, theatrical and athletic displays and mass demonstrations may also be examples, but often also have elements of conscious planning and rehearsal.

Unison breaks down when enough people realise something has changed or gone wrong and/or they want to be elsewhere doing something else. Instinctive coordination can't be forced, though it may be orchestrated. We tune into it. It lasts for as long as everyone present wants it to. Trust is like that too, but we can sustain and strengthen it by thinking about what we're doing, checking our mutual understanding and wanting to share what we learn. It is a model for the kinds of collective decision-making and action that are required to save our planet.

The Vagaries of Trust

Though many of our relationships and attempts at cooperating are spontaneous and tacit, they aren't all gratifying and successful. One partner or group can be trusting and another mistrustful. Mistrust and disrespect can be mutual, and, for as long as that's the case, there is no fulfilling relationship, no agreement and no effective working together. Our trust and mistrust may alternate, which is uncomfortable or unbearable. We may be sorry we distrust someone or a group—sorry for the offence we cause, or sorry for the opportunities we miss out on.

Have you known relationships in which trust and mistrust alternated?

If resolution was found, what helped that happen?

Trust isn't betrayed if someone or a group makes a genuine mistake. Thoughtful, informed and sincerely intended decisions and actions aren't to be condemned when they fall short or fail. We must understand that no one can be trusted never to falter, always to prosper. Religious and political leaders, successful sporting coaches, Nobel Prize winners and the people we most admire and love get things wrong. We all do.

If every scientist and academic were brought to book for their errors, there'd be no science or academic study. The same is true for military, business and community leaders, union officials, lawyers, doctors, inventors, pioneers, civil and public servants, in fact anyone who takes an initiative or responsibility.

Imagine we act in good faith, but things don't go as we intended or hoped. That doesn't have to mean we were negligent, incompetent or deceitful. If we're pilloried, we can try to say we acted with proper regard for what we understood to be the facts and in line with conscientious advice. We may have nothing to be sorry for except that we made mistakes and were unsuccessful. And we can be thankful when others accept that getting things wrong isn't wrong-doing.

Flawed performance isn't always dishonest, self-serving or malicious. We must expect others to make mistakes and fall short or fail, just as we do. This is something rival political parties would do well to remember. If we lose trust in those who make mistakes, we can trust no one—not even ourselves.

Is that the society you want?

Under those conditions, is society even possible?

A Way to Understand One Another

Hearsay and rumour aren't reliable. We take a risk if there's no clear, positive, objective evidence or reason to trust an individual, a group, situation or source. For us to benefit from trusting and working together, we have to be candid about what matters to us. We have to temper our antipathies and calm internal conflicts. Just as adversity is a spur to our physical and psychological development, and just as courage helps us to take warranted risks, so does inhibition play a vital part in social enterprises that depend on people's sinking their differences and working together.

Phillips (2013)[6] explained an aspect of this as follows. Our inhibitions can be constructive, allowing us to be 'self-preservative: conservative not innovative', helping us to choose 'safety in preference to transgressive excitement' and protecting us from danger and exhaustion. The keys are getting alongside one another, learning what each of us feels and thinks, finding ways to agree what to do and then acting accordingly.

We come to understand one another by sensing and imagining what each of us is driving at, which amounts to realising what questions we're answering and what questions we'd like answers to. When I say, 'I like apples', I answer the question 'What fruit do you like?' or 'How do you feel about apples?' When you say, 'We're going to do this', you answer the question 'What's to be done?' or 'Who's going to do this?' When they say, 'We're not sure about these new components,' they may want to know 'What are these for?' or 'How do these work?' And so on. It helps us to know that—with everyone's good will—we can put forward our needs, wants and suggestions and that we'll be responded to.

In everyday conversation, we may or we may not encourage one another to express our wishes, doubts and suggestions. 'Thought-tracking' is a drama-in-education convention[7] which allows us to explore what is left unsaid: we can pause the action and ask characters to voice their inner feelings and thoughts. We can do something similar in debates, asking speakers to check what's being proposed. It's by grasping one another's presuppositions and puzzlements that we come to understand one another better. This enables us all to merge our subjective worlds and share objective worlds—essential to our making scientific, social and political progress.

Blind Trust

Feeling at one with many other people sometimes makes us daring: we climb over the top and rush at an enemy; we shout or post things we wouldn't say to an individual's face; we pledge allegiance to symbols and pull down statues. Anonymity or mass euphoria may provide momentary or momentous feelings of identity and solidarity.

The Internet can facilitate our holding onto unhelpful frames of mind. Matthew Syed (2019)[8] described research which showed how neither hearing opponents' views nor having access to a range of sources moves us away from extreme positions or towards more nuanced in thinking; rather, our views tend to become even more polarised.

Our default option is to trust views we already hold: 'Alternative views are dismissed not after consideration, but on contact. Facts are rejected even as they are offered. Perspectives and evidence are repelled somewhat like a magnetic field repelling iron filings'. And, whatever our politics or beliefs, we are affected by individuals' or groups' being systematically undermined or vilified. This is what information manipulators, propagandists and authoritarian regimes promote and thrive on. Unscrupulous people and organisations prey on our susceptibilities and vulnerabilities.

Have you been badly misled by harmful one-sidedness?

Do you know other people who have suffered from seeing things from a single, narrow perspective?

The intention of those who operate Internet platforms seems to be to maximise the volume of clicks or hits we make on digital devices, so that advertising, sponsorship and sales revenues can be kept as high as possible. They do not necessarily set out to undermine public confidence. High visibility and profitability take precedence over the side-effects on people. This is reinforced and exacerbated by the algorithms and programmes that feed us with pop-ups, messages and postings relating to our history of browser searches and the websites we visit.

We may not realise this locks us into an echo chamber. Unless we take control of our digital devices—and how many of us know how to do that?—we become immersed in information we haven't asked for. Then, though we may feel we're increasingly well-informed, our small world shrinks further. We might be relaxed about this automated surveillance and conditioning because we value instant news and choices, delivered in a style we're used to, expressing opinions we get used to skipping over or accepting without thinking.

We forget we don't know who or what is sending us material calculated to suit our tastes and habits. We have an illusion of choosing, but our control of what we experience is partial and eroding. It takes determined efforts of self-assertion, critical enquiry, responsible governance, effective regulation and re-education to counteract this subversion.

Trust as Certainty

Trust can't be for ever, unchanging. It has to be renewed as something made and felt between us. We take it for granted or become complacent about it at our peril.

Shankar Vedantam and Bill Mesler (2021)[9] described three ways in which we experience a form of trust beyond our purely subjective, autonomous selves, beyond one-to-one relationships, beyond our close groups and beyond the making of specific contracts. The three ways are ritual, nationhood and religion: 'powerful drives that human beings possess to act in the service of things greater than themselves'. We may not want to realise that these are not guaranteed to be objective, valid or reliable. Their function is to give us enough certainty to fulfil commitments, though in the long run they may bring us hardship and suffering as well as intended or incidental benefits. Righteous causes and principles give us energy, focus and strength.

According to Vedantam and Mesler, rituals make use of synchronised, repetitive movements which reinforce group cohesion, as in the case of concert audience applause, just mentioned. Chanting, purifying and purging have similar features and effects. And a 'certain level of commitment and complexity is needed for a ritual to be psychologically and socially effective. This may be why rituals often seem to become more effective as the burdens they place on participants become more intense'.

About nationhood, Vedantam and Mesler wrote that populations are united when they link their personal and social identities with their native territory and history and commit to making a better future for generations to come. It is often seen in newly born nations or when nations are threatened with occupation or annihilation.

About religion, Vedantam and Mesler wrote that we humans have adapted to knowing or fearing that we are mortal 'by turning to a variety of mental defences, some of which involve invocations of supernatural forces'. Some religions personify their power in the form of ethereal, immortal gods. The neuroscientist V. S. Ramachandran (1996)[10] suggested we convince ourselves of something we have no proof of as a 'psychological defence mechanism … a coping strategy'. In this state of belief, we usually feel we don't need proof: conviction is all, giving us confidence, identity, solidarity and vocation to ward off doubts and fears.

Writers and film-makers have imagined worlds designed to be perfect, where truths are imposed by single, would-be all-powerful authorities, and where there is no spontaneous trust, hence no doubt and no debate. In his novel *Brave New World*, Aldous Huxley (1932) wrote about the eradication of error through technologies affecting human conception and reproduction, reinforced by brainwashing and indoctrination. In his novel *Fahrenheit 451*, Ray Bradbury (1953) invented a future society reminiscent of the McCarthy era in the USA from the late 1940s to the mid-1950s, when accusations of subversion and treason were made without regard for evidence. And George Orwell's (1962) novel *1984* gave a dystopian vision of citizens' 'thoughtcrime' and the sole, official, universal 'truth' of 'newspeak'.

Your Part in Politics

If politicians deny they have options, or if it's clear they act in bad faith, it doesn't make sense to vote for them or support them. If politicians implement policies you think misguided and you are free to express yourself, you can argue for alternatives. If politicians fail with their misguided policies and their actions do no harm or inadvertently do good, you can rejoice. If politicians fail with policies you approve of, you can try to find out why they fail and do what you can to help them work better in future.

When you judge politicians, you must weigh the evidence and your conscience. Suppose an individual or group shows interest in forming a partnership with you even though there's little or no trust between you. They might already have betrayed your trust or other people's. Their ways of thinking and behaving might be difficult for you to evaluate or stomach. They might feel the same about you. But suppose they have experiences, qualities or resources you could benefit from.

Can you be polite and watchful?

Can you ask them what they hope for?

Can you ask them what they fear?

If you're not sure that you trust them or that they trust you, you may have to let time pass and, in the meantime, seek opportunities elsewhere. The prospects of working together improve as confidence grows and mutuality and reciprocity develop.

Having values that differ from another person's or group's is not an absolute reason to withhold trust from them, unless their values are chaotic or pernicious and go against common decency and humanity. When you disagree with the values that are expressed by an individual's or a group's intentions and actions, and if you're free to do this, you may debate with them. You may ask questions to help you understand how they came by their views and preferences. You may explain yours. You may look for ground you and they can share. When it's essential you act, the pressure is on to find the most amenable compromise and consensus. Of course, it can happen that events turn out badly, even when all or the majority agree about what has to be done.

Do you know a better way?

Some societies base themselves on a belief that a special person or group of people has to decide for everyone else what is right. This book supports an opposite view: the wisest leaders and politicians appreciate they have to earn their people's trust and so are judged according to what they make happen, let happen and prevent from happening. The Prime Minister of Barbados Mia Mottley referred to this when she spoke in Glasgow, Scotland, on behalf of many of her fellows at COP26, the United Nations' 26th Conference of the Parties climate summit in 2021. She said that people across the world were watching, listening and wanting to see good results from the well-intentioned deliberations.

Trust in Decision-Making

One morning, I was at my desk in a large open-plan office in our organisation's headquarters. One of my bosses phoned me from his office 50 metres away on the same floor.

He said, 'I understand you had a meeting set up tomorrow with Sue and Rob.'

'Pardon?'

'I've cancelled it.'

'But it's a meeting for us to discuss a possible project between our teams.'

'Well, it's not going ahead.'

'No one has ever before said I can't meet colleagues to talk about our work.'

'I'm doing that now.'

'I don't understand.'

'There's nothing for you to understand.'

'That must mean you don't trust our teams to explore a promising topic.'

There was a silence. Then he said, 'That's the way it is.'

'That's really serious. We need to resolve this.'

'There's nothing more to be said.' He rang off.

That account presents me as cooler than I actually was. I vented frustration and outrage. When I put the phone down, there was an uncomfortable silence.

I thought I'd better set about finding another job. Perhaps that was what I was meant to think.

Should I have taken the matter to my boss' superior? What might he have said or done?

What might you have done in my place?

When do we opt out? When do we argue or protest?

We may be so opposed to a person's or group's values, ideas and action that we conclude we can't live or work with them, and we would rather they weren't responsible for anything to do with us. In a democracy, our options are to:

> Disagree and voice dissent
>
> Elect and support people whose values are as close to or compatible with ours as any we can find
>
> Stand for election.

Something to avoid is being offended or angry that others don't see things as we do.

Disagreement and dissent do not have to be failures. Agreement and concord are not what we should aim for above all else. Enquiry and discussion are essential to our decision-making, but needing too much to agree can lead us away from enquiry and discussion. Our goal is ideally to do what we have sound reasons to trust is good for us all.

We take decisions as individuals, as groups and as organisations. Many factors affect us—psychological, emotional, social, cultural, moral, economic and political. Few of us consistently apply scientific, statistical principles and methods when we consider probabilities and possibilities. This is especially apparent when we compare decisions we make with the decisions that classical or behavioural economics might recommend. We aren't beyond hope or help. There have been many changes in policies and projects that have introduced vital measures to protect and conserve our environment[11].

Trust and Authority

Sometimes, authority is embedded in a non-negotiable hierarchy. Sometimes by contrast, authority comes from recognising people's diverse experiences and merits. Sometimes, it's a mixture of the two. And wherever it comes from, authority may or may not be wisely used. Sometimes, there are enough people in a community or enterprise who value or fear authority so much that they won't challenge it.

Unless authority is exercised in such a way that it is shared, the experiences, insights and energies of most of the group or population are likely to be lost. When that happens, trust is lost too. Some organisations deliberately foster freedom and cooperation so that trust and responsibilities are felt by everyone and used productively. When that is the case:

> Authority is earned according to demands of specific situations
> Individuals' and groups' fitness to perform key roles is judged according to their closeness to action sites, the breadth and depth of their experience and vision and their capacities to take opportunities and meet challenges
> No one exercises arbitrary power over anyone else
> Everyone has a voice or representation in decisions.

(These characteristics of mutually constructed relationships are explored further in chapters 12 and 13).

Some leaders and politicians understand that every executive order or piece of legislation is an experiment. No one can say for sure how it will turn out. The US State Governor Andrew Cuomo declared during the 2020 Covid-19 crisis that he couldn't dictate events: the public's behaviour would determine the outcome of measures designed to safeguard and benefit the population.

The difficulties of controlling the spread of the Covid-19 coincided with public disorder following the murder of George Floyd. Governor Cuomo's view was that citizens pay through their taxes for their police. This recalls the principles on which London's Metropolitan Police was founded (referred to in the 'Learning for Everyone's Sake' section of chapter 5). Cuomo asked the public to be actively involved in deciding how to improve the service. He used the same approach to the two crises in the State of New York, enabling everyone to contribute to promoting public health and racial equality by asking:

> What are the facts?
> What do we want to happen?
> What can the people do, and what can government and authorities do, to help make that happen?

These questions about how to respond to emergencies and challenges are like the questions which the surgeon, writer and public health researcher Atul Gawande (2014)[12] found most helpful in discussing what matters as individuals approach the end of their life:

> What do you understand your situation is?
> What do you want to happen next and going forward?
> What can we do, and what can you do, to help make that happen?

Taking Part

Without trust, all kinds of relationship and activity break down. We need trust to play our part in and benefit from our society. To develop personally, socially and collectively, we have to deal with uncertainty and conflict, and be prepared to work at building and maintaining trust. We can't trust one another to know and understand everything, but we can be honest and clear about what we think is right and keep our word.

Dictatorships need people to distrust one another. They intend to eliminate the natural habit of debating and deciding, both inside our heads and as a part of talking with and against one another[13]. They do what they can to suppress or extinguish our true and better selves. Disrespect for others is tolerated or wilfully inflamed. Autocratic and authoritarian regimes have all the answers, pre-empt our questions and remove our doubts. Totalitarianism seeks to abolish uncertainty, surprise and spontaneity; it requires people to be converted—if not voluntarily, then forcibly—to whatever they're told to believe. And living in a democratic society is not guaranteed to safeguard us against pressures to believe and obey things against our conscience (explored in the 'Feeling Inner Conflict' section of chapter 10).

Politics is the framing and implementing of policies. Policies both constrain and enable our working together. They inhibit and assist our focusing on what might serve our living good lives. The more each of us engages in the framing and implementing of policies, the better we govern ourselves. The better we match our decisions and actions to the numbers of people involved and to the scope of our aspirations, the closer outcomes are likely to be to our goals. This applies when we're trying to resolve a disagreement as a couple, or deciding on how best to move forward as a team or company, or addressing conflict between nations.

Summing Up

However much we trust a source of information, we do well to test and try to improve what it proposes.

When we act in good faith, we give others good reason to trust and respect us. When others act in good faith, they give us good reason to trust and respect them.

If we lose trust in those who make mistakes, we can trust no one—not even ourselves.

The more each of us engages with the framing and implementing of policies, the better we govern ourselves.

We have to accept that any of us is capable of holding onto versions of events that are denied by *prima facie*, conscientious, well-attested, incontrovertible evidence, and so may be prepared to ostracise or defame whoever contradicts them. No race, religion, ideology, organisation, group or class of people is exempt from this. We must listen, check evidence and look out for how our prejudices and timidity might make us defend or obscure the indefensible.

---

[1] See 'Oxytocin increases trust in humans', published in *Nature*, 435(7042), pp 673-676, by the Professor of Business Administration at Frankfurt University Michael Kosfeld, the Director of the Laboratory for Biological and Personality Psychology at the University Freiburg Marcus Heinrichs, the neuroeconomist Paul J. Zak, the economist

and Professor of Applied Economics at the University of Konstanz Urs Fischbacher and the behavioural economist and neuroeconomist Ernst Fehr (2005).

[2] See Robert Sapolsky (2018), p 39.

[3] See Adam Phillips (2021).

[4] See Matthew Syed (2019), p 115, concerning different forms of authority.

[5] These are Philip Ball's (2005) 'curtain call' observations about audiences' applause in his *Critical Mass: How One Thing Leads to Another*, published in London, UK, by Arrow Books.

[6] See Adam Phillips (2013), pp 60-62.

[7] See Betty Jane Wagner (1976), referred to here in the 'Self-Reliance, Cooperation' section of chapter 6.

[8] See Matthew Syed (2019), p 62; and then pp 185, 189 and 200. About 'echo chambers', Syed referred to the senior lecturer in statistics Seth Flaxman's (2016) 'Filter Bubbles, Echo Chambers, and Online News', written with Sharad Goel and Justin Rao, published in the *Public Opinion Quarterly*, 80, pp 298-320.

[9] See Shankar Vedantam and Bill Mesler (2021), pp 147, 152, 161, 176-177 and 192.

[10] See Vilayanur Subramanian Ramachandran's (1996) 'The Evolutionary Biology of Self-Deception, Laughter, Dreaming and Depression: Some Clues from Anosognosia' in the journal *Medical Hypotheses*, 47, pp 347-362. Also his (1998) *Phantoms in the Brain*, written with the science writer Sandra Blakeslee; and his (2004) *A Brief Tour of Human Consciousness*, published in New York, NY, by Pi Press.

[11] Just one example was given by Peter Godfrey-Smith (2017), pp 201-203: the coast around Sydney, Australia, was over-fished for many years, but in 2002 'one small bay was designated a marine sanctuary, with complete protection of its wildlife'.

[12] See Atul Gawande's (2014) *Being Mortal: Illness, Medicine and What Matters in the End*, published in London, UK, by Profile Books.

[13] See Hannah Arendt's (1963) *Eichmann in Jerusalem: A Report on the Banality of Evil*, published in London, UK, by Penguin, pp xiv, 3 and 175; and (1951) *The origins of totalitarianism*, originally published in the UK as *The Burden of Our Time*, and then in New York, NY, by Schocken.

9 Finding Satisfactions

In this chapter we hear from Lord Martin Rees, Simon Winchester, Nicholas Shaxson, and Kate Raworth, among others.

How does compromise benefit our economy?

Wanting

Once I asked the independent consultant Keith Robertson what he was going to be doing the next day. He said, 'I'm going to report to the head of the civil service the results of a six-month job-enrichment[1] experiment in half of the UK's national insurance offices.' Job enrichment is an approach to leadership and management whose purpose is to increase 'both task efficiency and human satisfaction by means of building into people's jobs, quite specifically, greater scope for personal achievement and its recognition, more challenging and responsible work, and more opportunities for individual advancement and growth'.

The head of the civil service was perhaps expecting to hear that the majority of employees' job satisfaction had increased. But the reverse was the case: the most recent attitude survey showed they were now less happy at work than they had been before the experiment. When I wondered how that came about, Keith said, 'It may be that giving people a taste of better working practices made them more aware of their frustrations. It seems they've become more impatient and outspoken about what is wrong at work. We haven't solved problems; we've only begun to uncover them'.

We're born making demands. Adam Phillips wrote (1995)[2], 'desire is always in the form of a demand. To be a person is to be asking for something'. Our demands become questions—'I want' becomes 'Can I?' or 'Can we?'

Our questions arise from our needs and wants, and so may lead us to ideals and quests, hence triumphs and disappointments. About our needs Phillips (2013) noted that they 'may be more akin to directions than destinations', and our ideals propel us to do better than give way to inertia, habit and resignation.

Phillips (2002) described how this may evolve in each of us. Initially at least, our brain rushes to satisfy our wishes by making a fulfilment fantasy. We get the impression that we make things happen—like a cat sitting beside an empty food bowl. We become pleased with ourselves. But as we engage with other people, we're exposed to conflicts and disappointments, not least because other people are busy satisfying their needs and desires and have priorities other than fulfilling ours.

Our true and better selves can only be properly satisfied when we find what we want in the external world, or when we change our world or when our world is changed for us in such a way that it provides what we're looking for. Becoming who we want to be is our 'high road to happiness': 'Ideals should feel like affinities, not impositions'—helping us find what makes us and others healthy and happy.

Inertia, habit and selfishness stop us changing our behaviour, but not in the way that addiction holds us back. The philosopher Alain de Botton (2017)[3] spoke about the function of an addiction as something that distracts us from what troubles us. Addiction is a self-defeating wanting. It obscures anxiety and confusion and disrupts our capacity to manage stressful anticipation, and meet challenges. Phillips (2013) saw an addiction as 'an unarticulated frustration', pointing to an unmet need. Our addictions take us away from what would satisfy our true and better selves. If our addictions were good for us, they might lead us to reduce 'the distance between who we are and who we should be ... according to the dictates of our internalised morality'. We help ourselves by tracing and dealing with our troubles *en route to* finding the most reliable, sustainable ways possible to be healthy and content.

Accepting What Can and What Can't Be Changed

Ivan Illich (1973)[4] advocated: 'People must learn to live within bounds'. He thought that we have to realise what we can control or influence, but that understanding 'cannot be taught. Survival depends on [our] learning fast what [we] cannot do. [We] must learn to abstain from unlimited progeny, consumption, and use'. He warned that we can't be educated willingly to accept being poor; we can't be manipulated into self-control; we can't be taught happily to renounce things we want 'in a world totally structured for higher output and the illusion of declining costs'. More is not always better. Enough of what we need is sometimes ideal.

In his novel *David Copperfield*, Charles Dickens (1850) simplified domestic economics. Using the currency and vocabulary of the day—pounds, shillings and pence, and 'ought' meaning nothing—he gave these words to the character Wilkins Micawber: 'Annual income twenty pounds, annual expenditure nineteen pounds nineteen and six, result happiness. Annual income twenty pounds, annual expenditure twenty pounds ought and six, result misery.' Spend more than you earn, and you're unhappy. Spend less than you earn, and you're happy.

Wilkins Micawber believed 'Something will turn up'. But, when there was no reliable reason or evidence for his optimism, he brought calamity on himself and others. Many of us now have acquired the capacity to borrow money in unsustainable ways—without understanding the mechanics or the consequences. This is a short route to misery, though some of us profit by others' losses.

We can't take full account of events yet to happen, or of the part we may play in them or of our feelings about what unfolds. We have to improvise on a vast shifting stage. And we change too. As Phillips (2002) noted, we never quite know what we want: we have to 'find what it is about our wants that is possible'. Then, singly and together, we can work deliberately and determinedly to make a better present and future for all our sakes.

Most of us make demands on other people. Some of us choose to be activists. A. C. Grayling (2019)[5] defined activism as 'any form of protesting or campaigning aimed at bringing about change in the political, social, environmental, educational or other spheres of public concern … even if it involves deliberate inaction or passivity'. To improve how we do things, we usually have to oppose or change things, as well as decide what to aim for and how to go about it. There is encouragement in the example of people who have imagined how we might live better—people such as William Wilberforce, Florence Nightingale, Emmeline Pankhurst, Mahatma Gandhi, Bantu Stephen Biko, Rosa Parks, Martin Luther King, Whina Cooper, Nelson Mandela, Malala Yousafzai and Greta Thunberg. Activists express and display dissatisfaction with and resistance to things they can't reconcile themselves to. They may push dissent beyond words and propose alternatives. This promotes engagement and social change, but it also exposes divisions and causes antagonism and disruption.

Who are the people you admire for their efforts to enable us all to live better lives?

Compromising

Satisfaction with our lives seems to depend on there being a balance between what we let happen and what we make happen—between pleasures we get by consuming or receiving goods and services and benefits we receive by producing or providing goods and services. Achieving balance requires compromise. When we compromise, we offer up some of what we have—without losing too much of what we value. It is an essential element in our developing healthy, productive, profitable cooperation.

We can't cooperate if we don't find ways to compromise. Worthwhile sacrifices include changing our mind and adapting our preferred ways of doing things in favour of what we have reason to trust will be in our long-term interests. If we're to gain even a part of what we need and want—at home, school and work and in our communities—we have to be as open as we can be and adapt. This includes working with people and things we don't fully understand, and may not like. Most of us need help with this.

Phillips (2013)[6] observed, 'Education should be there to teach us—to give us a language to find out—which self-sacrifices are forms of self-betrayal, and which are all to the good'. We can learn to ask questions like these: Is this what you need to happen? Is this what you want to happen? How will that help?

De Botton's (2017) view was that compromise is at the heart of love: the challenge is to accept we're all strange and tricky and continue trying to find ways to be true to ourselves and respect one another. This entails learning how to how to trust and be trusted by others. It is to 'interpret another person's not very appealing behaviour' in a sympathetic and understanding way. It is to be kind and generous as often as we can be, accepting that we all have both good and not so good traits. It is to understand that everyone you love can't help both pleasing and disappointing you. We make healthy, fulfilling relationships by realising that perfection doesn't last: 'to be in the company of another person is to be negotiating imperfection every day ... It is through the work of love that we gradually accept the need to be compatible'. It is the work of love to help us graciously accommodate our incompatibilities. The fruit of love is to have the marvellous feeling that those we love are good for us and be intent on being good for them in return. It is the opposite of narcissism and dogma.

We help ourselves and other people too if, in our discussions and meetings, we ask: Why is this important? How does this seem to work and that doesn't? What do we think is crucial to our well-being? How will we coordinate our efforts and keep in touch? Reasons for asking such questions are given by Matthew Syed (2019)[7] as part of his distinguishing between 'rebels' and 'clones'. Rebels have an outlier's experience and outlook. Clones have, or act as though they have, experiences and outlooks that conform to what the majority expects or what authorities demand.

Syed gave examples of what has gone well when rebels are listened to and examples of what has gone badly when clones hold sway. His examples include teams' climbing Everest; some intelligence organisations' recruitment processes; economic forecasting; code breaking; the UK government's planning of the Poll Tax; and making decisions about social and health care and education policy. He reflected on his experience of working with the England Football Association's Technical Advisory Board, preparing for the 2018 World Cup: 'The most exhilarating moments occurred when someone in the room said something not known to anyone else; when they offered an insight drawn from experiences that were, in some way, unique'.

Evaluating and Trusting

To become and remain 'us', we have sometimes to disagree. As much as we may feel in sympathy with one another, if we are to be healthy, resourceful and resilient, we have at times to think not as one, but against each other and against the way things are. There have to be tensions and conflicts between us about what we can and should do, about what we will do and then about what we've done. Syed saw that 'Honest dissent is not disruptive, but imperative'; it opposes coercion and is a corrective to complacency and apathy.

Hannah Arendt (1978)[8] wrote about the benefits of seeing things from multiple points of view because no single perspective can be relied on or give us all the information we need. In her view, customs, laws and constitutions emerge from historical precedents, contested ideas and ongoing events. Testing established and would-be laws is our most dependable way of making, pursuing and amending decisions. Without new and sometimes hard-won theories and practices arising from difficulties, debates and divisions, we lack the benefits as well as the risks of disrupting what we're used to. And we should remember that disagreement and dissent can be amicable as well as constructive and don't have to be disrespectful or hostile.

This takes us beyond trusting one another for convention's or ideology's sake. It is a step towards being willing and able to work through problems and hard times together. It involves a combination of intuitive feeling and deliberate reasoning. None of us is able on our own to dismantle all of our prejudices and biases. All of this illustrates how disciplined we have to be, both cognitively and socially. We have to keep putting aside or resolving our surmountable differences. This applies whether we're out on a walk, or discussing family matters, or deciding what's best for our company or service or trying to find solutions to historically intractable political and environmental problems.

Picture this. A pivotal discussion is taking place. Everyone who is involved is present and free to speak. After sharing information, arguments and counter-arguments, the majority decision is for Plan C to be implemented. Suppose that those who favour Plans A and B reconcile themselves to Plan C because they know that the process of implementing it will be monitored with everyone's involvement. Progress will be regularly reported; it will be possible to amend planning and after six months there will be a thorough evaluation and it will be possible to amend planning. If the supporters of Plans A and B turn out to be vindicated and it's clear Plan C needs a radical overhaul or to be ditched, their voices will be strong when it comes to deciding next steps.

If you were in their shoes, would you think the process is fair, inclusive and reasonable?

Evaluation is much more than merely collecting data on how much people like or dislike things. As part of efficient, holistic development, evaluation invites us to be explicit about goals and success criteria, review timescales, adapt to events and continue learning. Committing to evaluation taking account periodically of how well you're doing and trying to do better. Systematic, transparent evaluation involving all stakeholders is-how we improve cooperative endeavours.

Defining Goals

In your experience, what makes drives for development helpful and effective?

What makes them unhelpful and ineffective?

I've known many people object to or complain about targets and far fewer object to or complain about goals. That may be because targets are often imposed and goals aren't often discussed. Many people I've worked with, young and old, have said that targets don't actually improve things and can easily be counter-productive[9]. They say targets should be part of a time-out, when you stand back from what you're doing in order to see how to do it better. They also say that when you're not responsible for targets, they tend to stop you being as committed as you could be, stop you taking initiatives and stop you thinking laterally or afresh.

Targets turn out to be more important to accountants, liquidators, investors, speculators, managers and leaders who want to feel they're in control and maybe take the credit for successes, and less important to the people who actually do the work at the centre of the enterprise or on the front line. Clients, service-users and customers don't benefit from many of the ways targets are used.

It isn't consistently helpful to think about targets while you're trying to save lives, treat someone in hospital, innovate and thereby increase production or profitability in a business, teach a class or improve performance in a public service or a sport. Poorly used, targets stop you finding the subtle balance you need between using your unspoken know-how and concentrating on immediate and changing realities. The more varied and multifaceted your activity is and the more complex, interactive and organic the context is, the less likely it is that targets will play an indispensable role in achieving what's wanted. Nevertheless, when you play an active part in defining targets and so understand and own them, they may help you improve your performance—personally and as a team.

Do you have goals that make clear what you intend to achieve?

If you have targets, do they include being clear about your group's goals?

Do they lead to everyone appreciating what's gone well and what can be improved?

Goals turn our hopes and wishes into visions of what to aim for and celebrate. They point us in directions we want to go, and give us yardsticks for gauging how close we get to what we want. They are inevitably limited because they can't express everything that might be conceived of as worthwhile: the goals we didn't pursue might have helped us achieve more of what we wanted—more quickly and/or more economically.

Having goals or targets is only one factor in our decision-making. In his BBC Radio 4 Reith Lectures, the cosmologist and astrophysicist Lord Martin Rees (2010)[10] spoke about science as 'organised scepticism'. He recommended that we 'tackle the tractable' and take careful account of the views of 'experts with good credentials' to help us make up our mind. He challenged us with two questions: can we think and act with the long term in view; and can we recognise others' interests?

What do you think helps us do those things?

Using Data in Everyone's Interest

Rees (2018)[11] wrote that 'human intuition evolved to cope with the everyday phenomena that our remote ancestors encountered on the African savanna', and that our brains haven't changed much since that time. He acknowledged there are important things 'we are not aware of', yet which are 'crucial to our long-term destiny and to a full understanding of physical reality'. Through the power of computers, it is 'becoming possible to calculate the properties of materials, and to do this so fast that millions of alternatives can be computed, far more quickly than actual experiments could be performed'. We should harness this power to help us calculate how to reduce carbon emissions and air-, land- and sea-pollution, for example.

To achieve this, though, enough of us have to be capable of creating, assembling, sharing, interpreting and applying relevant and potentially unsettling data. Rees advocated we be humble enough to understand that there may be 'some fundamental truths about nature ... too complex for unaided human brains to grasp fully'. Machines can help us: 'Any process is in principle computable. However, being able to compute something is not the same as having an insightful comprehension of it'.

Any universe that's complicated enough to have allowed us to emerge and evolve must be too complicated for us to understand fully, especially without masses of data and the means to interpret it. Our task is to act on what we continue to learn. One great fork in the road is whether or not we value immediate or vested interest and selfishness more highly than we value long-term cooperation with nature, with our environment and with one another.

Can we choose more sympathetic, responsible, sustainable options than private gain?

If we can make progress toward doing those things, we will create an economics to match the ideal and goal of cooperation in society and between societies. We need the help of a range of mathematicians, scientists and professionals, including those with experience and understanding of groups' behaviour and decision-making. Susie Orbach (2016)[12] wrote that, 'Like other disciplines such as sociology, economics and social psychology, psychoanalytic thinking should have a place at public policy tables as its insights speak to the mismatch between people's inner and outer—the gap between what they say and what they feel, which no other discipline addresses'.

People with experience and expertise in information technology and its continuing evolution are vital to our trying to make a better future. Such individuals were interviewed for the docudrama *The Social Dilemma*, written by Jeff Orlowski, Davis Coombe and Vickie Curtis (2020)[13]. It showed how social media are specifically designed to maximise the profits of platforms' sponsoring companies and organisations by nurturing addiction to information-feeds, by manipulating our feelings, thoughts and behaviour and by spreading conspiracy theories and disinformation. The film saw linked those covert subversions of our minds and ways of being with the alarming rise in adolescents' mental ill-health and teenagers' suicide rates.

Living Economics

Economies are the economics we live by and live with. Economies are made up of unstable moving parts having several essential elements: funding, ownership, labour, trade and consumption. Included are both costs and benefits to our climate, environment, health and well-being.

Labour, trade and consumption are the means by which goods and services are produced, exchanged and procured. Funding is the provision of necessary means to sustain activity and enterprise. Ownership bestows rights and obligations on people and organisations. Proxies for ownership include trusteeship which is an extension of and alternative to exclusively private ownership, and stewardship which similarly grants rights to individuals and organisations and often emphasises public service. An illustration of this is how we come to own land and fund its use.

The author and journalist Simon Winchester (2021)[14] gave the negative example of 16th and 17th century Europeans' occupying Mohicans' land in the Hudson Valley, New York State: they 'had no knowledge of the land and its needs, and ... regarded it only for its potential for reward'. A positive example is seen in how shared land ownership developed in some places. In 1604, the English Dorset village of Radipole began a 'revolution in the social order, a cataclysmic change like few others before or since'. Up to that point there had been 'no concept of ownership', no common or formal understanding that 'some especially motivated individual might assume direct responsibility for, and an interest in, a specified piece of enclosed land'. This was a relatively late development which in some places has made the 'sharing and distributing' of land a powerful expression of trust.

Enclosure meant that pieces of land were removed from 'the common ownership of many to that of one or more private individuals', incidentally giving the concept of 'private' unprecedented meaning. The incentive some people feel to promote and engage in a region's economic development became 'a virtue common to owners rather than tenants'. Common ownership became 'an axiom that goes to the heart' of what it means to own land or be its trustee or steward.

We can do better than 'live in the same place'. We can give 'home' a broader, richer meaning when we share where we live. The elementary distinction between 'private' and 'public' becomes complicated and enriched when we set out to benefit everyone by suspending or moderating our purely private interests.

Rocky Narrows consists of 274 acres of 'unspoiled Massachusetts landscape ... given for the public good in 1897 to a body that had been established six years previously as the Trustees of the Public Reservations'. It has 'the distinction of being the oldest surviving possession of the oldest privately run and not-for-profit land conservation trust in the United States'. It was founded by a landscape architect, Charles Eliot, 'a man with the vision of a community as trustee-owners of the land around them, for all to enjoy and for none to keep private', thereby making the land 'communally owned, and doing so organically and apolitically, and not enforced artificially'.

There are now trusts that 'operate on a state-wide level; those that work solely within a county; there are town and village trusts; and ... community land trusts, the much smaller-scale groups [being] less involved with landscape and prettiness and leisure, more with affordability and want and social need'. County-level trusts are currently enjoying the greatest success, there being about 1300 of them across the USA. In Britain, 'the popularity of the movement is growing at similar speed'; at the time of Winchester's writing, there were 255 of them—slightly more than in all of the United States. And in the 1950s, a voluntary land reform movement, called Vinoba Bhave, 'established the idea of … a voluntary land reform movement' which has thrived in parts of India.

Costs and Benefits of How We Live

Proximity seems to be crucial to owners' caring for property, whether it be goods or enterprises. When owners, trustees and stewards are absent or distant, they tend to lose interest and stop seeing it as something both living and life-sustaining. We might say that having something is only beneficial up to the point when owners, stewards or trustees become disconnected and negligent; then the good and the enterprise it sponsors fall into disuse.

This brings us to 'finance'. Finance gives a person or group a motive and means to take on and promote a good, a service or an enterprise. According to the economist John Maynard Keynes (1936)[15], finance is good, but only until it becomes harmful. It fuels conventional capitalism and, in so doing, spawns profit, one part of which may be fed back through taxes as social benefits, a second part of which is re-invested to sustain companies and their workforce and facilitate their growth and development, and a third part of which is enjoyed by share- and stakeholders.

Profit isn't in itself good or bad, any more than possessing property or organising labour is. What matters is, first, how helpful or otherwise the processes are of making a profit and, second, how well benefits and proceeds are used so that no one is harmed and those involved and others too may benefit.

In the words of the journalist and investigator Nicholas Shaxson (2018)[16], finance is constructive when it creates wealth for the community and its economy, and destructive when it extracts wealth from the community and its economy. Because sharing of responsibility, social well-being and public health all have to be funded, they should be included in what we mean by 'wealth'.

The more effectively finance providers and receivers communicate, the better off everyone is. When providers and receivers of finance communicate transparently, each may check the other's credentials and performance. At their most effective, enterprises support the sharing of monetary surpluses and the distribution of benefits and welfare to balance social inequalities and compensate for people's disabilities and misfortunes. Wealth and well-being not only depend on but also contribute to our capacities for individual and collective resilience, cooperation and ingenuity.

In the 1990s, transnational monopolies became dominant and finance across the world was made less transparent. By 2008, Russian-doll-like systems of insurance, ownership and franchising had put byzantine barriers to communication and understanding between insured parties and insurers, tenants and owners, debtors and lenders, lessees and lessors, hosts and visiting or distant entrepreneurs. As a result, it became all but impossible to survey, understand and regulate many kinds of market activity. More than that, inflated government subsidies helped businesses to expand and exploit social and public services in unwarranted and unchecked ways. They haven't been immune to market instabilities, yet have been treated as though they were too big to fail. Private banks and other institutions have been bailed out with taxpayers' money.

Shaxson described how selfish profitability, left to its own devices, can maximise the wealth of certain companies' owners and directors at the expense of whole populations. This makes for an extortionate economy and an untenably unequal society. Financial engineering has served shareholders' interests without any apparent social or public rationale or ethic. Ways have been found for taxation not to feed benefits back to society, island tax havens being one example. In this world, compensating for individuals' difficulties and balancing groups' inequalities have little or no priority.

Are people who try to steer economies unable or unwilling to consider, or just not care about and disown, the effects they have?

What might we do to prevent the same or similar things happening again?

Investing in Mutual Interest

When selfish profit and greed drive social and public change, many people are made to suffer and the costs are borne by communities and societies. It is often those with the fewest resources who suffer most. And the further those who damage our world are from the immediate and ongoing consequences of their decisions and actions, the more oblivious and negligent they are likely to be.

What has to happen for financial regulators to have the will and means to manage the complexities and risks of transnational systems?

Phillips (2002)[17] observed that to make our lives democratic we have to create ways of feeling, thinking and acting that grant us all a voice in decisions: 'The whole notion of extending effective political power to more and more people; the idea of people having a right to choose their own government and, in some sense, rule themselves by themselves—by their own consent—without the need for people (or deities) of extraordinary and superior status; this, as an ideal and a political struggle, turns the world upside down. And it does this in part by making new kinds of association between people both possible and necessary. The whole idea of an extraordinary or superior person, or group of people, has to be re-described ... Hierarchy becomes a matter of consensus rather than a divine or any other kind of right. Agreement and disagreement have a whole new status'.

This depends on a fusion of the private and public dimensions of our lives. It points to how we must combine business interests with considerations of public health and well-being. The researcher Miranda Hall and head of co-production Lucie Stephens (2019)[18] at the New Economics Foundation reported how effective childcare is as a cornerstone of a healthy society, and how effective public investment in social infrastructures has significant environmental and economic benefits. Norway, New Zealand and Quebec are examples. There, political action has been made to serve society by accommodating and developing goals, partnerships and services that do no harm, protect the most vulnerable and promote the common good: 'Instead of trickling money into the demand side, the state should direct funding into the supply side, investing in providers who meet established standards of excellence and equality. This approach enables local and national governments to play a stronger role in driving up standards and ensuring equitable provision'.

The economics journalist Martin Wolf (2014)[19] analysed how we might counteract the serious ill-effects of 'rigged capitalism'. He made these suggestions:

> Use policies to constrain monopolistic practices and promote competition between businesses, for example, requiring public justification for mergers and acquisitions

Make finance less selfishly focused, for example, requiring bank intermediaries to have much greater capital and making it no longer possible for interest to be tax-deductible

Introduce laws, rather than merely stricter regulation, to check corporations' maximising value for shareholders against the public interest and innocent, vulnerable parties

Devise a range of policies and changes to reverse growing social and economic inequalities, for example, attacking tax avoidance and evasion

Reduce the power of money in politics and the media, for example, using public revenues to fund political parties while making private funding completely transparent

Develop community-based forums to consult local people and interests.

Repairing and Reforming Economies

In a Zoom Talk attended by 300 people in many countries, the economist Kate Raworth (2020)[20] outlined her approach. She characterised conventional economics as 'male, solitary, money-in-hand, ego-in-heart, calculator-in-mind, knowing the price of everything and the value of very little'. Its current goal couldn't be simpler; it is for gross domestic profit to grow and, unrealistically, to continue growing indefinitely. This fails to address the difficulties posed by economic cycles, the short-term nature of many politicians' tenure and the imperative in some markets to make a profit, sell on and move on. She argued that together we have to change how we value things.

Across the world, many societies are 'falling short on needs and overshooting on consumption of resources. We need our industries to move from a degenerative to a regenerative economy, from a divisive to a distributive economy'. How we live should not cost the Earth. So these are recommended steps towards an increasingly equal, hospitable, satisfying and sustainable world:

Engage with what each of us values

Share ownership and use trusteeship in as many ways as possible

Play our part in governance

Define our purposes

Make open, transparent networks and coalitions

We can do these things within existing social arrangements and within political systems. But when little seems to be achieved through argument or the ballot box and when opposing ideologies can't be bridged, activism spreads, intensifies and sometimes brings violent conflict. We can promote constructive change by acting against or outside existing arrangements, by writing, publishing and blogging independently, through street demonstrations, civil disobedience and occupations of space or property to highlight protest.

A. C. Grayling (2019)[21] suggested Western politics are 'now about small arguments between managerial parties in an age when big decisions about (especially) economics are no longer wholly in the hands of governments, but of global trends and factors'. Conflicts may be provoked, steered, usurped or modified by the interventions of governments or self-appointed individuals and groups. Tragically, sometimes, conflicts become wars and innocent people suffer and die.

What might can we do differently to share responsibility for institutions and enterprises via representation, trusteeship and stewardship?

What can we do better to promote justice and equality, locally and globally?

The writer and journalist Johann Hari (2021) wrote that we achieve our best when we have a sense of flow. This comes when we choose to focus on just one concern at a time—something that has significant meaning for us—and when we choose to work at the limits of our individual and collective capabilities. As many of us as possible have to put other people's well-being alongside and, if necessary, above our selfish, private, sectarian desires. None of us has a right to harm or be a risk to others. We help ourselves and improve our prospects, if, as Hannah Arendt (1958) advised, we 'think what we are doing'. Finding solutions to our economic and environmental problems requires cohesive efforts on the part of significant majorities of people who are moved by empathy, connectedness and imagination to want better for us and our planet.

It is in everyone's interest to narrow the gap in income between people, so that as far as possible everyone may support their families and participate in and contribute to their communities.

Summing Up

We can turn our demands into questions and our questions into ideals and quests.

The purpose of education and government, we can say, is to enable as many people as possible to participate in and contribute to society.

When little seems to be achieved through negotiation, argument or the ballot box and when opposing ideologies can't be bridged, activism spreads and intensifies, sometimes bringing violent conflict.

Finding solutions to our economic and environmental problems requires cohesive efforts on the part of significant majorities of people who are moved by empathy, connectedness and imagination.

---

[1] See Alain de Botton's (9 May 2017) Google Zeitgeist talk *Why You Will Marry the Wrong Person* via YouTube: https://www.youtube.com/watch?v=DCS6t6NUAGQ.

[2] See Ivan Illich (1973), p 78. His philosophy is referred to in the 'Learning from Experience' section of chapter 2.

[3] See A. C. Grayling's (2009) *Ideas that Matter: A Personal Guide for the 21st Century*, published in London, UK, by Weidenfeld and Nicolson, p 4.

[4] As many of us as possible have to put other people's well-being alongside and, if necessary, above our selfish, private, sectarian desires.

[5] See Matthew Syed (2019), p 45; then pp 54, 56, 61 and 65; and about dissent, p 267. See also Caroline Criado Perez's (2019) *Invisible Women: Exposing data bias in a world designed by men*, published in London, UK, by Chatto & Windus.

[6] See Hannah Arendt's (1978) *Life of the Mind*, published in San Diego, CA, by Harcourt Brace Jovanovich.

[7] See chapter 8 of my (2002) *Teaching and Targets: Self-Evaluation and School Improvement*, published in London, UK, by Routledge/Falmer, and chapters 3, 11 and 12 of my (2017) *Inside Teaching: How To Make a Difference For Every Learner and Teacher*, published in Abingdon, UK, by Routledge.

[8] See Martin Rees' (2010) 'Scientific Horizons: 2010', *The Reith Lectures,* on BBC Radio 4.

[9] See Martin Rees' (2018) online *Prospect* magazine article 'What are the limits of human understanding?' Go to www.prospectmagazine.co.uk/magazine/martin-rees-what-are-the-limits-of-human-understanding.

[10] See Susie Orbach (2016), p 287.

[11] The film *The Social Dilemma* (2020), directed by Jeff Orlowski and written by him, Davis Coombe and Vickie Curtis, shows interviews with the following: Tristan Harris, the former Google design ethicist, co-founder and CEO of Apture and co-founder of the Center for Humane Technology; Tim Kendall, the former Facebook executive, former President of Pinterest and CEO of Moment; Jaron Lanier, the American computer philosophy writer, computer scientist, visual artist, composer of contemporary classical music and author; Roger McNamee, an early investor at Facebook and venture capitalist; Aza Raskin, the employee of Firefox and Mozilla Labs, co-founder of the Center for Humane Technology, founder of Massive Health and inventor of the infinite scroll; Justin Rosenstein, the Facebook engineer, Google engineer and co-founder of Asana; Shoshana Zuboff, the Professor Emeritus at Harvard Business School and author; Jeff Seibert, the former executive at Twitter, serial Tech Entrepreneur and co-founder of Digits; Chamath Palihapitiya, the former Vice President of Growth at Facebook; Sean Parker, the former President at Facebook; Anna Lembke, the medical Director of addiction medicine at Stanford University; Jonathan Haidtof, the social psychologist at the New York University Stern School of Business and author; Sandy Parakilas, the former Operations Manager at Facebook and former Product Manager at Uber; the data scientist and author Cathy O'Neil; Randima Fernando, the former product manager at Nvidia, former executive director at Mindful Schools, and co-Founder of Center For Humane Technology; the former experience design consultant at Google and author Joe Toscano; Bailey Richardson, an early team member of Instagram (2012–2014); Rashida Richardson, the adjunct professor at the New York University (NYU) School of Law and director of policy research at AI Now Institute; Guillaume Chaslot, the former engineer at YouTube, CEO of Intuitive AI, and founder of AlgoTransparency; Renée Diresta, the research manager at the Stanford Internet Observatory and former Head of Policy at Data for Democracy; and Cynthia M. Wong, the former senior Internet researcher at Human Rights Watch.

[12] See Simon Winchester's (2021) *Land: How the Hunger for Ownership Shaped the Modern World*, published in London, UK, by William Collins, pp 17, 23, 172ff, 337ff and 389-396.

[13] This view is explained in John Maynard Keynes' (1936) *The General Theory of Employment, Interest and Money*. His theory refers to interacting demands in society for saving, investment and access to usable assets.

[14] See Nicholas Shaxson's (2018) *The Finance Curse: How Global Finance Is Making Us All Poorer*, published in London, UK, by Bodley Head/Random House. He is a co-founder of the Balanced Economy Project and a member of the Tax Justice Network. See also: the journalist and novelist John Lanchester's (2010) *Whoops! Why Everyone Owes Everyone and No One Can Pay*, published in London, UK, by Penguin; the author and

financial journalist Michael Lewis' (2010) *The Big Short: Inside the Doomsday Machine*, published in New York, NY, by W. W. Norton and Company; and Richard Wilkinson and Kate Pickett (2009)

[15] See Adam Phillips (2002), p 25.

[16] See Miranda Hall's and Lucie Stephens' (2019) *Who's Holding the Baby: Democratising Ownership and Control of England's Childcare*, published in London, UK, by the New Economics Foundation, pp2-3 and

[17] See Martin Wolf's (2014) *The Shifts and the Shocks: What We've Learned—and Have Still to Learn—from the Financial Crisis*, published in London, UK, by Penguin Press, and his regular articles for *The Financial Times*, for example, 5 December 2019.

[18] Kate Raworth's (5 June 2020) talk was called *Doughnut Economics: an idea for Oxford?* Visit www.doughnuteconomics.org and www.kateraworth.com/doughnut.

[19] See A. C. Grayling (2009), p 5.

[20] See Johann Hari's (2021) *Stolen Focus: Why You Can't Pay Attention*, published in London, UK, by Bloomsbury. His ideas incorporate many other people's insights and experiences, including Mihaly Csikszentmihalyi's 'flow' (referred to in the 'Becoming Resilient' section of chapter 1), Lev Vygotsky's 'zone of proximal development' (referred to in chapter 3's 'Drawing Together' section) and Fritjof Capra's and Pier Luigi Luisi's work (referred to above in the 'Working with Nature' section of this chapter and in the 'Working with Nature' section of chapter 11).

[21] See Hannah Arendt (1958).

10 Doing the Right Thing

In this chapter we hear from Thomas Blass and Stanley Milgram; Stephen Gibson and Kathryn Millard; John Darley and Bibb Latané; Richard Philpot and his colleagues; and Richard Baldwin, among others.

How does dealing with inner conflicts help us make good decisions?

Feeling Inner Conflict

In 1945-46, Hannah Arendt attended war criminals' trials in Nuremberg, Germany. She wrote (1951)[1] that, when a society is reduced to having just one way of thinking, it creates conditions that compel every citizen to submit to a 'rule from within'. Then the state takes precedence over individuals, making some people's identities and lives 'superfluous and expendable'. Arendt's (1963) insights reflected[2] a change in international law, designed to help us avoid social harms and atrocities. Previously, state leaders had been exempt from legal responsibility for inhumane actions. And the same had applied to people who obeyed leaders and officers of the state. The Nuremberg trials made it possible to prosecute offences against humanity and to hold people accountable whose crime involved carrying out orders.

Thomas Blass (2004)[3] gave an account of his fellow social psychologist Stanley Milgram's experiments on obedience, carried out in the 1960s. In his original investigation at Yale University, USA, Milgram aimed to find out 'when and how people would defy authority in the face of a clear moral imperative'. Volunteers aged between 20 and 50 from a range of occupations and with varying levels of education, answered a newspaper advertisement and were paid four and a half US dollars just to turn up. 740 men and 40 women applied and participated. Milgram expected the volunteers to defy authority.

They were shown to a space resembling a laboratory and were invited to act as teachers for the purposes of an experiment. An accomplice was present throughout to observe each volunteer participant. Wearing a white coat and holding a clipboard, he posed as a laboratory scientist and kept to a rehearsed script as far as he could. He explained the aim was to find out whether we become better learners if we are punished for our mistakes.

Each volunteer was given a script and asked to read it into a microphone and operate a dial said to control the transmission of electric shocks. The volunteers didn't know that no electric current would actually be conveyed. The 'learner', like the 'experimenter', was an accomplice and followed a script. He appeared to forget words the volunteer 'teacher' dictated, and he wasn't really punished. The 'teacher' and the 'experimenter' couldn't see but could hear the 'learner' via a speaker relay from the neighbouring room.

When the 'learner' 'made a mistake', the 'experimenter' instructed the 'teacher' to administer progressive shocks up to a level which would normally cause serious distress and pain and then beyond to a lethal 450 volts. The 'learner's' script included escalating signals of discomfort, distress and agony. When the 'lethal limit' was reached, the 'learner' fell silent.

The experiment found that 65 percent of participating volunteers fully obeyed the instructions. Milgram hadn't expected these results at all, but they have been replicated across the world. At the end of her or his session, each volunteer was told what the work was actually about and could talk through what had happened. Most reported that putting themselves in the hands of an authority who required them to do apparently harmful things made it difficult afterwards to re-establish their normal sense of self-control. For many years after the experiments there were arguments about the ethics of deceiving and disorientating volunteers, even for scientific purposes.

Milgram (1974) concluded that 'the essence of obedience' consists in a person's coming to view herself or himself as an 'instrument for carrying out another person's wishes'. When we do what we're told to do, sooner or later we seem to lose touch with our normal values and even our sense of humanity. We might say we lose touch with our true and better self. In this scenario, it's not aggression which leads to violence. We feel conflicted and, when we lack the encouragement and solidarity of peers, the likelier it is we'll bow to authority. We lose capacity to do what we'd normally feel to be right or decline to do what we'd normally feel to be wrong. Military and other forms of training, including induction to clubs and societies and initiation to gangs, may exploit equivalent mechanisms.

When Obedience Becomes a Problem

Milgram suggested *obedience* means accepting what authority requires, whereas *conformity* means falling in line with what peers do.

Under conditions that lead to obedience, it seems, we become more concerned about whether or not we live up to what others expect of us, and less concerned to be true to our better selves. This dynamic takes on its own momentum. Our tendency to divide people into 'them' and 'us' comes into play (referred to here in chapter 3). Those of us who do as we're told against our conscience may try to rationalise or justify our actions by downgrading or dehumanising 'others'. The psychologist Phillip Zimbardo's (2007) *The Lucifer Effect: How Good People Turn Evil?* published in New York, NY, by Random House is a study of this. Volunteers in Milgram's experiment denied they'd conformed but agreed they'd obeyed. They insisted that their freedom of choice hadn't been reduced.

It seems we can feel we are in control of ourselves even when we're doing things we'd ordinarily find abhorrent. Obedience seems to come from our being part of a hierarchy: a person 'above us' has a right to tell us what to do. According to Milgram's analysis obedience tends not to diminish us: we don't seem to be any less of a person when we obey, though we may suffer internal conflicts. This may be explained by its having been advantageous to us in our evolution to be disposed to accept and act on advice or instruction. It seems that 'We are born with a *potential* for obedience, which then interacts with the influence of society to produce the obedient [person]'.

When we're part of an organisation or system, many of us let others choose for us and we stop expecting to use our own moral standards. Of course, acting on someone else's behalf may prove to be beneficial for others and ourselves but, when an authority dictates our actions, it can be an excuse for, or cause of, wrongdoing. Conscience comes into play when we act autonomously, or independently or according to critically considered agreement with our peers and/or as many of the people as possible who will be affected by what we intend to do.

Most of the time, many of us internalise the social order we inhabit. Once we consent to 'authority's definition of the situation' and begin to obey instructions, we find it difficult to change tack; internal conflict and guilt are a price we pay if we deviate.

Some of us are likelier to obey than others. Some of us draw lines we try not to cross. Some of us feel comfortable being obedient and enjoy how obedience rewards us: we grow in confidence about our role, feel appreciated by people in important positions, develop solidarity with others and gain special attention and/or privileges. For us to feel responsible for our actions, we must sense that what we do expresses who we truly are or who we aspire to be.

We don't feel responsible for ourselves when our overriding concern is how high or low we are in someone else's estimation. When we choose to doubt or challenge instructions but still follow them, we tend to remain troubled and struggle to rid ourselves of uneasy feelings or outright guilt. As Blass explained, 'The price of disobedience is a gnawing sense that [we have] been faithless'. This applies as much to our intimate and interpersonal relationships as it does to our social and public interactions. It is a symptom of our true and better self's wanting what's good for us and for others.

Milgram thought it a catastrophic failure that a culture creates a morality based on obedience to authority. Destructive authorities and leaders have a limitless source of servants and followers for as long as we feel we have little or no option but to be pliant and stick to the rules we're given. Automatic deference is as great a danger to human survival and well-being as ignorance and indifference are.

Feeling Responsible

Attention is key to being responsible for what we do. Daniel Kahneman (2011)[4] wrote that 'Our emotional state is largely determined by what we attend to and, when we are focused, it is usually on our current activity and immediate environment'. Other people can direct, manipulate and exploit but not control our attention and interest[5]. It's in our power to choose what matters most to us and what might be done about it. Yet neither elaborate moral reasoning nor feeling great empathy translates necessarily into doing something compassionate, difficult or brave.

What helps us take responsibility in a healthy, productive way?

What seems to be required is that we be free to question, debate and choose how to live our lives. We have first to accept that we can't be protected from making mistakes; then we have to seek to govern ourselves. We can't be free by denying others their freedom. We must embark on our good intentions and act in good faith, intending to succeed and taking strength from wanting to learn. Every situation is unique and so demands we be ready to adapt and be inventive. To succeed in humane, social, economic and political projects we have to stretch our thinking and data-bases. We have to look for patterns in our error-making. We have to self-diagnose tendencies toward impatience, lack of concentration, short-term thinking, absent-mindedness and aversion to careful preparing, criticism and checking. We have to want to be imaginative *and* realistic, autonomous *and* cooperative. As Matthew Syed (2019) explained, some of our worst problems occur when easy options are taken or default responses are given: 'Workers capable of altering the script are more likely to fix problems, and make changes to their jobs that make them happier and more productive'.

Can you alter the script in your personal relationships and everyday interactions?

Can you contribute to decision-making about how your business is conducted, how your service is provided or how it's experienced by your clients or customers?

The statistician and economist Ernst Schumacher (1973)[6] wrote that the strongest reason to be hopeful about our capacity to act together in our best interests is that ordinary people often take a wider and a more humanistic view than experts: 'The power of ordinary people ... does not lie in starting new lines of action, but in placing their sympathy and support with minority groups which have already started'. When we work together, we may counter flawed and undesirable practices and help construct reasonable, viable, fruitful alternatives.

One example Schumacher gave was a private, voluntary organisation. From the late 1940s onward, the Soil Association has explored vital relationships between soils, plants, animals and human beings. It undertakes and assists research, and does what it can to listen to and keep the public informed. Its ethos and methods are collaborative, its purposes socially intentioned. It is humble and respectful toward 'the infinitely subtle system of natural harmony' which 'the lifestyle of the modern world' does much to disrupt. Another of his examples was also a not-for-profit non-governmental organisation which provides 'practical answers to poverty' and technical assistance in many countries. The

Intermediate Technology Development Group, now renamed Practical Action, carries out systematic studies and helps people to help themselves. As an international development organisation, it aims to serve 'production by the masses instead of mass production'.

Taking up the Challenge

Multinational organisations committed to working with new technologies for the survival and health of our planet may help us alter the script we feel we have to follow. Jaron Lanier said in an interview (2013)[7], 'I am still hoping VR might lead to a new level of communication between people: for instance, with simulations that embody feelings and sensibilities. There have also been experiments in filtering virtual worlds so that one gets a sense of what it's like to be dyslexic, colour-blind or face blind.'

To be better than average, we must look to create the best possible unique practice to suit the situation we're all dealing with. This is the opposite of making a prescriptive rule out of a pattern we've observed, the opposite of having pre-emptive bureaucratic requirements and the opposite of prioritising strict bottom-line accountancy.

Mass-production is focused on making economies of scale by lowering the costs and quality of the product or service as far possible—taking those down to the point when customers or clients defect to competitors. Reducing costs—without passing benefits onto clients or customers—risks lowering the quality of goods or services to unacceptable levels. In social endeavours, we can't afford to neglect what customers or clients expect and deserve; we can't afford to defer to producers' and providers' margins and convenience. Doing what's right and good for human beings means being honest with ourselves and others and being adaptable and flexible. These are serious challenges for all of us.

Toby Ord (2020)[8] wrote about two major contexts in which we may influence communities and organisations. Each of us may choose to discuss vital issues affecting our future, on the one hand, with the people who are closest to us and, on the other hand, with the people we meet at work or as members of the public. Most of us communicate most with immediate family, friends and colleagues, and 'Each of our careers is about 80,000 hours devoted to solving some kind of problems, big or small'. To thrive as a community and species, we have to strive to be 'informed, responsible and vigilant', staying abreast of crucial issues and 'urging [our] political representatives to take action when important opportunities arise'. Exceptionally healthy family units, groups, communities, companies and services tend not to see 'best' practice as prescribable or universal; they see it as the 'best so far'. Highly effective partnerships, teams and organisations encourage and enable everyone to look for ways of improving what they do. This means being free to examine, update and regenerate core processes and systems affecting how we live.

Between 2002 and 2007, in a project led by the professor of education Michael Fielding and Fiona Carnie for the University of Sussex and Portsmouth local education authority in the UK, many schools found it transformative for students to use the reminder EBI, standing for 'even better if ...', when they gave and received feedback[9]. They benefited by building on achievements and looking for what they could improve. And governors, administrators, school leaders and teachers found the same applied to them.

Better perhaps than 'even better if ...' is 'even better when ...'. Sometimes it is especially productive to focus on something that happens and falls short of what you aimed for; alternatively, on something that simply has to be done and might as well be done to the very best of your abilities. The keys are focusing and being deliberate.

Having Confidence to Disobey

Many of us seem to be primed to accept instructions and commands. And it's sometimes easier to obey than face the embarrassment or conflict of speaking up or following our conscience. There are plenty of examples of cults where members were ostensibly free to disagree or leave, but did neither[10].

A young man told me he was having flashbacks and feelings of uncontrollable panic. He was taking mood- and perception-altering drugs with friends most Friday or Saturday evenings before they went out to a rave, club, concert or party. We stood in the room and I asked him to show me what the ritual was.

'The drugs are handed out', he said.

'Show me', I said. He acted the part of the leader, reaching into his pocket. I took the part of a recipient, holding out my hand.

'So everyone accepts it and puts it in their mouth?'

'Yes.'

'Can I ask you to do something different? Let me show you.' On my turn, I turned the palm of my hand toward the leader signifying 'Stop. No'.

The young man began to tremble, saying, 'I can't. I can't.' He had to sit down.

'Why is it hard to say no?'

'I don't know.' I wish I had asked him what would have to happen for him to think and say 'No thanks'. I wish I'd asked him 'What are you afraid of?'

We've evolved to be suited neither to being completely autonomous nor to being completely submissive. There's tension between self-determination and compliance, and we're bound to want to resolve it or find relief from it. When the factors that tie us into authority, hierarchy and peer pressure are greater than our drive to govern and decide for ourselves, we comply or obey. But, when the strain of doing what we feel is wrong is greater than the forces that bind us in, we dare to assert ourselves. The strain tells us we have a problem. Before we can resolve it, we have to acknowledge it. We can't deal with addictions, health problems, repeated failures, emergencies, inequality, injustice or oppression unless we recognise their dangers and harms.

Most of us feel stress when:

> we're instructed to do something that doesn't fit with the kind of person we feel we are
> we're prevented from doing what we feel is right
> there is a threat of retaliation against us.

We find some relief when physical symptoms absorb the psychic tension: we sweat, tremble or laugh nervously, for example. If we can't deflect, dissipate, tolerate or escape the strain, and if we *can* summon up an alternative script, we may disagree or dissent. If the stress persists and debate and dissent don't work, we may rebel or escape.

Milgram highlighted something dangerous about us: we have a capacity for acting inhumanely without wanting to. When we set aside our humanity, we can't help but merge our 'unique personality into larger institutional structures … This is a fatal flaw … It is ironic that the virtues of loyalty, self-discipline and self-sacrifice that we value so highly in the individual are the very properties that create destructive organisational engines of war and blind [us] to malevolent systems of authority'. In the long run, it 'gives our species only a modest chance of survival', because suppressing our humanity entails losing commitment to one another, along with our potential resourcefulness and ingenuity.

Becoming Assertive

Harm and atrocities happen when we:

> do things we can't defend
> defer to those who are 'above' us or feel we must obey, whatever the cost
> don't question instructions or take issue with decisions which trouble us
> do a job with a purely technical, administrative or bureaucratic attitude
> use euphemisms and/or deceit to hide the moral implications and effects of our actions.

What can we do to avoid apathy, denial and harmful obedience in situations that affect our own and others' well-being and health?

In 2018, the social psychologist Stephen Gibson and the film-maker Kathryn Millard[11] made a film, *Experiment 20*, about the increasing numbers of researchers drawn to Stanley Milgram's archive at Yale University, which includes audio recordings of many of his experimental sessions. They found that '*Milgram's experiments do not show that people naturally follow orders*. If anything, they show the opposite.' Some of the participants defied the experimenter, 'argued, questioned and challenged him, and tried to find clever and inventive ways of getting themselves out of the experimental situation'. And the 'experimenter' had to go off-script to find 'increasingly creative ways of trying to persuade people to remain in the experiment'.

It may also have been the case that the 'experimenter' was seen by the volunteers not so much as an authority figure but as a human being and much like themselves—wanting to help research and so benefit society. Perhaps some of the volunteers too confidence from the 'experimenter' who was trying to help them play their part in a worthwhile venture. Overall, the picture is more complex and nuanced than that participants were 'blindly' obedient: 'Participants could—and did—argue, resist, and fight back. This is not to deny that lots of participants *did* keep going with the shocks, but rather to assert that "obedience" is only part of the story.' In Gibson's and Millard's film, three women are shown as having different ways of challenging the experimenter—sometimes displaying anger, sometimes exasperation, sometimes calm determination, but most still ended up obeying.

Harm and atrocity may be averted and humanity is more likely to be sustained or recovered when we:

> Talk to one another honestly about our feelings and doubts
> Challenge wrongdoing
> Commit to relationships and actions which have humane purposes, methods and outcomes.

Our challenge is to choose what is good for as many of us as possible, and then set about achieving it, using as much knowledge, imagination and commitment as we can muster. Autocratic and totalitarian leaders and states make our feelings irrelevant by dictating how we should live. Their bureaucracies curtail the potential we have to ask and pursue questions. Questions and their answers are passed 'down' from authority. When we tolerate incompetents, bullies and authoritarians, we help sustain forces which demean us and impoverish our lives. An authoritarian individual or group has to acknowledge *they* have a problem before change can be achieved.

At the opposite end of a spectrum from a rigged or dictatorial form of governance is a pluralist society, that is, one in which two or more kinds or sources of authority coexist. Stuart Hampshire (2000)[12] wrote that in a free society people have different practical values and ideas about how best to structure institutions and facilitate commerce and services. Vigilance and commitment to inclusive, constructive attitudes and behaviours build everyone's capacity to benefit from transparent negotiation and collective autonomy. Then, in the interests of the common good, conflicting views and interests are arbitrated openly, peacefully and fairly. And what applies to individuals and groups locally also applies internationally.

Standing Out from the Crowd

As an anonymous member of a group, it seems, we tend not to call for help or respond to a call for help because we feel others will. There's solid research about 'diffusion of responsibility': being part of a crowd veils or dissipates ill-feeling about what we're doing and/or what we're not doing.

The social psychologists John Darley and Bibb Latané (1968)[13] used staged laboratory experiments to study how people who were either alone, with a friend or with a stranger, responded to a woman apparently in distress. Believing she had fallen and was hurt, 70 percent of the people who were alone called out or went to help the woman, but of those who were paired with a stranger only 40 percent offered help. The finding was that we are less likely to assist an apparent victim when other people are present; and the more bystanders there are, the less likely it is that any of them will act.

How passive we become seems to depend on how cohesive we feel as a group; on how long we we're exposed to the tension of not knowing whether or not to speak up and intervene; on the extent to which we interpret someone else's lack of response as a lack of concern for the victim; and on our feeling that, if no one responds, the situation can't be serious. When what is happening is open to a range of interpretations, it can take individuals in a group of bystanders up to five times longer to react than when the gravity of the situation is more obvious. Darley and Latané suggested that, when it isn't clear what is happening, we look to one another and misinterpret inaction as lack of concern.

This research was revisited by Richard Philpot, Lasse Suonperä Liebst, Mark Levine, Wim Bernasco and Marie Rosenkrantz Lindegaard (2019)[14]. At the time of its publication, theirs was 'the largest systematic study of real-life bystander intervention in actual public conflicts captured by surveillance cameras'. Cross-national video datasets were analysed from South Africa, the Netherlands and the UK, showing that in nine out of ten public conflicts, at least one bystander, and typically several bystanders, did something to help. It was found that the more bystanders there were, the likelier it was that someone would intervene: 'Taken together these findings allay the widespread fear that bystanders rarely intervene to help'. The authors argued that 'it is time for psychology to change the narrative away from an absence of help and toward a new understanding of what makes intervention successful or unsuccessful.'

The value of these and similar studies is not to fix a description of how we behave or how we should behave. Rather, they encourage us to think about what affects us in groups and crowds, and how we might prepare to respond to our own or others' need or to an opportunity for us to contribute to our own or others' well-being.

A difficulty many of us face from time to time is managing our feeling that something isn't right in our organisation or community. Should we speak up?

How can we help one another accept and share responsibility?

These are some of the things we can do to help resolve conflicting feelings:

> Make safe spaces for everyone to speak as openly as possible
> Check where views come from and their evidence base
> Avoid or challenge indefensible forms of authority and influence
> Record and celebrate satisfaction when we fulfil our autonomous and properly agreed humane intentions.

Acting in step with those we respect and trust helps us feel we're doing the right thing. Paradoxically, we may also feel we're doing the right thing when we step out of line and take responsibility for ourselves. If staying in the mainstream makes us feel uneasy or conflicted, we do well to stop and consider. Non-conformity, dissent and disobedience can help us bring an end to inner conflict and avert widespread violence.

Finding Your Voice

At home, at work and in your community, sharing responsibility for important decisions helps you and others become used to saying what you think is going well and what is not. You might use a strategy suggested by solution-focused therapy (referred to in the 'Getting Back on Track' section of chapter 1). You might ask about what is happening when things are going relatively well. Envisaging how you'd rather live stimulates and sustains your efforts to make changes.

It's healthy to be ready to revise your understanding of what is good and what might be even better, hence of what you need to do to move towards it. You can't definitively pin down what it means to be well, what it means to be equal and what it means to be fair and just. If quality of life matters to you, you have no choice but to keep critiquing and refining what you mean by well-being, equality and keep working to achieve all three.

Stuart Hampshire (2000) proposed that the best that can be achieved in a free, pluralist society is to ask such questions, explore desirable and feasible answers, then negotiate how best to proceed. If politicians and other people think it's possible to arrive at a finite conception of what equality and justice are, they are mistaken. We have to take each situation as it uniquely appears.

Since the signing of the English Magna Carta in 1215, jury members have been able to propose new interpretations of or amendments to laws according to the peculiarities of the cases they address. So, with judges' support and guidance, ordinary people have contributed to improving legal procedures and instruments. One of the charter's purposes was to prevent King John from ridding himself of nuisances and enemies by having them imprisoned or sentenced without trial. Clauses 39 and 40 have had the most practical and enduring consequences, first, guaranteeing all 'freemen' the rights to hear what they are accused of and to have a fair trial and, second, insisting that defendants be assumed to be innocent until proven guilty. It gave rise to Common Law which has continued to evolve over centuries through precedence.

Some legal theorists have argued that Magna Carta's genius lay in sharing with juries some of the Crown's prerogatives[15]. Since then, in England and subsequently in the UK, the USA, the British Commonwealth and elsewhere, juries have been authorised not merely to use existing laws to decide defendants' innocence or guilt. By enabling jurors to play their part in updating and refining the law, Magna Carta shows that justice can be made to serve us all better. The same principle is seen in policing that is informed by public cooperation and dialogue (referred to in the 'Learning for Everyone's Sake' section of chapter 5).

An essential element in this is that everyone benefits when each of us has a voice and wherever possible a role in how our communities, companies and services are run and how they evolve[16]. This is a specific, concrete way for us to realise our mutuality and shared interests. By tackling less than satisfactory public services, injustice and inequality, we come to understand better what unites us and how together we may be stronger and enjoy a better life. It's our duty towards our fellow human beings to feel, think, speak up and act.

Tele-technology and Interdependence

In our efforts to devise respectful, compassionate, satisfying, sustainable, efficient and effective ways of living, we often reach for technology.

Up to the time of the first agricultural revolution around 12,000 years ago, when humans began to settle as farmers, relocation had been their way of life. Mobility had been as intrinsic to living as breathing and foraging. Now they needed logistics—ways of moving things from place to place. The professor of international economics Richard Baldwin (2016)[17] wrote about challenges and opportunities of logistics which have driven down costs of relocation. Because they are subject to both private and public arrangements, strictly technological considerations tend to be trumped by markets, cultural customs and politics. For example, governments have sometimes subsidised means of communication and sometimes left them to fend for themselves, sometimes funded and sometimes not funded transport systems, sometimes encouraged and sometimes discouraged migration ...

What some economists call the Great Divergence refers to events which began in the early 19th century, widening and then entrenching gaps between the haves and the have-nots within and between societies. The driving force was steam power which enabled goods to be produced and moved quickly, cheaply and in volume. One effect of this was to concentrate economic, political, cultural and military power in the hands of small numbers of people, thereby consolidating and increasing societal disequilibrium and inequality. It led to exploitative richer nations' feeling downsides as well as advantages and to poorer nations' being exploited and losing quality of life as well as gaining access to innovations.

Then, from 1990 onward, national and international efforts have been made to reverse the growing imbalances and tensions within and across societies—a trend which Baldwin dubbed the Great Convergence. As ever, outcomes have not wholly matched intentions, in part because it's difficult to attract lasting commitment to highly complex undertakings across large and widespread territories. Now, 'Despite the Great Convergence, salaries and wages are much higher in rich nations and there are billions of people who would like to earn those wages', but they can't easily move there and unregulated migrations ensue. So further changes have been set in motion.

New technologies increasingly allow people to work at a distance from colleagues, from their headquarters and from those they're serving. Through computer-integrated manufacturing, workers now help machines make things where previously machines helped people make things. All 'the basic manufacturing functions—machining, forming, joining, assembly and inspection—are supported and integrated by computer-aided manufacturing systems and automated materials-handling systems. Inventory control is automated for tracking inventory movement, forecasting requirements and even initiating procurement orders'. The costs of face-to-face interaction are also likely to continue falling, enhanced by, for example, instant language translation, telebotics and holographic telepresence. The Covid pandemic has also contributed to increased digital communication.

Current trends mean that many tasks that used to require in-person presence can now be performed at a distance, and there is virtual rather than physical traffic of high- and low-skill work between nations. Baldwin foresaw that low-skilled workers in developing nations are increasingly likely to telecommute to rich nations and high-skilled workers in rich nations to telecommute to developing nations: 'Virtual presence will make the fractionalisation and offshoring much easier to coordinate'. But managing and coordinating are not bound to promote effective listening, empathic understanding or equalising of opportunity and wealth-sharing.

As wages increase in developing nations, more and more unskilled work transfers to them and, when wages there get high enough, offshoring of production by rich nations spreads further and further afield. Some people predicted that, as the gap between wage-levels in richer and poorer nations narrowed, trade would decrease the difference between the 'North' and 'South'. Baldwin took the opposite view, believing that global trade 'will come to resemble the trade that occurs today among rich nations, namely lots of two-way trade in manufactured goods'.

In this evolution, 'Routine low-skill tasks are bundled into high-skill occupations, while the remaining low-skill tasks will typically be highly labour intensive but less routine. The resulting broader [production] stages will involve more capital-intensive, more technology-intensive, and more skill-intensive processes. This tends to favour their location in developed nations'. Is this another example of the haves keeping ahead of the have-nots?

Sharing Information

Can we join together to address challenges that affect us all?

We respond automatically to what we see in front of us, to what we hear, smell and sense. Technical, mathematical and statistical information doesn't easily make sense to many of us. Changing our world for the better will require us to interpret and respond to data in ways that were unimaginable only a generation ago. It's challenging but necessary for us to bring data to bear on our desire to promote autonomous cooperation as a means of improving everyone's prospects for a good life.

To be thoroughly effective, organisations and businesses need to be alert and creative enough to avoid making messaging contextless, formulaic or algorithmic, and so enable the receiving of messages to be better than a passive, prescriptive, confining experience. It takes social awareness, insight and skill to reach out, hear and taken in information from people and cultures we're unfamiliar with, then communicate accessibly, interact bilaterally and check shared understanding. That is how we connect with and enrich one another. We're helped in this by effective leadership and organisation.

Even so, cultural and political distances have to be overcome if we're to cohere and cooperate. It may seem surprising, but many more of us across the globe are involved in keeping everyone going than in producing goods. Something like two-thirds of jobs in the global economy are in service sectors—preparing, maintaining and repairing things, people and systems—and rich-nation workers could increasingly find themselves in competition with poor-nation workers who currently provide such services remotely. A major flaw in the systems we've evolved is that those who discover, invent, change, own or invest in things can have too little contact with those who are hired to make, mend and keep things going, and tend to have limited contact with customers and users of common services and goods.

A premise of this book is that the better we understand processes of socio-cultural change, the likelier we are to overcome the arrogance of power and privilege and the destructiveness of neglect and exploitation. We need to be humble enough to trust appropriate experts and advisers and respect information which, on the one hand, we can't easily verify by our senses alone and which, on the other hand, we may wish we didn't have to face up to. We can be heartened by human beings' extraordinary accomplishments, and we can combine what we suspect, intuit and hope with what we've learned from the sciences, the humanities, the arts, technologies and our common experience.

Being committed to working together enables us to survive, live well and make a worthwhile future for generations to come. In their different ways, spirituality, humanitarianism and technology help us commit to learning and working more closely together. We increase our chances of succeeding when we play our part in establishing and monitoring the work of international organisations whose mission is to safeguard and benefit humanity and our planet.

Summing up

Automatic deference is as great a danger to human survival and well-being as ignorance and indifference are.

We can't deal with addictions, health problems, systemic failures, emergencies, inequality, injustice or oppression unless we recognise their dangers and harms.

We all benefit when each of us has a voice and a role in how our communities, companies, services and representative bodies are run and evolve.

We have to be humble enough to trust appropriate experts and advisers and respect information which, on the one hand, we can't easily verify by our senses alone and which, on the other hand, we may wish we didn't have to face up to.

---

[1] See Hannah Arendt's (1951, 1976) *The origins of totalitarianism*, originally published in the UK as *The Burden of Our Time* then in New York, NY, by Schocken.

[2] See Hannah Arendt's (1963) *Eichmann in Jerusalem: A Report on the Banality of Evil*, published in London, UK, by Penguin.

[3] See Thomas Blass' (2004) *The Man Who Shocked the World: The Life and Legacy of Stanley Milgram*, published in New York, NY, by Basic Books, pp 4, xii-xiii, 6, 7-10, 68, 72, 113-115, 125, 130-164, 186-188 and 204. Also see Stanley Milgram's (1974) original work *Obedience to Authority: An Experimental View*, published in New York, NY, by Harper & Row.

[4] See Daniel Kahneman (2011), pp 394 and 674.

[5] See Adam Phillips (2019), p 9.

[6] See Ernst Schumacher's (1973) *Small Is Beautiful: Economics as if People Mattered*, published in New York, NY, by Harper, chapters 10 and 12. The title 'Small Is Beautiful'

came from Schumacher's teacher the economist, jurist and political scientist Leopold Kohr (born 1909, died 1994) who proposed that small, appropriate forms of social organisation, technologies and policies can be superior to mainstream thinking that 'bigger is better'. This relates to 'Dunbar's numbers', referred to in the 'Numbers Make a Difference' section of chapter 3, and to Maximilien Ringelmann's work (1913), first referred to here in the 'Teamwork' section of chapter 3.

[7] Jaron Lanier's interview (19 June 2013) 'Virtual reality: Meet the founding father Jaron Lanier' was with the news editor of *MIT Technology Review* Niall Firth and published in the *New Scientist*.

[8] See Toby Ord (2020), pp 214 and 216.

[9] See my (2009) *Teaching, Learning and Assessment*, published in Maidenhead, UK, by the Open University Press, p 107ff.

[10] See Anthony Storr's (1996) *Feet of Clay: A Study of Gurus*, published in London, UK, by HarperCollins.

[11] See Stephen Gibson's and Kathryn Millard's (2018) blog 'The women who defied the Milgram Experiment about their creative documentary film Experiment 20', available at www.thebritishacademy.ac.uk/blog/women-who-defied-milgram-experiment/#:≈:text=Of%20the%20780%participants%20in,behaved%20during%20the%20experimental%20sessions.

[12] See Stuart Hampshire's (2000) *Justice is conflict*, published in Princeton, NJ, by Princeton University Press.

[13] See John Darley's and Bibb Latané's (1968) 'Bystander intervention in emergencies: Diffusion of responsibility', published in the *Journal of Personality and Social Psychology*, 8, 4, Pt.1, pp 377–383. Go to doi:10.1037/h0025589. PMID 5645600.

[14] See Richard Philpot's, Lasse Suonperä Liebst's, Mark Levine's, Wim Bernasco's and Marie Rosenkrantz Lindegaard's (2019) 'Would I be helped? Cross-national CCTV footage showed that intervention is the norm in public conflicts', published in the *American Psychologist*, 75, 1, pp 66–75, available at https://doi.org/10.1037/amp0000469.

[15] This was the view, for example, of the philosopher Lysander Spooner (born 1808, died 1887).

[16] See, for example, Fiona Carnie's (2018) *Rebuilding Our Schools from the Bottom Up: Listening to Teachers, Children and Parents* published in Abingdon, UK, by Routledge.

[17] See Richard Baldwin's (2016) *The Great Convergence: Information Technology and the New Globalisation*, published in Cambridge, MA, by The Belknap Press of Harvard University Press. Also his (2019) *The Globotics Upheaval: Globalisation, Robotics, and the Future of Work*, published in London, UK, by Weidenfeld & Nicolson, pp 1, 283-288 and 292-301.

11 Taking Responsibility

In this chapter we hear from Madeleine Bunting; Fritjof Capra and Pier Luigi Luisi; Ute Frevert; and June Tangney, Jeff Stuewig and Logaina Hafez, among others.

How can we work with nature and care for one another?

Caring

One balmy summer's evening in the late 1980s, I was on my way from the Vaudeville Theatre in London to catch a train, walking down Villiers Street, up steps and across Hungerford Bridge. About 30 metres ahead, I saw a dishevelled young man looking down over the barrier at the full tide running dark below. I took in that he had a loaded British Airways travel bag slung over his back. The shape and weight told me there were house bricks in the bag. He clambered onto the barrier and dropped into the River Thames. If I'd run straight away, could I have pulled him back? I've asked myself that question many times.

I had no mobile phone. I knew there was usually an attended police river boat moored under the bridge. Less than a minute later I reached the South Bank and looked back. No boat had been launched. I doubted he could have survived. I had read the situation, but had done nothing to help. Perhaps you've experienced something like that. Do you know what your response would be to seeing someone in danger?

We have increasing exposure to news and mobile-phone video clips showing that some people respond quickly and bravely. Could it be that now many of us are better prepared to intervene in a crisis?

Conscious preparation and practice make it likelier we'll be ready when the need arises. Perhaps you've been trained or you've rehearsed what to do in your head or in conversation.

Can we be prepared to respond to social and global issues?

Does inertia or indifference stop us? Or are we overcome by feelings of hopelessness or lack of resources?

Wanting to do something for someone else and for the common good springs from an empathic impulse and social conscience. Caring is the opposite of narcissism and dogma. A good number of us sense we've a better chance of being safe and well when our fellow human beings are safe and well. That sense is a part of wanting to work in war zones, emergencies, search and rescue, aid and charity, education, and for security, judicial, mediation and reconciliation, medical, welfare, social and end-of-life services. We are sometimes altruistic and selfish at the same time, and by turns. It seems that we discover in the moment whether our first response to alarm is to freeze, flee or fight[1]. And, in the case of bigger social, environmental and climatic problems, there are issues of consensus-building, funding, administration and collaboration between organisations to contend with. Turning fellow feeling into practical action is a challenge.

The writer and broadcaster Madeleine Bunting (2016)[2] said that professional caring draws on 'instinct and judgement' as well as on 'competence derived from rigour and emotional engagement with the individual' who is cared for. It 'rests ultimately on a combination of training, organisational culture and the disposition of an individual and their personal motivation'. When circumstances allow, the intention is to make a connection with whoever needs care because 'caring involves a relationship over time'. Bunting said its hallmarks are 'continuity, spontaneity and autonomy', but not at the expense of diligent planning or coordination. Holding those capabilities in fruitful tension is something we have to work on. It goes wrong when carers exploit the power or opportunity the role gives them to abuse susceptible and vulnerable individuals or groups, or when providers forget or misunderstand their essential purpose.

Does it take exceptional human beings to do what's right for individuals and communities?

If it does, we should enlist their energy and expertise in the biggest possible of all causes: saving our species and planet and improving our quality of life—without losing sight of the fact that each of us has contributions to make.

Caring that expresses both empathic spontaneity and consideration leads to altruism. And, when we care about others as much as we care about ourselves, the fusion of caring and altruism is love.

Altruism

Brian Boyd's analysis (2010) was that altruism works when we:

> Have sympathy for one another
> Are grateful for kindness
> Treat one another fairly, that is, as we would like to be treated
> Are remorseful when we fail to respond to others' needs.

Negative emotions, such as regretting our own omissions and failures and speaking out against unkind behaviour or poorly managed essential services, are a vital part of our caring and becoming altruistic, just as adversity is crucial to our becoming resilient and not knowing inspires us to learn.

Remember Michio Kaku's (2021) observation (referred to in the 'Becoming Resilient' section of chapter 1) that we have to struggle to achieve anything meaningful and worthwhile. Boyd described how, when we try to do the right thing, conflicts arise because some of us vehemently oppose what seems ideal to others. We don't all agree on how to go about what we want to achieve, and there may always be some of us who exploit cooperative efforts for their own selfish ends and 'accept the benefits without paying their share of the costs'. Where there are beneficiaries of generous and social initiatives, there may also be freeloaders, some of whom exploit privileged, powerful positions.

Our evolution equips us for *and* counteracts our empathising and working well together. Because our feelings about ourselves aren't always in harmony with our feelings about others, and our instincts can be at odds with our decisions. So we help ourselves and others when we:

> Focus on others' feelings as much as our own
> Check our ideas against reliable facts and verifiable sources of information

Are as alert to our medium- and long-term goals as we are to our initial ideas about what to do

Notice what goes well as much as what doesn't go well

Replace unhelpful habits with conscientious, updateable routines

Are as prepared to challenge wrong-doing and injustice as we are to celebrate kindness and fairness.

Looking forward to being satisfied moves us to act. Robert Sapolsky (2018)[3] observed that positive anticipation makes us more responsive than the prospect of reward does: 'If you know your appetite will be sated, pleasure is more about the appetite than about the sating … This explains the context-dependent craving in addiction'.

Over millennia, we have both followed and forsaken principles and ways of behaving which might have countered our seeking merely selfish or short-term gratifications. We blind ourselves to mistakes and mishaps, or rationalise and argue them away. We struggle to learn from occasions when we've not resisted actions our better selves knew we shouldn't have let happen.

We're not the only species willing to help those in need. And we're probably not the only species to be glad when we're helped. Reciprocal altruism among non-kin is seen in vampire bats, capuchin monkeys, baboons, chimpanzees, bonobos and dolphins, for example. In Brain Boyd's[4] account, 'All social species prosper more together than alone, or they would not remain social, but humans take this to another level, ultra-sociality, the most intense cooperativeness of all individualised animal societies'. Our challenge is to help one another get the best out of this capacity. On a relatively small, local scale, sometimes we have an urge to 'pay it forward'[5]: rather than simply returning a kindness, we take time and trouble to repay someone else's good deed by being considerate, neighbourly or helpful to other people. This goes beyond reciprocating and actively propagates generosity. Sometimes, it becomes a conscious practice, for example when we choose to carry out random acts of kindness, smiling, say, at three more strangers when one smiles at us. When we manage to do those things we come to regard what is extraordinary as natural.

Strands in civilised codes of behaviour and customs guide us toward doing what our culture or better judgement tells us is right. As Boyd wrote, things that 'seem morally obvious and intuitive now weren't necessarily so in the past; many started with non-conforming reasoning'.

Working with Nature

By the 1930s, Gestalt psychologists, ecologists and biologists had opened new fields of study and applied research, focusing on prolifically diverse evolutionary interrelationships. Attention was drawn to the significance of context and connectedness in and between living organisms and between their constituent elements and communities. Of particular interest were patterns of dynamically evolving interdependences and networks. It became a priority to focus on complementariness and interplay between systemic and materialist approaches to questions about all complex forms of life, including our own. As much as this thinking was developed to advance scientific understanding, it was developed with ethical concerns in mind.

Individuals, groups, communities and societies holistically came to be seen as much more than the sum of their parts—but without losing sight of their specific characteristics and functions. Fritjof Capra and Pier Luigi Luisi (2014) and Capra (2019)[6] described how 'Revolutionary discoveries in quantum physics in the realm of atoms and subatomic particles led physicists to see the universe as an interconnected web of relationships whose parts can be defined only through their connection to the whole.' It became possible to think of patterns in all forms of living matter not as statically or mechanistically regular but as infinitely varied, ever-changing, ever-changing, intentional and communicative. Reinvention—both organic and structural—emerged as one of life's essential features.

Matter equates to structures, and mind equates to processes. Both matter and mind become proportionately and increasingly complex over time. This 'thinking about life in terms of patterns, relationships and contexts', uses a 'mathematics of non-linear dynamics', leading us to realise we have to work with nature 'not through domination and control but through respect, cooperation and dialogue'. In this way, Capra and Luisi highlighted a sophisticated exchange between contingency and determinism: 'Every living organism continually renews itself, as its cells break down and build up structures, and its tissues and organs replace their cells in continual cycles', all the while maintaining 'its overall identity or pattern of organisation'. It's a paradox that mutations and gene mixing are random, yet 'evolution as a whole does not proceed randomly at all'.

All living bodies—as individuals and collectively—are moved by and act on their environments. Environments don't specify or direct changes; they trigger adaptive responses. Organic systems deal in variation and novelty and are architects and drivers of their evolutions. Networks of cells and units generate new structures and processes by responding to their internal, constitutive dynamics and as well as to external linkages and disturbances. The human brain illustrates such natural, highly complex networking. Our feeling alone may be dispelled by our discovering that we depend on all kinds of natural phenomena and they depend on us. And human communities, companies, services and species undergo the same kinds of systemic transformations that individual organisms perform.

Consciousness is a special kind of cognitive process which emerges when certain levels of complexity arise. By developing our appreciation of natural interdependences we learn about our own and others' needs and wants, and so are readier to live better lives. Mutual, reciprocal and coordinated relationships grow from our optimistic, constructive interactions, enabling both individuals and communities to benefit and grow. As we study and seek to protect and enhance our lives, we can learn to bring together these four dimensions of life—the biological, cognitive, social and ecological—and so work *with* nature. We can learn to pay attention both to relatively unalterable structures—like laws or rules—and to possible alternatives and options—like moves in a game. We can learn to avoid tackling social and environmental problems as though they were entirely amenable to self-evident, contextless, settled, finite, guaranteed or universal solutions. We are then better prepared to conceive of the most courageous life-enhancing goals and address unwanted outcomes resulting from our efforts.

Becoming Part of It All

In Iain McGilchrist's (2021)[7] view, 'The way of understanding things is to see how [we] are in relation to as many other things as is possible, because it's in those relationships that [we] exist ... Relationships are prior to the things that are related'. Yet we tend to have an everyday, default image of the world as being made up of things which are put together in the way that a bicycle is assembled. This is not how our world is made up. So, for as many of us as possible, it has come to be essential to take a multiplicity of viewpoints[8] into account and be as flexible and context-conscious as we can manage. The 2020 film *My Octopus Teacher*[9] richly illustrated dialogue and cooperation between humanity and nature. It documented the forging of a relationship between the filmmaker Craig Foster and a wild common octopus in a kelp forest off the Western Cape of South Africa.

Merlin Sheldrake (2020)[10] wrote that so far there have been five major extinction events on Earth, each of which eliminated between 75 and 95 percent of all species. None of those cataclysms was caused by humans. Fungi survived, and some 'even thrived during these calamitous episodes'. Fungi's exemplary characteristics 'might help us by restoring contaminated ecosystems'. We've always had a symbiotic relationship with fungi, currently, for example, using alcohol, soy sauce, penicillin and fizzy drinks to assist our digestion. This should encourage us to foster stronger partnerships with microbes as well as between us as we try to secure our survival and better ways of living.

Can we find ways to innovate and so avoid a sixth major extinction event—this time, one of our own making?

McGilchrist saw that some of our habits stop us from responding to things. For him, our role is to be part of all there is and so counter the temptation to see ourselves as separate, superior or indispensable. We need to appreciate quality as well as quantity, recognising that the world is both beautiful and terrible. He noted that we tend not to listen when we're told what to do. We have to see for ourselves and internalise what we need to do. This connects strongly with themes in this book: to live better lives we must use our abilities to be empathic, symbiotic and adaptive in our relationships to one another and our complex, anomalous world. Without those qualities we're unlikely to respond to one another's and our common needs and wants, still less likely to meet them.

We're all strange and tricky. On a personal level, our best hope is to find someone intriguing and willing enough to face life's opportunities and challenges with us. In our groups and as a species our best hope is to find as many people as possible who are willing to work together to live as considerately and happily as we can.

Tackling Problems

Some of our problems come from the wrongs we do and the mistakes we make.

Toby Ord (2020)[11] observed that the refuse human beings have dumped will take thousands of years to decay away. It will take 100,000 years for the Earth's climate to be 'mostly restored and rebalanced', provided 'we can learn to care rightly for our home'. He hoped and believed that 'we can address pollution and biodiversity loss much more quickly than this—that sooner or later we will work to actively remove the pollution and to conserve threatened species'.

Some of us infect ourselves by eating animals already infected by coronaviruses. Viruses also jump to our cells from cells in the bodies of wild, feral or farmed animals, and then from infected humans' bodies. We have much still to learn about human vulnerability to diseases, including those that arise from viruses initially transmitted as a result of 'wet market' practices in some areas of Asia and meat production methods in a number of regions across the world. We continue to learn about how to limit and vaccinate against the transmission of lethal and life-limiting diseases.

When viruses sense threat or opportunity, they seek out cells in new hosts and feed on them. It's not just wild animals that are involved in this zoonotic transmission. Chickens, pigs, pangolins and civets are examples of intensively farmed animals, bred with reduced genetic variety, making them more susceptible to viral infection. Companies producing and distributing these foods get big returns on these kinds of investments and in the process create conditions for pandemics.

We could take measures to reduce our being infected by fruit bats. We could stop destroying fruit bats' forest habitats which causes them to eat our fruit crops. We could stop bats from eating fruit crops by covering whole orchards in fixed nets[12]. Legislating and regulating against deforestation and harmful husbandry and farming practices would be effective ways of combating viral diseases. Every country could be required to make bats a protected species and enforce the law. But there are commercial and political temptations and/or pressures to turn a blind eye to ecological negligence and abuses. So we need to have the collective courage and determination to apply pressure where it's needed. In the meantime, might we help by not buying meat produced in damaging ways?

It appears also to be the case that some human populations are more susceptible to Covid-19, and, most seriously, if they have conditions such as obesity. How might nations work together to reduce levels of obesity, now increasing exponentially across the globe but not in every country? 40 percent of the population of the USA is obese, compared with 4 percent in Korea.

At the time of writing this, the root cause of the Covid-19 pandemic had not been established. It might not have been zoonotic transmission from bats or other animals. It might have been that, without anyone's realising or acknowledging the significance of this chain of events, the virus was produced in a laboratory, infected one or more scientists or technicians and spread through the community and then from community to community, helped by airtravel[13].

Sharing Responsibility

What enables and encourages us to share responsibility for the health and well-being of communities, companies and services[14]?

The more intimately and intricately we affect and need each other, the more important it becomes for us to develop and maintain constructive ways of communicating and cooperating. We might apply the lessons of Maximilien Ringelmann's (1913)[15] investigations into teamwork. His research and its later verifications gave these pointers:

> Recognise that each of us has to play a part in protecting and promoting worldwide health and well-being
> Acknowledge how profound and complex the challenges are
> Emphasise the necessity of coordinating our efforts.

When we act together with sincere, informed, collegial inventiveness, satisfaction tends to follow—up to the point when respect is forfeited, when trust is broken or when unforeseen calamity strikes. It's a different matter if we believe an individual, a group, community or government acts in bad faith. Then, it's right to challenge them and do what we can to reduce or limit their power. We may continue to look for and encourage signs that they will be prepared to develop mutual trust with us. It is part of acting in good faith that we do our best to establish and maintain open lines of communication. We increase our chances of succeeding by strengthening our resolve not to be selfish or partial but to work toward what is good for all of us. Doing those things, we avoid feelings of shame and guilt that we haven't done enough or that we've neglected our common humanity.

We all struggle with the tension between the two poles of being certain and needing to ask questions. Susie Orbach (2016)[16] saw that 'Out of that tension comes enormous creativity … [C]omplexity and category-making are the dialectical prerequisites of being human'. It is crucial therefore that we're free to put questions to anyone we live and work with, and that we appreciate that the 'right' answers enable us 'to get ahead with the process of questioning and answering', as R. G. Collingwood (1939)[17] put it. The 'right' answers are ones that help us work through our conflicts and differences to find goals and methods we can agree on. We need answers that do more than make us feel better for a while.

Good answers help us lead healthier, more enjoyable and more effective lives. We achieve this by acting together with sincere, informed, inventive intent; then satisfaction tends to follow—up to the point when respect is forfeited, when trust is broken and when there is bad faith or unforeseen calamity strikes.

It's a different matter if we believe an individual, community, government acts in bad faith. Then, it's right to challenge them and do what we can to reduce or limit their power. We may continue to look for and encourage signs that they will be prepared to develop mutual trust with us. It is part of acting in good faith that we do our best to establish and maintain open lines of communication. We increase our chances of succeeding by strengthening our resolve not to be selfish or partial but to work toward what is good for all of us. Doing those things, we avoid feelings of shame and guilt that we haven't done enough or that we've neglected our common humanity.

Safeguarding

What do you do if care for one person or group conflicts with care for others?

What do you do if an individual or group puts others' safety, health or well-being at risk?

When safety and protection are at stake, there are few single, absolute, right answers. There are occasions when forceful confrontation has to be considered. Taking someone out of society for rehabilitative treatment is an example. And, as a pre-emptive resort, national leaders may have to be deterred from waging war by having their military capability and supply lines disabled.

The following is a case study of how people who are responsible for a community's safety, health and well-being approached a serious dilemma. The governors, senior leaders and staff members in a school for students with moderate learning difficulties including autism at Westfield Arts College in Weymouth, Dorset, UK, were struggling to manage a small number of students who were abusing others. Over the course of nearly a year, led by the head teacher Phil Silvesters and the chair of governors Kath Gould, the school developed processes which set out the ambitions and limits of what they would do to safeguard everyone.

They realised they were neither helping certain troubled, troubling students nor fulfilling their duty of care toward everyone else. They understood that their community is sustained by everyone's assenting to conventions and rules in relation to safety and respect for persons and things. They were clear that they were responsible for sponsoring and promoting relationships that allow everyone to learn and grow. They saw it as their role to help each student to accept her or his responsibility for herself or himself and so share responsibility for everyone.

If they had asked 'What do we fear?' I think the answer would have been 'We're afraid we're not protecting our community.' And if they had asked 'What do we hope?' I think their answer would have been 'We hope we'll succeed in helping students we're currently failing and, if necessary, help them transfer to places better able to meet their needs.' The governors and staff understood that inclusive learning depends on creating conditions that allow individual discipline and collective discipline to reinforce one another.

When a student wasn't held by healthy bonds and boundaries, the adults' first response would be to remind her or him of what most of their peers were doing successfully, that is, planning the curriculum and events and making, reviewing and updating rules, sanctions and rewards. A line would be drawn, inviting the student to make a fresh start, if necessary elsewhere. A halt would be called, temporarily in the first instance, possibly more than once, and, as a last resort, permanently. Exclusion would signal that provision had been failing and had to be improved, and, when the danger was no longer present, the person or persons responsible for it could be welcomed back.

This has to do with wanting to do everything possible to make communities inclusive and so help everyone realise two essential things: that there are consequences to our actions and that we all are responsible for how we live together. Healthy development, shared understanding, well-being and rehabilitation were the objectives. So contingencies were put in place.

When a decision was made to exclude a student from part of a lesson or longer, the message to her or him was 'You can't carry on doing what you've been doing—hitting, swearing, running off—and be part of what we do. You're going to have to change what you do. You have to choose how much you want to be with us. We like having you with us when you are part of how we all do things together. If there are things we can do to help you, please, tell us. We're here to do all we can to help you learn and grow with us. But you're the one who decides how you behave.'

Implementing Protocols

When I showed this case study to Phil Silvester, he gave me his retrospective summary of the school's thinking and approach. Their plan and process had been to allow everyone 'a safe space and precious time to think, reflect, analyse, discuss and communicate'; to work with agencies beyond the school; to 'take charge' of what was already or was likely to become 'a destructive, disruptive and potentially dangerous spiral'; to de-stress everyone 'by laying out clear boundaries and consequences'; to provide 'tailored pastoral support or clinical supervision'; to address difficulties head-on and come to agreements about ways forward; and to 'support everyone in becoming their own advocate'.

The school was determined to maintain an environment which wouldn't jeopardise anyone's security or well-being, and just as determined to give troubled and troublesome students and their parents and carers opportunities and support to recover enjoyment and achievement. The leadership, governors and staff became explicitly committed to improving their provision. Because the processes demanded maximum attention from those responsible, a senior leader stayed at a remove from the action, carried out periodic checks and communicated what was happening to interested parties, often informally.

Ostracising and shaming were not to be resorted to. Dignity was not to be enjoyed only by those who played their proper part in the community; it was also to be enjoyed, for as long as it was tenable, by those who were at odds with both their peers and those responsible for everyone's well-being.

Exclusion had not to undermine anyone's responsibilities, so what senior personnel did, for example, had not to take anything away from the role and status of front-line colleagues or from parents' or students' learning about how to benefit from one another's contributions. Policies and strategies were kept under review and reported to supervisory, funding and inspecting authorities. Concise, plainly expressed documentation, including planning for re-integration, was sent to the student's home, care and teaching staff, a nominated member of the governing body and welfare agencies.

The following protocol was used. A senior leader met with everyone involved, enquired into the precipitating events, checked what had happened and facilitated a decision about what should be done. If in the first instance an exclusion was recommended, a senior leader convened a formal meeting with the student, parents or carers, members of staff and other relevant parties including social services, focusing on causes and consequences of actions. If necessary, the purpose and terms of limited exclusion were discussed and made clear, along with details of immediate and continuing support and arrangements for a post-exclusion meeting and re-admission.

While a temporary exclusion was in place, care was taken to counsel and support students, staff members and others who were affected by the events which could be distressing. Re-admission following temporary exclusion was structured so that all concerned attended a meeting which addressed what had taken place.

If these processes didn't help students re-integrate successfully, permanent exclusion would follow according to a similar protocol, involving negotiations and arrangements for students to transfer to another school or form of educational provision. The justification was that the care-providers have to protect the community by excluding an individual if, and only if, processes which meet all stakeholders' needs and most stringent requirements are carried out conscientiously and lead to an overwhelming conclusion that the community rigorously does everything it can to keep everyone safe in its care.

Can you see how this might apply in national and international political situations?

Safety First

The intention can be to:

> Be honest with yourself
> Be honest with others
> Keep focused on acting in the interests of safety, equality of opportunity and justice.

These then are processes that inform humane, effective governance and practice:

> Living up to our view of our better selves
> Reviewing intentions and setting goals
> Creating and updating protocols for everyone to be aware of and use
> Being answerable for outcomes.

Of course, communities, organisations and countries aren't given into one another's care in the way that young people are to their school and social services. A voluntarily and cooperatively constituted body such as the United Nations would have to bear responsibility for actions taken in everyone's interests. Institutions such as the International Court of Justice in The Hague can be empowered to investigate and prosecute states suspected of crimes and facilitate their rehabilitation.

Without international worldwide cooperation, we lack the means to isolate and properly engage with offenders. Forums for investigation and courts of prosecution and appeal have to have legal and ethical frameworks and operate outside spheres of political representation. The threats we face include dangers associated with rising carbon dioxide levels, our planet's declining biodiversity, highly contagious diseases, people trafficking and enslavement, infringements by one state on another, the use of armaments on civilians and the threatened use of biological, chemical and nuclear weapons.

We have to feel responsible, contribute to finding ways of working together and play our part. Safety and survival are our first goal. Our ultimate goal is to flourish through our sense of responsibility for one another.

We make choices, and doing the right thing depends on what we learn about the practical, social, moral and legal consequences of our decisions and actions. Acting with a conscience entails acknowledging our reliance on one another. This was an important aspect of an edition of BBC Radio 4's *The Life Scientific* in which Jim Al-Khalili (2021)[18] spoke with the epidemiologist Dame Anne Johnson. She explained that public health is a relatively recent phenomenon.

The sciences of epidemiology, population surveillance, statistics and genomic sequencing form part of the basis of an informed and socially responsible government's policy and practice, aiming to respond to and guide people's behaviour. Shortly after the emergence of AIDS, for example, Johnson began The National Surveys of Sexual Attitudes and Lifestyles in the UK. It is now a cornerstone of many people's and governments' efforts to protect and promote hygiene and well-being in society[19].

A Role for Guilt

Feeling shame, initially at least, we transfer our sense of inadequacy or wrongdoing onto others and imagine they judge us badly. In guilt, we don't transfer our feelings onto others. A part of feeling guilt is recognising we're not always perfect or right. The historian Ute Frevert (2020)[20] explained that recognising our mistakes and feeling remorse have a function both in our individual emotional maturing and in our communities' and societies' sharing responsibility for the quality of our interdependent lives. Narcissists and sociopaths know neither shame nor guilt.

Frevert explored the history of social shaming as a way of leading people to behave according to what a group or an authority requires and expects: 'All forms of shaming entail stigmatisation and exclusion, even when the primary aim is to reintegrate and improve recalcitrants and delinquents'. Shaming carries the threat that we might be put beyond the pale, depriving us of redemption and belonging.

There is an argument in favour of appealing to offenders' purely selfish self-interest while helping them realise that they need other people. Frevert observed that 'Ideas of honour and dignity play a divisive, albeit often overlooked and under-estimated role'. When we realise we might feel honour and dignity by acting a certain way, we can know there's a risk of our forfeiting those rewards if we don't do the right thing. Feeling shame or guilt prompts us to seek reconciliation and make reparation. Shame and guilt come from knowing we've lost our bearings. Respect, compassion and wanting to make amends put us back on the right path.

As societies have evolved, the practice of publicly embarrassing the convicted has become less tolerated. States and jurisdictions have tried 'actively to protect citizens from being humiliated', in part because 'the new citoyen demanded that their honour be protected against attacks by other citizens, but also from encroachments by the state'. The goals of modern penal policy have become improvement and re-socialisation—'acknowledging the dignity of all, including those who [have] violated the law'—through our values, attitudes and actions.

Guiding and Reforming

In the 20th century, the power of many small groups and communities was transferred to larger units: peoples, nations and alliances. Sovereign states took responsibility for moral re-education by sanctions and/or removal from society. When citizens were uninhibitedly sanctioned, shamed and humiliated, it was at the hands of agents of the state. Frevert explained, 'Generally speaking, societies that place primacy on the social embeddedness of the individual and their obligation to act in accordance with the common good tend to give secondary status to the rights of the person and to their entitlement to respect ... The official justification was always that the shamed had to be taught a lesson so that they could successfully be reintegrated into society'.

If we don't accept the norms or the sense of the rules we're charged with transgressing, we can't be shamed, though we may be made to suffer inconvenience or punishment. So, if a recalcitrant or an offender has no regret or feels justified in her or his actions, shaming has no socialising or rehabilitating effect: 'Public humiliation only works in the context of asymmetrical power relations', with at least one party displaying its power for everyone else to see. To be humiliated is to be made to feel humble, with the risk that the feeling won't last very long. Humility is an essential ingredient in our developing affiliation, allegiance, empathy, trust and cooperation.

It's not only formal authorities that want to humiliate. Disadvantaged or oppressed individuals and groups have sometimes turned the tables and committed self-sacrificial acts designed to shame those who have public power. The 1936 Jarrow Marches in the UK, the 1975 Māori Land March in New Zealand and self-immolation by protesters in India and China and across Asia can be seen as examples.

Social cohesion breaks down when sections of society feel they're persecuted while others seem to be protected, for example, by selfish or sectarian privilege and power. It's an unending challenge, first, to have law enforcement treat everyone equally without fear or favour, and, second, for everyone's experience of justice to be that it is fairly administered.

The psychologists June Tangney, Jeff Stuewig and Logaina Hafez (2011)[21] wrote that, when we feel guilt, we ruminate over our misdeeds and wish we'd behaved differently. Their research showed that increasing offenders' shame tends to be socially counter-productive, because it contributes to their denying personal responsibility for their actions and to their wanting to escape or hide from consequences, for example, by abusing prohibited substances and drugs.

Shaming offenders fails to address and instead compounds their psychological difficulties and is likely to lead to their re-offending. Good evidence was found of successful reform when judicial sentences and conditions were 'designed to foster constructive feelings of guilt by focusing offenders on the negative consequences of their behaviour, particularly how their behaviour affects their communities, their friends and their families'.

The former education psychologist, trustee and director of the Restorative Foundation Schools Partnership Tom Macready (2009)[22] recommended a specific way of guiding social and public responses to anti-social behaviour. He saw that we can prompt and support offenders to talk about how what they did has affected them and to learn about how those who were harmed have been affected. And we can help them talk about what they can do to make amends and how they might try to make a better future for themselves and those they come into contact with.

The goals of restorative justice are to guide and support offenders' learning to develop their moral emotions: 'to see, first-hand, the potential or actual destructiveness of their infractions, to empathise with their victims, to feel behaviour-focused guilt, and importantly to actively involve them in constructive solutions … to enhance their capacity for adaptive guilt and to reduce their propensity to experience shame'. Community-service sentences are an example.

The emphasis is on 'the need to acknowledge and take responsibility for one's wrongdoings, and act to make amends for the negative consequences of one's behaviour'. The principal rationale is that there are many risk factors rooted in offenders' history—for example, their age when first arrested and their parents' courses through life—but moral emotions have been proved amenable to the right kinds of intervention in rehabilitative centres and prisons, particularly when promoted and supported by well-trained and well-managed staff.

Summing Up

Part of caring is being ready not to accept situations as given.

We must learn to work with nature 'not through domination and control but through respect, cooperation and dialogue'.

Suffering guilt after we've done wrong helps us learn from consequences. Anticipating we'll feel guilty helps us learn to promote justice and well-being.

Doing the right thing depends on what we learn about the practical, social, moral and legal consequences of our decisions and actions.

---

[1] The fight-flight-freeze response was identified by the physiologist Walter Bradford Cannon (1915) in his *Bodily changes in pain, hunger, fear, and rage*, published in New York, NY, by Appleton-Century-Crofts. It was part of his theory of homeostasis, popularised by his (1932) *The Wisdom of the Body*, published in New York, NY, by W. W. Norton and Company, pp 177–201.

[2] Madeleine Bunting's (2016) essay 'Crisis in Care' was broadcast on BBC Radio 3 as *The Essay*, Episode 4.

[3] See Robert Sapolsky (2018), pp 671-672, 45, 71-72 and 674.

[4] The phrase 'paying it forward' was probably coined by Lily Hardy Hammond (1916, 2009) in *In the Garden of Delight*, published in Whitefish, MT, by Kessinger Publishing, LLC. It was popularised by the science fiction writer Robert Heinlein, and then became even better known through Catherine Ryan Hyde's 1999 novel and then a film *Pay It Forward* (2000), directed by Mimi Leder, adapted for the screen by Leslie Dixon.

[5] See Brian Boyd (2010), pp 57-58, 63-64 and 101.

[6] See Fritjof Capra and Pier Luigi Luisi (2014), pp 59, 79-80, 180, 214-215 and 255-257. The analogy with game-playing, rules and players is explored here in chapter 7.

[7] Iain McGilchrist gave a talk (30 Mar 2021) about this via Zoom from the Arthur Conan Doyle Centre, Edinburgh, Scotland.

[8] See, for example, E. H. Carr (1961), referred to in the 'Learning Together' section of chapter 4.

[9] The film was produced by Craig Foster and directed by Pippa Ehrlich and James Reed.

[10] See Merlin Sheldrake (2020), pp 18 and 117, referred to here in the 'Evolving' section of chapter 2.

[11] See Toby Ord (2020), pp 219-220.

[12] See Sheema Abdul Aziz's, Kevin Olival's, Sara Bumrungsri's, Greg Richards' and Paul Racey's (2015) essay 'The Conflict Between Pteropodid Bats and Fruit Growers: Species, Legislation and Mitigation', edited by Christian C. Voigt and Tigga Kingston, published by Springer Open, pp 377-426; available via https://link.springer.com/content/pdf/10.1007%F978-3-319-25220-9.pdf.

[13] See Dr Sanjay Gupta's (26 Mar 2021) edition *Autopsy of a pandemic: 6 doctors at the centre of the US Covid-19 response* on the Cable News Network (CNN), including

interviews with Doctors Deborah Birx, Anthony Fauci, Brett Giroir, Stephen Hahn, Robert Kadlec and Robert Redfield.

[14] See the 'Becoming Inclusive' section of chapter 3 here, referring to Michael Tomasello's (2016 and 2018) works on intentionality.

[15] See chapter 3's footnote 22 here, regarding Maximilien Ringelmann (1913).

[16] See Susie Orbach (2016), p 84.

[17] See R. G. Collingwood's (1939) *An Autobiography*, published in Oxford, UK, by Clarendon Press, p 37.

[18] Dame Anne Johnson (2 February 2021) spoke to Jim Al-Khalili in the edition of BBC Radio 4's programme *The Life Scientific* entitled 'From HIV to influenza and Covid-19, why prevention is better than cure'.

[19] See the British Channel 4 television drama serial *It's a Sin* (2021), written and created by Russell T. Davies and directed by Peter Hoar.

[20] See Uta Frevert's (2020) *Die Politik der Demütigung: Schauplätze von Macht und Ohnmacht*, published by S. Fischer, then translated from the German by Adam Bresnahan as *The Politics of Humiliation: A Modern History*, and published in New York, NY, by Oxford University Press, pp 19, 206, 208-210, 217-219, 221-222, 224, 229 and 231-233.

[21] See June Price Tangey's, Jeff Stuewig's and Logaina Hafez's (2011) 'Shame, guilt, and remorse: implications for offender populations', published in *The Journal of Forensic Psychiatry and Psychology*, 22, 5, pp 706-723; available via https://doi.org/10.1080/14789949.2011.617541.

[22] See Tom Macready's (2009) 'Learning social responsibility: A restorative practice', published in *Educational Psychology in Practice*, 25, 3, pp 211-220: https://www.tandfonline.com/doi/abs/10.1080/02667 360903151767. Tom Macready built on work by the practitioner and professor in restorative justice Paul McCold and the founder and former first president of the International Institute for Restorative Practices Ted Wachtel (2003), for example, their *In pursuit of paradigm: A theory of restorative justice*, a paper presented at the XIII World Congress of Criminology; available at https://www.iirp.edu/pdf/paradigm.pdf.

12 Leading

Here we hear from Kurt Lewin, Ronald Lippitt and Ralph White; Donald Schön; Stuart Sutherland; Frederick Herzberg, Bill Paul Jnr and Keith Robertson; Gary Klein; Chesley Sullenberger; and Sabrina Cohen-Hatton, among others.

How does leadership help us participate and contribute?

How Leaders See Their Role

Who are leaders you have admired and respected?
What are their qualities and skills?
What qualities and skills do they look for in the rest of us?

Some of us seem to believe there's one sure way to have everyone do what's right. It is to tell people what to do, praise them when they do it and withdraw approval or penalise them when they don't. Under that kind of regime, we tend to be less productive, less successful and to put up with rather than enjoy what we do. Under that kind of regime, we lack opportunities, motivation and encouragement to improve what we do and how we do it.

What applies to leaders applies also to managers, coaches, trainers, mentors, teachers, doctors, advisers, consultants, therapists and any of us who accepts responsibility. We see what kind of leader someone is by how she or he treats people and responds to challenges.

Some leaders and managers are confident they know what problems arise and feel success comes from their taking controlling people and things. At the opposite end of a spectrum, there are those who understand that they have limited and infrequent access to the unique and dynamic situations which practitioners face on the front line. They realise that everyone has to adapt to events or call for assistance which may or may not be available. They understand that a fair measure of their success is not what they achieve but what the people they're working with achieve. They try to enhance cooperation between individuals and between teams.

A strength of leaders who are open to their people is that they gain invaluable information from as many sources as possible. The corresponding weakness in dictators and autocrats is that, because they tell people what to think and believe, they tend to be told what they want to hear, and so know less and less about what is really happening.

Kurt Lewin, along with his fellow practically oriented psychologists Ronald Lippitt and Ralph White (1939)[1], defined and experimented with three leadership styles. *Authoritarian and autocratic* leaders have a vision of themselves at the top or centre of their group, organisation or society and don't need anyone else's input. They tell people in their care or team or employment what to do, and don't ask them for their input. *Laissez-faire* leaders ~~want~~ leave people to make their own decisions. *Participative* leaders involve as many people as possible in deciding goals and ways of working.

How do you like to be led?

How do you like to lead?

Effects of Leadership

Michael Polanyi (1951)[2] explained that organising a group under a single authority limits and sometimes blocks dialogue and cooperation. Top-down hierarchies and centre-to-periphery systems deter individuals and teams from having their own sense of purpose and using their own initiative. Such structures make it difficult to respond spontaneously in the present and difficult to improve our prospects as societies and a species. These kinds of governance and management are usually the mark of leaders who—for whatever reasons—are more interested in exercising or bolstering their power than they are in serving the well-being and effectiveness of their people and those they serve. They put their own dignity above everyone else's.

For leaders who want what might seem in the short term to be a quiet life, the simplest thing to do is to tell everyone what to do, and ignore what happens when everything isn't fine; or move on. For workers and citizens who want what might seem in the short term to be a quiet life, the simplest thing to do is to keep a low profile, behave as though they're doing what they've been told to do, and ignore what happens when everything isn't fine; or move on if they can. Wanting a quiet life, we explain low morale and poor performance by blaming other people, bad luck, fate and/or conspiracies.

Leaders, who can't accept people 'below them' having a voice in choices about policy and practice, treat differences in power and responsibility as though they were natural and necessary. They believe or pretend that adhering to hierarchical roles protects us from chaos and failure. It may bring clarity and prestige to some people, but basing authority and leadership on status has serious weaknesses. Too little account is taken of individuals' capabilities, circumstances and fitness for specific roles and too many of us are likely to have too little opportunity to offer our perceptions and ideas. Understandably then, many of us tend not to speak up and, when things go wrong, there's little we can do to help.

Sharing decision-making doesn't have to mean we can't have different job descriptions and levels of seniority and pay. Leaders who know they need everyone to play their part expect us all to contribute. They don't go through charades of asking people to express their views and then ignore whatever is said. They treat consultation as one element in an inclusive, constructive culture, not as a one-off or short-term exercise. Inequality is a kind of bondage, pushing us to depend unilaterally on others for essential needs, consolation or empowerment.

Leaders who listen and respond to their people and those they serve realise they help their community and organisation more by guiding and supporting than by dominating or micromanaging. They realise that everyone has to play their part and be actively involved if work is to be satisfying and beneficial. They set up routines and systems so that whoever has ideas to offer can speak up. Such leadership promotes individuals' mental health and social well-being.

Have you seen that kind of leader in action? What were your impressions?

Have you been that kind of leader? How has it worked out?

Autocracy may sometimes have a measure of integrity as a short-term response to frustrations, difficulties or emergencies. But ultimately the imposition and exercise of unilateral power can't be expected to address complex issues. Someone who has strong narcissism, psychopathy or sociopathy might be interested in what unites people, but it's likely to be chiefly in order to exploit it for their own ends. For most of us, combining autonomy with interdependence increases our security and enriches our lives. If we are to develop as a mature democracy capable of securing a life worth living in a sustainable future world, we have to be free and equal enough to share leadership and work together.

Leading by Increasing Participation

The philosopher and professor in urban planning Donald Schön (1983)[3] wrote that, when we express our perceptions and ideas, we tend to become committed to our group's cause. In groups whose hierarchy is based on voluntary respect, we feel psychologically safe because we know we can 'offer suggestions and take sensible risks without provoking retaliation'. Leaders of communities, companies and services whose hierarchy is based on status or force 'don't feel they need other people, so don't tend to take their perspectives or read their emotions'. Healthy, constructive leaders need and want their teams and communities to join forces in the pursuit of shared, worthwhile goals. Enabling others to cooperate autonomously may be leadership's most significant aim and achievement.

In the mid-1960s, John Harvey-Jones was a junior manager with Imperial Chemical Industries (ICI) on Teesside in the UK. He became chairman and then Sir John. Keith Robertson was in one of Harvey-Jones' teams responsible for identifying and training individuals to become leaders in the company. He told me about the ICI project. The team's first step was to define social and psychological qualities and skills they predicted would mark out apprentices with the potential to become leaders. They went on to devise and run programmes for those selected, involving teamwork and trust, for example in the contexts of problem-solving and challenging outdoor activities including rock-climbing.

After several months, it became apparent that what they were looking for and wanting to promote were characteristics possessed, to a greater or lesser extent, by many of us, if not everyone. Rather than trying to focus on an exceptional few, the company needed to find better ways of managing working relationships and conditions so that everyone would be able to play their part. They began investigating and experimenting with ways of tapping into people's personal and shared motivations: what do we find engaging, and what do we find rewarding? This orientation in management theory and practice was an extension of the concept of job satisfaction and became known as job enrichment.

Robertson, along with his colleague Bill Paul, collaborated with the psychologist Frederick Herzberg (1968)[4] to record case studies of job enrichment projects in the UK. This approach proposed that everyone's decisions and actions are vital, and, when we do the following things, we're all encouraged and enabled to:

> Pool information and expertise
> Frame goals and reinforce a shared commitment to them
> Adapt to events as they unfold.

Organisations' health and effectiveness are seen to depend less on communication 'downward', far more on consultation 'upward', from the people working on the front lines to those who have oversight and obligations beyond the immediate and practical. This gives a green light to bilateral communications between peers in and across teams and networks, initiated by and involving anyone—whatever their status and role. Management and leadership then become services whose purpose is 'to enable, encourage, assist, and reinforce achievement by employees', and 'the job itself becomes a true learning situation, its ingredients the motivators'.

Here we have a dynamic framework which affords everyone opportunities to improve what they do and how they do it. It draws on the motivations each of us feels, and is in keeping with Rutger Bregman's (2019)[5] work. He quoted the psychologist and social scientist Edward Deci who, with his colleagues Takuma Nishimura, Emma L. Bradshaw and Richard M. Ryan (2021)[6] concluded that we should stop thinking so much about how to motivate others and focus on shaping society so that we motivate ourselves.

Quickly and without great fanfare, job-enrichment methods were adopted in some leading industrial, commercial and public service organisations in many countries, and have continued to evolve, but without radically transforming mainstream culture. 50 years later, Matthew Syed (2019)[7] noted, 'No amount of commitment can drive decision-making in a situation of complexity when diverse perspectives are suppressed, when critical information isn't flowing through the social network'. In poorly functioning organisations, what flows through the social network is chiefly gossip and mere 'noise' that detracts from what our main concerns should be. It's a considerable obstacle to progress and success that we fail to challenge our assumptions and address crucial questions.

This is because enough of us—at every level—continue to see and hear what we want to see and hear, and struggle to grow out of an attachment to top-down hierarchy.

Being Organised and Involved

Effective leaders don't act as though they had no relevant prior experience. Nor do effective practitioners or front-line workers. None of us should expect our most important problems to come packaged as standard or be amenable to off-the-shelf solutions. Rather, as Schön explained, our 'situation is complex and uncertain' and 'there is a problem in finding the problem'.

We can look for patterns and peculiarities, decide what to do, follow through in good faith, and then expect to have to adapt and innovate. Things change. We change. More change happens. Sometimes we're overtaken by events and tasks we struggle to handle. Some of us seem to want assurances that leaders are in charge and guarantee our security and progress. When we hear politicians and public health officers say good outcomes may not follow conscientious actions, some of us feel let down or take offence.

Being ready for any kind of action entails some guesswork, inevitably with the risk of getting things wrong. Disappointments and errors are a price we pay for the freedoms of having hopes, expectations and ambitions and making our own predictions and simulations. Schön saw this as being acknowledged and even encouraged by *reflective* organisations insofar as they have 'flexible procedures, differentiated responses, qualitative appreciation of complex processes and decentralised responsibility for judgement and action'. *Unreflective* organisations, with their 'uniform procedures, objective measures of performance, and centre/periphery systems of control', aim to prevent or dissuade the majority of us from making decisions, and so neglect individuals' and teams' insights and expertise.

We whose role is principally to interact with service-users, clients, customers, patients and learners can be enabled and empowered to do our best. Then, like leaders, we try to solve problems we set ourselves as well as problems we run into, 'seeking both to understand the situation and to change it'. In that way, we achieve much more and feel greater satisfaction than when we wait to be incentivised, instructed, managed and rewarded. As Syed underlined, knowledge that has a bearing on morale, motivation, strategy and practice should be shared: 'It is no good having useful information that never gets aired'.

Leaders and managers are bound to have no better than intermittent and/or indirect contact with front-line workers and practitioners. Remember Robin Dunbar's (2016)[8] observations: a relationship's strength correlates strongly with the consistency and authenticity of its partners' interactions. Kinship and social attachments are useful shortcuts to mutual understanding and cooperation. But beyond close family and friends, we depend on negotiation and cooperation to sustain relatively impersonal and public relationships and transactions. We have to invest time, imagination and energy in creating different ways to deal with organisational, societal and political issues.

Groups of about 15 and more people form layers because of our need to 'create coalitions or alliances that protect individuals against the costs of living in large groups ... The sub-structuring of human communities will have arisen for the same reasons: at each level, the smaller grouping makes the existence of the next layer possible'. What binds us into constructive efforts are emotional, thoughtful and moral commitments. But, of course, there can be no guarantee that all leaders and citizens will make such commitments, or abide by them.

Sharing Leadership

Picture a group of about 15 people. Most of them know one another by sight; some know one another as friends; a couple are siblings. In Robin Dunbar's terms, most of them are in one another's widest circle of around 150 people with whom they have positive, ongoing relationships. They're taking a casual walk across an open stretch of land. As they go, conversations develop and shift. The patterns of the ambling sub-groups change fluidly and spontaneously. Without a word being said, they come to a halt. The question hangs in the air: what direction to take?

If you were to read a transcript of their brief discussion, you'd see that two or three of them take an informal leading role. One makes a suggestion that others like; another summarises the flow of the short debate about whether to take this or that path; a third concludes, 'Let's go this way.' If you could see a film of the walk, you'd notice that those three were most connected to members of the group not so much because they approached others but because others approached them. Much of the time, one of those three individuals happened to be positioned at the back of the group with a view of everyone. They all felt safe and involved; they enjoyed one another's company and the experience they shared.

Groups that have no formal or permanent leader or leaders tend to be led by different individuals according to the situations they find themselves in. Because informal leaders tend to anticipate and appreciate others' inclinations and preferences, their perceptions and suggestions are listened to and often lead to fruitful decisions. Groups and societies work well when those who lead and those who are led understand one another's intentions and purposes, often implicitly, but also, when it matters, explicitly.

Dialogue and having an overview enable us all—not just designated or self-appointed leaders—to respond to options and challenges. Cohesion grows out of shared commitment and is strengthened by open, honest communication. To manage large-scale cooperation, we have to invest in a range of dynamic relationships without diminishing or side-lining individuals' or groups' autonomy. Social unrest arises when numbers of us feel we have little or no influence in decision-making and no control over our prospects. When we decide things together, it helps if at critical moments we explain our thinking and clarify what we understand and decide.

When the English, drama and special educational needs teacher Steve Parker read drafts for this book, he wrote to me, saying he recognised many of the techniques I outlined as being part of best practice in schools:. He wrote 'During my career, I came to realise how giving students the opportunity to be "experts" brought rewards for all. Not only did it help them consolidate their own learning and understanding, but it often made for a free-flowing process between the "expert" and the rest of the class, without the teacher—me—being at the helm. I replicated this idea in all sorts of permutations so that students could lead or support or be "official observers" of group dynamics. It helped them become aware of roles, collaboration, what it is to learn, and how they were learners as well as leaders and/or experts.'

Steve described his experiences in Namibia and Kenya with groups of 16-17 year-old students[9]. He and his colleague Richard Bossart had some training to prepare for their expeditions: 'The focus was on how to help students learn from one another about leadership. In practice, this meant rotating the roles of leadership and co-leading each day. Every night, we'd sit around the campfire and review the day. Everyone was encouraged to contribute something about their day and on any aspect of the day relating to leadership. A ban on direct criticism of anyone in their group was an unwritten rule, and followed by all; but reflections about things that didn't work or didn't go well etc. were encouraged. At the end of each day, the co-leader would become leader; and so on. It worked brilliantly. The routine became so well established that, on a couple of occasions, when Richard or I forgot to call the review, we were called out to attend!'

Enjoying Work, Feeling Rewarded

Narrowing the demands made on each of us is supposed to ensure that everything will be attended to. But there's poor evidence that this works consistently. It has been normal to believe that groups typically need a leader who tries unilaterally to prevent conflict or indecision. We're left with the conundrum that leaders make wise choices when they access their group's diverse views and develop their thinking beyond what they're used to thinking. Many leaders seem either not to know this, or deny it, or lack the trust and/or the qualities and skills to do something about it.

Having dominant leaders and stratified roles may simplify problems, but solves too few of them. It is striking that successful teams in sport tend now to have coaches who promote an explicit culture of having many leaders on and off the field of play. A weakness of hierarchically structured organisations was summed up as the Peter Principle, articulated by and named after the educator and psychologist Laurence Peter (1969)[10]: 'People rise to the level of their incompetence, and stay there'. He set out to satirise this feature of many workplaces he observed, and his perceptions resonated with so many people that the principle became part of some academics' and business leaders' vocabulary.

With her colleagues Alan Benson and Danielle Li from the Massachusetts Institute of Technology (MIT), the behavioural scientist and professor of finance Kelly Shue (2019)[11] explored empirical evidence for the Peter Principle. Their conclusions were that outstanding workers aren't necessarily well suited to or equipped for a formal management roles but are promoted nonetheless; and this reduces productivity along with client- and customer-satisfaction.

Does that chime with your experience?

Using micro-data on the performance of sales workers at 131 firms, Shue and her colleagues found that a high cost is paid by firms where there's a belief that doing your current job very well means you're bound to do well in a role at the next level 'up'. To avoid succumbing to the Peter Principle, the recommendation is not to promote people inappropriately, but to do more to incentivise front-line workers and, when considering potential promotions, to address what is specifically required at every 'level'.

Financial rewards might act as an incentive for some of us, but Herzberg's, Paul's and Robertson's work indicated that job satisfaction, morale and social recognition are for many of us more significant than money or status. If people feel intrinsically rewarded, they're less likely to want promotion for status' sake or simply to earn more money at the expense of job satisfaction. For informal leaders to be pleased to continue without official recognition, they need to have enough job satisfaction and not feel excluded or overlooked by policy-makers and executives.

Those of us who are closest to the action tend to have a different sense of responsibility compared with those who are at a remove from the action and concerned with schedules, policy, strategy, representation, public relations or marketing. Without a sense of responsibility for what we do, we have a diminished sense of time: our experience is detached from proper feelings of intention, duration and fulfilment. To work, rest and play well we need to feel present and alive in our experience.

Moving Away from Dominance

Dominance produces a primitive hierarchy and usually has to be maintained by status, tokens of approval, punishments, superficial concessions, charades of 'consultation' and 'participation', force of character, flattery, manipulation, nepotism, intimidation, humiliation, blackmail, bribery, brutality, corruption, hypocrisy, misinformation, deceit, divide-and-rule politics, indoctrination and/or relentless propaganda[12]. The temptation for dominant leaders is to exploit any means to maintain the *status quo* at least insofar as their power is concerned. Coming from indifference, helplessness or fear, a community's or workforce's inertia supports crudely hierarchical systems.

Syed suggested that 'Hierarchy is, indeed, an inevitable aspect of most human groups. We cannot ignore it. But our species, uniquely, doesn't have just one form of hierarchy. We have two': one based on dominance, the other on prestige deriving from merit. The more dynamic and flexible an organisation is, the likelier its hierarchy is to be based on prestige deriving from insight and skill, rather than on mere status, deceit, intimidation or violence. Leaders who are respected for their knowledge, skills and character are followed because they earn their people's trust.

Communicative, participative, reflective leadership is the most reliable path to our working together to govern our lives well. The relevant qualities and skills have to be recognised, learned about, promoted and developed. Democracy which does not rely on there being a subordinate, serf or slave class is a relatively recent political system with three main features: citizens can express their views, privately, publicly and via the ballot box; transparent constraints limit the power of the executive; and civil liberty is enjoyed by everyone. In autocratic or totalitarian systems, citizens can't see government's workings, can't express their political views and have no guaranteed civil liberty. To participate in and contribute to motivating, fulfilling ways of working, we have first to express our feelings and thoughts, keep listening to one another, agree goals and ways forward, then persevere and learn from events.

In 1900, close to 12 percent of the world's population lived in democracies; in 1950 close to 32 percent; and in 2015 close to 56 percent. Free universal education tends to promote individuals' political participation and foster a collective sense of civic duty. Democratic processes have tended to promote social confidence and autonomy in people's lives[13]. But, over the past century and a quarter, the extent and power of companies and corporations have rapidly grown, accompanied by rapidly increased carbon emissions and warming of the Earth.

Improving Decision-Making

Many of us are more motivated when we're enjoying our experience and receiving social recognition than we are by financial reward alone. Dunbar noted that we ensure we 'stick to the rules of the community' when we commit ourselves to 'a sense of obligation to the other members of the group'. Non-kinship groups cohere when both formal and informal connections are made between hierarchical layers and networks. This is something that resourceful colleagues and willing community members are well placed to promote and lead. These leaders—sometimes called 'leaders in the middle'[14]—are integral to the daily working and lives of many of us.

Informal leaders have relevant experience and specific expertise in a given situation. They apply what they know by taking critical 'vantage points' from which to survey the scene, and by instigating and responding to 'process points' which allow information and options to be sifted and prioritised. They may or may not be designated team leaders. Their influence is fed 'from below' by colleagues and community members who trust them, and in turn feeds 'upward' to people in senior positions and outward to partners, other organisations and wider communities.

Does your community or organisation have leaders for different situations and purposes?

A notable example of people's finding their own leaders was Denmark's fierce and dogged opposition to occupation and cruelty in World War II. Bregman (2019)[15] quoted Hannah Arendt (1963) who wrote that 'It is the only case we know in which the Nazis met with open native resistance, and the result seems to have been that those exposed to it changed their minds. They themselves apparently no longer looked upon the extermination of a whole people as a matter of course. They had met resistance based on principle, and their "toughness" had melted like butter in the sun …' Ukrainians' response to being attacked and invaded in February 2022 was another example of widespread refusal to lie down.

Effective leaders and groups tend to be aware that everyone has biases and these can undermine our effectiveness. We all have a part to play in being critically reflective about our assumptions, attitudes, ambitions, actions and achievements. Daniel Kahneman, together with the writer, educator and consultant Olivier Sibony and the legal scholar Cass Sunstein (2021)[16] have a powerful checklist for 'bias observation'. It alerts us to the advantages of helping one another to:

> Ask searching questions
> Take a range of views, including those of outsiders
> Avoid prejudgements and premature closure of discussion and enquiry
> Be guided by statisticians' best practice.

We shouldn't let group pressure make us do what we don't want to do. Extrinsic rewards, punishments, strong emotions and stress make it likelier we'll be irrational and undermine the potential we have to think flexibly and seek what is good for everyone. Each time we resist an immediate impulse or an ingrained habit, we exercise self-control.

The psychologist Stuart Sutherland (1993)[17] suggested ways of thinking about and improving our decision-making. In his view, decisions are good if they draw practical theories from experience, if they lead to our finding new solutions to problems and if they bring benefits both to us and to other people. These are tips I've drawn from Sutherland's work:

> When someone tells you what to do, ask yourself what good reasons there are for doing it
> When you're forming an impression of someone or something, don't let one or two apparent blemishes or virtues make up your mind, and don't base your choices on single cases or isolated experiences
> If you're faced with doing something unpleasant or against your better judgement, don't make it easier by pretending you don't mind doing it
> Don't let your decisions take you further and further away from what you're aiming for
> Don't stick by a choice because you've spent time, effort and/or money on the process so far: be prepared to revise plans and change what you're doing.

Using Appraisal

One of the most useful things leaders and managers can do is enable everyone to find out how others see their efforts. Performance reviewing has a role to play in almost any working and learning situation. In a formal setting it's often called appraisal and is a way of monitoring and promoting individuals' and organisations' development, whether it be for a business, a public service, a community project, a charity or an independent initiative. The intention is to understand one another's perceptions about how to make a better present and future for us all.

Appraisals relate to all aspects of personal, career, social and organisational development, and so have a bearing on initial qualification, induction, promotion and team and institutional advancement. For that reason if for no other, appraisees' team leaders, managers and seniors are well placed to be appraisers.

When it's thought advantageous, appraisers may be appointed from outside the locality or organisation. Appraisal systems are distinct from disciplinary procedures, inspections and investigations. So if matters of competence, health, safety, legality, equality or justice need to be addressed, appraisal stops and different systems come into play.

What experiences have you had of appraisal or monitoring?

The professor of education and educational leadership Christopher Day (1988)[18] spelt out how easily the value of appraisals, monitoring and evaluation can be reduced and wrecked. We lose the potential benefits if arrangements are imposed without consultation, if procedures are introduced that are ambiguous, unrewarding or unpleasant, and/or if we fail to take account of the time and commitment needed for reflection and development. Using audio or audio-visual recording can enrich colleagues' learning with and from one another, for example, but appraisal's benefits are put at risk if the participants lose control or involvement in how recording is carried out and who has access to the resulting material.

Appraisals have the potential to be constructive when processes:

Are negotiated by appraisees and appraisers together

Take account of participants' concerns as they see them

Reinforce the importance of everyone's having time and support for critical, collaborative reflection.

All of this applies to every person in every role and at every level. When appraisals work well, there are evident benefits, recognised by appraisers and appraisees alike. These include that appraisees and appraisers develop mutual understanding and respect and are motivated to continue learning. Appraisals also bring practical issues to light that can then be addressed as part of goal-setting, planning, research and development.

Analysis and Intuition

Syed[19] gave this illustration of attending to a problem and choosing how to tackle it.

In the late 1940s, the US Air Force couldn't explain the high numbers of crashes that were happening. Careful research found the root cause to be that one size doesn't fit all: standardised cockpits fail most pilots. The Air Force had to rethink how it went about their design. Instead of requiring pilots to conform to fixed measurements which suited almost nobody, cockpit spaces and instruments had to be made to fit the range of real people who became pilots. The changes that were made brought down the rate of incidents dramatically, saving lives and money and improving morale and overall performance.

This echoes what the activist and journalist Caroline Criado Perez (2019)[20] reported. There are countless examples—military equipment; police body armour; car drivers' instruments, seats and space; and piano keys, for example—all of which have supposedly been designed in the knowledge that women would use them; all of them are unsatisfactory and some are lethal. And few medicines prescribed for women in the UK have been tested on or trialled by women before they're prescribed.

If we're to respond well to complex dynamic situations, we can't rely on gut feeling alone. Nor are we well served by being calculatedly rational or procedural all or even most of the time[21]. We need moments and phases of instinctive insight and inspiration as well as periods of cyclical planning and reviewing, because we can't expect always to predict or simulate *when* or *how* threats and opportunities will crop up and change.

The research scientist in naturalistic decision-making Gary Klein (1997)[22] wrote about using a blend of intuition and analysis. He described how effective decision-makers begin by quickly recognising how to respond to their situation. They follow this up by simulating[23] a selection of possible responses and projecting how each might work out. They often do this on the spot and, the more they learn from their experiences, the more automatic and confident their choices and actions become.

Analysis checks out and builds on spontaneity. Calculating and evaluating aren't merely linguistic, mathematical or clinical processes. *Practical theorising* includes visualising and lateral or outside-the-box thinking. Klein and his colleagues found that expert decision-makers debrief their experiences and build a resource they know they can draw on. Working in difficult, unpredictable circumstances and under time pressures, they adapt to having to 'trade accuracy for speed' and 'allow errors'.

Experienced, skilled, resourceful individuals aren't born in a director's or an executive's office; they aren't bred in a laboratory; they aren't trained to rely on theory, authority or instruction. They don't dwell too long on what's gone well, but continue to learn and look forward to challenges. They are prepared to take charge and use their understanding of conditions on the shopfloor, on-site, at the 'coalface' and in the 'heat of battle'.

Are those leadership qualities you have seen in action?

Have you been able to show such leadership in areas of your life?

Intelligent Leadership

Chesley Sullenberger (2009)[24] is an international speaker on leadership and culture, risk and crisis management, high performance systems improvement and aviation and patient safety. On January 15, 2009, he was captain of Airbus A320, his co-pilot Jeffrey Skiles and crew Sheila Dail, Donna Dent and Doreen Welsh. At 3.24, they were cleared for take-off from LaGuardia Airport. At 3.27, the plane hit a flock of Canada geese and lost power in both engines. Quickly calculating that they couldn't safely reach an airport, Sullenberger decided to make a forced landing on the Hudson River. He did so at 3.30. He'd had no more than a few minutes to make an assessment and act.

Computer simulations at the Airbus Training Centre Europe showed that the plane could have made it back to LaGuardia, had they begun the manoeuvre immediately after the collision with the birds. The simulations didn't take account of how urgent the emergency was or consider the human cost of alternative decisions. The computer programme was not set up to weigh the risks of steering a plane without engines carrying 160 people over a densely populated area. The National Transportation Safety Board's investigation took 15 months to dissect the five-minute flight, and made 35 recommendations. One recommendation was that a checklist of procedures should be developed for dual-engine failure at low altitude. Another was that such a checklist should refer to the time needed to complete tasks in critical situations. (The role of checklists is a focus here in chapter 13.)

The Board concluded that normal procedures for engine loss were designed for cruising altitudes, not for conditions a few minutes after take-off, so returning to LaGuardia could not have been recommended. In case this wasn't already evident in the fact of everyone's having survived the emergency, Sullenberger was found to have made the right choices. The situation in real time was more complex than what all of the relevant models and protocols were designed to address. The challenges were specific, unique, profound, extensive and extreme. Sullenberger, Skiles and their crew negotiated them calmly, conscientiously, creatively and successfully.

Would you want to have people like Sullenberger and his crew responsible for your safety on a flight?

Would any of the 155 passengers that afternoon have liked a computer programme or computer programmers or board of enquiry personnel to have been in charge?

The most humane, intelligent decision-makers respond intuitively *and* rationally to a force field that has three points of tension: what is wanted by most if not all of us; what is compatible if not actively helpful to our individual and collective well-being; and, given our situation and resources, what is feasible. This echoes the conclusions reached by the firefighter and psychologist Sabrina Cohen-Hatton (2019)[25]. She became the first female firefighter commander in the UK. Like Klein's, her findings can be applied in many contexts that affect individuals', groups' and societies' problem-solving responses to health, safety and well-being challenges. These are key elements in her research and professional experience:

> Situational awareness combines information gathering and processing with anticipating what could happen next and later
>
> Individuals and groups take good decisions when they combine intuition, analysis, evaluation, dialogue, cooperation and learning
>
> Effective organisation and performance combine clear briefing with careful listening
>
> Being able to share and swap roles supports individuals' coming together and working as a team
>
> Personal resilience and group resilience alike combine thinking-time with managing stress and fatigue.

It is *combinations* of skills and qualities, not stand-alone factors that make the difference between on-the-spot capability and hesitancy or inadequacy. Cohen-Hatton's list helps us understand how Sullenberger was able to take charge so successfully.

How do you think those factors apply in areas of your life?

It follows from Klein's and Hatton-Cohen's research and Sullenberger's story that we are more likely to strive for what's in all our interests and thrive, if we combine breadth of sympathy and vision with humility and respect for considered experience and evidence.

Summing Up

The more dynamic and adaptable an organisation is, the likelier its hierarchy is to be based on prestige deriving from insight and skill, rather than on mere status, deceit, intimidation or violence.

Enabling others to cooperate autonomously may be leadership's most significant aim and achievement.

Good leadership produces humane, intelligent decisions designed to match what is feasible with what most of us agree we need and want.

To survive and live well we depend on leaders who have breadth of sympathy and vision combined with humility and respect for considered experience and evidence.

---

[1] See Kurt Lewin's, Ronald Lippitt's and Ralph White's (1939) 'Patterns of aggressive behaviour in experimentally created social climates', published by the *Journal of Social Psychology*, 10, pp 271-301.

[2] See Michael Polanyi's (1951) *The Logic of Liberty*, published in Chicago, Il, by the University of Chicago Press.

[3] See Donald Schön's (1983), *The Reflective Practitioner: How Professionals Think in Action*, published in London, UK, by Temple Smith, pp 129, 134 and 338.

[4] See Frederick Herzberg, Bill Paul Jnr and Keith Robertson (1968), pp 77-78. The concept and practice of job enrichment are defined in chapter 9's 'Wanting' section.

[5] See Rutger Bregman (2019), p 280.

[6] See Edward Deci's, Takuma Nishimura's, Emma L. Bradshaw's and Richard M. Ryan's (2021) 'Satisfaction of basic psychological needs in an independence model of

fathers' own aspirations and their adolescent children', published in *Social Development*, 30, 1, pp 293-310. Go to https://doi.org/10.1111/sode.12473.

[7] See Matthew Syed (2019), pp 62, 91, 107, 122-123, 112-113, 115 and 117-118.

[8] See Robin Dunbar (2016), pp 42, 268, 271, 276, 293, 312-4, 40, 78, 268 and 293.

[9] Steve Parker (2018) included details about his African experiences along with observations about family, everyday economics, commemoration, defiance, conciliation, loss and commitment, in his *Rememberland*, published in King's Lynn, UK, by Biddles Books Limited.

[10] See Laurence Peter's (1969) *The Peter Principle: Why Things Go Wrong*, written with Raymond Hull, published in New York, NY, by William Morrow and Company.

[11] See Alan Benson's, Danielle Li's and Kelly Shue's (2019) 'Promotions and the Peter Principle', published in *The Quarterly Journal of Economics*, 134, 4, pp 2085–2134.

[12] See Niccolò Machiavelli's (1532) *The Prince*, published by Antonio Blado d'Asola.

[13] See the professor of economics Francisco Gallego's (2010) 'Historical origins of schooling: the role of democracy and political decentralisation', published in *The Review of Economics and Statistics*, 92, 2, pp 228–243.

[14] See the professor for educational leadership, education policy and school improvement Alma Harris' and the professor of leadership and professional learning Michelle Jones' (2012) *Managing to lead?*, published in Nottingham, UK, by the National College for School Leadership; available at www.nationalcollege.org.uk/cm-mc-let-op-harrisjones.pdf. See also *Inside-out and downside-up: How leading from the middle has the power to transform education systems* (2016) by the consultant and speaker on leadership and system reform in education Steve Munby and the Global Leadership Director of New Pedagogies for Deep Learning Michael Fullan (2016), published in Reading, UK, and Thousand Oaks, CA, by the Education Development Trust and Motion Leadership, p 11.

[15] See Rutger Bregman (2019), p 180.

[16] See Daniel Kahneman, Olivier Sibony and Cass Sunstein (2021), pp 370-374.

[17] See Stuart Sutherland's (1993) *The Enemy Within*, published in London, UK, by Pinter and Martin.

[18] See Christopher Day's (1988) 'The Relevance and Use of Classroom Research Literature to the Appraisal of Teachers in Classrooms: issues of teacher learning and change', published in the *Cambridge Journal of Education*, 18, 3, pp 333-346.

[19] See Matthew Syed (2019), pp 213-217 and 228-230 about web browser users; and p 232 about adaptability and flexibility.

[20] See Caroline Criado Perez (2019).

[21] See Michael Polanyi (1958), referred to here in chapters 6 and 7, and Donald Schön (1983), referred to above. Also Iain McGilchrist's (2010) account, given here in the

'Self-Efficacy' section of chapter 5 relating to how our left and right brain hemispheres function.

[22] See Gary Klein's (1997) *Sources of Power: How People Make Decisions*, published in Cambridge, MA, by the MIT Press, pp xxii and 289-291.

[23] See the 'Becoming Resilient' section of chapter 1 here about the function and value of simulation.

[24] See Chesley Sullenberger's (2009) *Highest Duty: My Search for What Really Matters*, published in New York, NY, by William Morrow. Also the film (2016) *Sully: Miracle on the Hudson*, directed by Clint Eastwood and written by Todd Komarnicki.

[25] See Sabrina Cohen-Hatton's (2019) *The Heat of the Moment*, published in London, UK, by Doubleday/Penguin Random House.

13 Deciding

In this chapter we hear from Kate Orkin; Richard Thaler and Cass Sunstein; Theresa Marteau; Leidy Klotz; and Olivier Sibony, along with others we've already met.

How can large numbers of us change our behaviour for the common good?

Changing Behaviour

Have you sometimes made important changes in your behaviour, and benefited?

Did you act on your own, or were you one of many who made changes?

In chapter 7's 'Making up Your Mind' section, I quoted Cailin O'Connor's and James Weatherall's (2019b) answer to the question 'How do we come to believe something, and then act on it?' According to their analysis, our actions are affected by our beliefs, and our beliefs are affected by many people, organisations and cultural factors.

They proposed that the mental processes that take us from decision to action have two crucial elements. These processes may be relatively conscious or relatively unconscious. First, we identify the focus for the choices we're going to make: what are we trying to do; will we do this or that or nothing at all? Second, we decide how autonomous or how directed by others' influence we will be: how free and self-assertive, how compliant and obedient will we be?

Stories, images, videos and pieces of texts frame our experiences and responses and influence our deciding and acting. Few of us can escape entirely from the fact that we are moved to a greater or lesser extent by our sense of what the majority thinks, by the Internet, newspapers and televisual media, by key figures in our group or charismatic leaders.

Authorities, organisations or institutions are agents of potential change. The behavioural economist Kate Orkin's analysis (2020)[1] was that, when behaving normally is incompatible with public safety, would-be agents of change are advised to point people in the direction of doing what's good for themselves and for their communities. One of her key findings summarising statistical evidence was that, if you highlight people doing a bad thing, there's an implication that 'it isn't that bad' and people may do it more; it is 'much more effective to highlight positive behaviour or ask people to do the right thing.'

In times of a pandemic, alternating and combining approaches tends to be most effective—sometimes setting a default such as 'Stay at home', sometimes asking us to protect our health services and the vulnerable. It helps to motivate people to do the right thing by appealing to a spirit of allegiance and solidarity. Enforcement would always be a last resort.

When asked, many people said they agreed it's reasonable for government and the law to prompt compliance by giving advice and instructions and using sanctions. Orkin reported surveys that showed '82 percent of Britons would support the police being able to arrest or prosecute anyone who should be self-isolating but isn't'. Penalties and fines can be used to register disapproval alongside rewards and bonuses as signals of approval.

The environment and urban and rural planning play a crucial part in changing attitudes and behaviour. In the Netherlands, for example, there is now less reliance on road signs indicating 'stop', 'give way', 'slow down' and so on, and traffic-calming has been achieved through changing the road surfaces and layouts: one colour and more generous lanes for cycles, another colour, chicanes and narrower lanes for cars. And car drivers are held liable for accidents. The result is by and large cycle-friendly towns and cities[2]. But there will always be challenges. In the Netherlands still, cyclists are not obliged or expected to wear protective headgear; and serious accidents happen on frozen lakes where there is nothing to help ice yacht sailors be aware of skaters.

The economist Richard Thaler and legal scholar Cass Sunstein (2008)[3] explored and proposed a concept of 'nudging'—unobtrusively pre-disposing or shifting us toward beneficial ways of feeling, thinking and acting. Making lift doors close more slowly increases the numbers of people taking the stairs. Chevrons painted on the road create an illusion of speed, causing many drivers to slow down. When men have the image of a housefly printed on the base of a urinal to aim for, floors and walls tend to be drier and cleaner.

Changing our Environment

It seems that our feelings and associations are conditioned more by our environment than by our 'free will'. The health psychologist Theresa Marteau (2018)[4] wrote that it would help us all if our environments were redesigned so that cities encouraged us to take exercise, and restaurants and food-outlets helped us eat and drink smaller servings.

For a population to change its behaviour, policy makers and researchers do well to abandon supposedly sensible ideas about 'personalising risk information'. We can know what's meant to be good for us, but do something else: the sofa beckons, stopping us from taking 10,000 steps a day; against our better judgement, we drink alcohol on weekdays; and while we go about our business and pleasures, our planet is over-heating and species are dying out. Just being told something may not change our awareness and is unlikely to trigger enough of a change.

Marteau wrote that 'Most of us value our health highly yet act in ways that undermine it'. Cancers would be reduced by 40 percent and 75 percent of diabetes and cardiovascular disease would be avoided if we ate and drank less, didn't smoke and were physically more active. Making these changes would 'halve the gaps in life expectancy and years lived in good health between the rich and the poor'. There is a strong case for policy makers', governments' and public servants' targeting our non-conscious processes which are 'readily activated by the cues that surround us'.

Because risk information often 'targets the conscious set of processes least involved in regulating our routine or habitual unhealthy behaviours', many of us feel that general advice doesn't apply to us. More effective approaches to changing how we feel and think—hence what we do—appeal to non-conscious processes that 'effortlessly activate most of our behaviour, particularly routines and habits'. It has been shown that taking larger sizes of food portions and tableware out of circulation can reduce adults' daily energy intake in the UK by 12 to 16 percent or up to 279 calories a day, in the USA by 22 to 29 percent or 527 calories a day.

Marteau focused on the emerging evidence that governments can influence people's attitudes toward improvements in the environment and public health by gently or indirectly advising and steering them. Effective advice is most likely to link informing people about their unhealthy habits with changes in policy and taxation. Tacit or oblique persuasion is a more pragmatic, promising way of enabling us to stop doing harmful things and start or return to doing healthy things.

Have you resisted changing your behaviour when many others have changed theirs?

Do you understand the reasons others have had for changing their behaviour when you haven't changed yours?

Our Self-Deceiving Brain

When it comes to changing what you do, you're more likely to be open to suggestion than to commands or appeals to sense or tradition, and you're more persuaded by stories than by facts or logic.

Shankar Vedantam and Bill Mesler (2021) asked, 'How do you get large numbers of people—most of whom are strangers to each another, and all of whom have strong incentives to look out for their self-interest—to work together in the service of the common good?'

They referred to experiments[5] which showed there are ways to 'reduce false pattern recognition and the erroneous generation of conspiracy theories'. It is better achieved, not by 'hectoring volunteers with logic and reason, or by telling them they were "morons" for subscribing to fantasies, but by addressing the problem at its emotional root—providing people with ways to boost their self-esteem and restore their feeling of being in control. Paradoxically, we sometimes become more likely to listen to the voice of logic and reason when we turn away from logic and reason, and pay closer attention to people's unmet, underlying emotional needs'.

Vedantam and Mesler showed that 'Many people hold false beliefs not because they are in love with falsehood, or because they are stupid—as conventional wisdom might suggest—but because those beliefs help them hold their lives together in some way'. They argued that to achieve socially constructive results, 'you have to work with the algorithms of the self-deceiving brain, rather than ignore them'. Advocates and leaders are most likely to help us take or keep our heads out of the sand, when they concede to our need for reassurance and comfort.

Marteau acknowledged that governments are not helped by some powerful forces. Industries have brought cases against governments in the USA, Scotland and England, for example, 'to prevent effective policies' which were designed to cap the size of fizzy drink bottles sold in places other than shops. She observed that reducing the availability, styling and sizing of foods and drinks achieves more positive results than asking or telling us to eat or drink less; and concluded that changing behaviours for a healthier world 'will need many different interventions operating at the same time'.

In Marteau's view, governments and public authorities have, first, to realise that the environment we inhabit determines how we behave at least as much as, if not more than, than our individual 'free will' does. Second, they have to realise how regulations and economic measures strongly influence us; we tend, for example, to buy fewer heavily taxed items and buy more lightly taxed items. Third, they have to realise that social benefits come from regulating and intervening in the market without deception and without infringing or diminishing anyone's rights to pursue their interests within local, regional and international laws.

Whether our concerns are personal or institutional, parochial, local, regional or global, we are bound sometimes to find it hard to set aside our prejudices, biases, vested interests and preferences. We help ourselves and one another when we work together for the common good. Cooperation works best when everyone becomes a potential source of ingenuity and determination. Then, there are many centres of decision-making and leadership, and personal and collective achievements are celebrated by everyone. Under these conditions, order, dignity and inventiveness are sustained by spontaneous and caring interactions as much as by formal arrangements and statutory, legal systems.

Making Discussions Count

In a pluralist democracy, people can be expected to have different, sometimes antagonistic values and ideas, for example, about how to educate children and young people, how to care for the vulnerable, how to respond to wrong-doing, how to make organisations efficient, effective and fair and how to deal with perceived threats and dangers. When everyone plays their part in protecting and serving the interests of society as a whole, we come as close as we can to making a society in which no single or partisan group or power can exclude, dominate or destroy another. Those are the ethics, politics and practicalities of forming healthy coalitions, fairly arbitrating conflicts and living together constructively.

Lord Martin Rees (2018)[5] suggested recent discussions about how to influence our future have been characterised by short-term and polarising thinking and lazy pessimism. He advocated that nations empower supra-national institutions to improve global collaboration. His analysis and recommendations showed that there are at least three dimensions to the challenges of working together on solving global problems. As citizens we have to take account of the quality of our lives and the health of our planet. And then governments have to come together to commission, launch and steer working parties, forums and processes for mediation, conflict-resolution, reconciliation and reparation. Further, enterprises, universities and organisations with every possible kind of expertise have to work together.

Daniel Kahneman, Olivier Sibony and Cass Sunstein (2021)[6] focused on how we may be more measured and so more accurate in our thinking and decision-making. Their concern was to help us avoid 'noise' and bias. 'Noise' is defined as 'variability in judgements that should be identical' and it is extremely difficult to check, let alone remove from judgements made, for example, in business and medical diagnosis and treatment. It applies equally in criminal justice, fingerprint analysis, all kinds of forecasting, awarding patents, personnel ratings and decisions about asylum and child custody. Bias, on the other hand, shows consistent flaws in thinking, including over-optimism, risk-aversion and prejudice against certain people or ideas. Bias is as difficult to avoid or dismantle as 'noise'.

We have to work to negate the effects of 'noise' because 'It is unfair for similarly situated people to be treated differently, and a system in which professional judgements are seen as inconsistent loses credibility'. That is why it takes courage, expertise and determination to identify and counteract flaws in our judgement-making: 'a statistical view of the world enables us to see noise, but that view does not come naturally—we prefer casual stories'.

Kahneman, Sibony and Sunstein gave principles that help us be actively open to new ways of thinking and doing things:

> Be as accurate as we can be about the matter in hand

At crucial points, consider similar cases and situations and think statistically

Break judgements down into independent tasks

Be alert to possible risks of following our intuitions too early in our decision-making

Collect judgements from as many people and sources as possible

Pay attention to details and avoid making global judgements.

Meeting, Focusing

Stopping doing things, inhibiting certain impulses and conserving resources are threads running through this book, reflected in the work of the professor of engineering and retired soccer player Leidy Klotz (2021)[7]. He illustrated this with an enlightening experience he had one day while he and his son Ezra were playing with Lego bricks. At a crucial point in their construction, they needed to bridge two columns, one column being taller than the other. Instinctively, Klotz senior added a brick to the shorter column, but Ezra removed a brick from the taller one.

This opened up and crystallised a whole field of study for Klotz senior. Through his experiments he came to show that subtracting is 'not the same as doing less' and that we underestimate and neglect subtraction 'as a way to change things'. This may be in part because making changes by subtracting occurs less readily to many of us, and 'Even when we do manage to think of it, subtracting can be harder to implement'. Doing and getting less can be very useful and sometimes essential. In Klotz's view, by failing to take opportunities to subtract 'we're missing ways to make our lives more fulfilling, our institutions more effective, and our planet more liveable'. This resonates with Ivan Illich's, Robin Dunbar's and Ernst Schumacher's work (referred to in chapters 2, 3 and 8).

Have you had experiences which show that less can be better?

Matthew Syed (2019)[8] reported that 'in a typical four-person group, two people do 62 percent of the talking, and in a six-person group, three people do 70 percent of the talking. It gets progressively worse as the group size gets bigger. Perhaps the most remarkable thing is that the people doing all the talking don't realise they're doing it.' Syed's summing up was that, in many meetings, 'communication is dysfunctional. Many people are silent. Status rigs the discourse. People don't say what they think but what they think the leader wants to hear. And they fail to share crucial information because they don't realise other people lack it'. When we think about what we want to say and say it concisely, more of us get the chance to speak.

The kinds of informal and formal meetings you have reflect how your group, organisation or institution carries out its business. We help ourselves when we see the shortest route to take and cut to the chase. In other words, our effectiveness depends on focus and discipline.

One method is for a volunteer to write on a flipchart, black- or whiteboard questions, concepts, details and possible actions as they emerge. Everyone can see the 'picture' and flow of the conversation. This can stand as a lasting record, or be transcribed and posted or circulated.

Kahneman's (2011)[9] advice is that it's better to elicit information from a group 'not by starting with a public discussion but by confidentially collecting each person's judgement'. His research showed that 'The standard practice of open discussion gives too much weight to the opinions of those who speak early and assertively, causing others to line up behind them.' And if brainstorms have a role to play, they're most likely to be helpful early in a discussion or meeting and when they have an explicit purpose and deliberately enable those who have least status to speak. Such strategies foster openness, engagement and reflectiveness.

You tend to have effective meetings when:

> Everyone is thanked for participating
> Everyone understands what your meetings are for
> Time isn't wasted
> You consider information from a range of sources and points of view
> You challenge assumptions, express doubts and check what's agreed
> By the end, everyone understands what the goals and next steps are.

How might you improve that list? Would you add any features, or take any away?

Checking

Well-run meetings and effective ways of working include the voicing of doubts and difficulties—essential to high-quality performance and job satisfaction. In their research into attitudes to error, stress and teamwork, J. Bryan Sexton, Eric Thomas and Robert Helmreich (2000)[10] reported that 'Highly effective cockpit crews use one third of their communications to discuss threats and errors in their environment, regardless of their workload, whereas poor performing teams spend about 5% of their time doing the same.' They are prompted to do this in part because they routinely use checklists.

What have been your experiences of using checklists?

If they were productive, why was it? If they were unhelpful, why was it?

Lazy, dishonest and oppressive practices have given checklists a bad name in some places. Ticking off items to indicate we do certain things diverts us from what we're trying to do there and then. But Atul Gawande (2009)[11] has shown that using intelligent checklists sensibly supports high-quality performance and saves lives and money—in surgery, medical care, building construction, aircraft piloting, space travel, food preparation, auditing and investment. We can do much better than merely doing what we're told to do or what we've always done.

Sensible checklists work as follows. We pause to note key components in the task before us. Items are listed in brief, precise and practical terms. Crucially, everyone involved in the actions being checked takes part and has an equal voice. Everyone is asked periodically to update the checklist by considering what it means to do well and focus on whatever might enhance success.

In an edition of BBC Radio 4's *Desert Island Discs* with Kirsty Young (2015), Gawande said that what matters most is that you 'work as part of a good system and try to influence it for the better'. His ideas may seem to be plain common sense, but it takes great discipline and determination on everyone's part to put them into practice: 'Groups of people working together are far better than the smartest, most experienced, most trained and hardest working individual in the system. If you aren't part of a whole group of people who are all pulling in the same direction, communicating with the same consciousness of what a good outcome is, you don't get anywhere.'

Our lives are now more complicated and complex than at any time in history. Checklists, well used, help us work together in situations that combine simple, complicated and complex features. Simple situations can be responded to with prescribed methods or 'recipes', because mastering a few basic techniques brings a strong likelihood of success. Complicated situations throw up unanticipated difficulties, and require many people's involvement covering many areas of expertise. Complex situations are unique, meaning we have to understand that outcomes are unpredictable.

Complication requires us to consult or depend on many people and organisations. Complexity requires us to prepare systematically, make periodic checks and be alert to the need to respond creatively to inevitable surprises and disappointments. In difficult and unforeseen circumstances, we must be free to follow our judgements and find new paths. Remember the pilot Chesley Sullenberger (referred to in chapter 12): he instinctively and quickly assessed his situation and averted disaster.

Checklists Worth Using

A command-and-control paradigm may rescue us in the short term, but it doesn't help us when we face unique, dynamic, ongoing challenges. Gawande wrote (2009) that complexity makes it necessary to 'push the power of decision making out to the periphery and away from the centre': we need 'room to adapt' how we think and act; we need to 'talk to one another and take responsibility'. Checklists are based on our experience and enhanced by reputable research and practice. They spell out concisely what has to be done for us to measure up to success criteria we've set for ourselves *and* had formally recognised by stakeholders and public authorities. They enable everyone involved in key tasks to share responsibility and accountability. While they're being developed or used, no one is allowed to ignore, belittle, overrule or silence anyone else.

To use checklists effectively, everyone has to:

> Define essential elements and steps in key processes—preferably no more than half a dozen items per checklist
>
> Make the wording of checklist items exact and straightforward
>
> Make sure every person has an equal voice in devising and using checklists
>
> Use checklists as a tool for improving both job satisfaction and effectiveness

Agree when to use checklists, including at the beginning of research and development projects and to launch innovations and improvements
Revise checklists periodically.

Checklists don't dispense with guidelines, routines or protocols, but do allow for and encourage our being focused, flexible and innovative. We are clear about what we intend to achieve, but don't pretend we're certain to succeed. There are benefits to everyone's well-being and prospects when everyone involved has an equally respected voice in creating, using and revising protocols and checklists.

Imagining and Reasoning

We're bound to have diverse values and divergent views about what we should do to safeguard ourselves and live well. Especially when the stakes and/or our aspirations are high, we must aim for better than average, better than normal. If we carry on behaving normally, we will change too little.

The more we become used to acting considerately and responsibly together, the better we're able to protect and develop our understanding, skills and confidence. The better we develop our understanding, skills and confidence, the more we become used to acting resiliently and responsibly together.

Stuart Hampshire (2000)[12] saw that it is via ethics and politics that we serve equality and justice. He wrote that ethics deal in 'Conceptions of the good, ideals of social life, [and] visions of individual virtue and excellence, [which] are infinitely varied and divisive'; and the 'proper business of politics' is to afford 'protection against the perennial evils of human life—physical suffering, the destructions and mutilations of war, poverty and starvation, enslavement and humiliation'. Our prospects are brightest when in our ethics and politics we combine our collective wisdoms, when we respect rational, evidence-based, dialectical argument and then act decisively. Both our ethics and our politics need to be served by our imaginations and intellects.

Imagination expresses our natures and instincts by being 'creative and unmethodical'. It tells us about what we wish and hope for. Intellect filters our spontaneity by being 'critical and methodical'[13]. It tells us about how we might live up to our ideals, avoid what we fear and fulfil our aspirations. Imagination, we might say, comes naturally, but intellect has to be worked for. Imagination apprehends problems and possible solutions, while intellect enables us to cooperate in agreeing, monitoring and improving what we need to do.

A Bill Withers[14] lyric urges us on:
> 'Good things come to those who wait
> Not for those who wait too late
> We gotta go for all we know.'

Together we can find our best answers to the following questions. What is happening? How is it happening? How can we make something better happen?

How well we live depends on how well we develop our thinking. At its most powerful, thinking is deliberate and collective and involves feeling, imagining, experimenting and observing as well as reasoning.

Summing Up

When everyone becomes a potential source of ingenuity and determination, there are many centres of decision-making and leadership.

Use meetings to foster openness, reflectiveness and decisiveness.

Everyone benefits when everyone involved has an equal voice in creating, using and revising goals, plans, protocols and checklists.

Our prospects are brightest when we combine our collective wisdoms and when we respect rational, evidence-based, dialectical argument

---

[1] Thanks to Steve Parker for the example.

[2] See Kate Orkin's (2020) *Don't tell people off, tell them how to help*, available via **www.research.ox.ac.uk/Article/2020-03-27-dont-tell- people-off-tell-them-how-to-help**. This resonates with the case study in the 'Safeguarding' section of chapter 11.

[3] See Richard Thaler's and Cass Sunstein's (2008) *Nudge: Improving Decisions About Health, Wealth and Happiness*, published in New Haven, CT, by Yale University Press.

[4] See Theresa Marteau's (2018) 'Changing minds about changing behaviour', published by *The Lancet*, 10116, pp 116–117. Also her (2011) 'Judging nudging: can nudging improve population health?' written with David Ogilvie, Martin Roland, Marc Suhrcke and Michael P. Kelly, published in *The British Medical Journal*, 342. Go to doi:https://doi.org/ 10.1136/bmj.d228. Details of such cases are made available by the London-based Cochrane Collaboration, founded in 1993 by Sir Iain Chalmers to inform choices about health interventions.

[5] See the professor of management and organisations Jennifer Whitson's and the social psychologist Adam Galinsky's (3 Oct 2008) 'Lacking Control Increases Illusory Pattern

Perception', published in *Science*, 322, 5898, pp. 115-117, available via DOI: 10.1126/science.1159845, and discussed by Vedantam and Mesler (2021).

[6] See Martin Rees' (2018) *On the Future: Prospects for Humanity*, published in Princeton, NJ, by Princeton University Press. His (2010) Reith Lectures and (2018) article in *Prospect* are referred to here in the 'Defining Goals' section of chapter 9.

[7] **See Daniel** Kahneman's, Olivier Sibony's and Cass Sunstein's (2021) *Noise: A Flaw in Human Judgment*, published in London, UK, by William Collins, pp 361-374.

[8] See Leidy Klotz's (2021) *Subtract: Why Getting to Less Can Mean Thinking More*, published in New York, NY, by Flatiron Books. Leidy co-founded and co-directs the Convergent Behavioural Science Initiative at the University of Virginia. CBSI brings together researchers, designers, teachers, engineers, doctors and psychologists to 'address climate change, systemic inequality, and other issues'.

[9] See Matthew Syed (2019), pp 108-109 and 119-120.

[10] See Daniel Kahneman (2011), p 245.

[11] See J. Bryan Sexton's, Eric Thomas' and Thomas Helmreich's (2000) 'Error, stress, and teamwork in medicine and aviation: cross sectional surveys', published in ***The British Medical Journal*, 320, pp 745–749**.

[12] See Atul Gawande's (2009) *The Checklist Manifesto: How to Get Things Right*, published in London, UK, by Profile Books, p 73. He appeared on BBC Radio 4's *Desert Island Discs* on 11 December 2015.

[13] See Stuart Hampshire (2000), pp xi-xii, 87, 91ff, 92-94 and 98.

[14] There are parallels between Hampshire's ideas and those of other writers quoted in this book: e.g. Cailin O'Connor's and James Weatherall's (2019b) writing (referred to in chapter 7) about our sometimes conscious and voluntary, sometimes unconscious and involuntary drives and actions; Daniel Kahneman's (2011) writing about Systems 1 and 2 thinking (referred to in 'Learning to Learn' section of chapter 4); and Iain McGilchrist's (2010) writing about left- and right-brain ways of seeing the world (referred to here in the 'Self-Efficacy' section of chapter 5).

14 Living Well

What can we do to help protect ourselves and our planet?

We increase our chances of living well when we consult widely, plan carefully, act responsibly, keep track of progress and keep learning.

We can:

Be emotionally intelligent

Combine intuition with calculation and analysis
Be prepared to be surprised as well as determined
Seek harmony

Value integrity

Question authority and apparent consensus
Be honest with ourselves
Be true to our better selves

Be rigorous and resourceful

Pay diligent attention to facts and truths that are open to scrutiny and revision
Cooperate across boundaries of cultural and social background, status and expertise
Share and swap roles

Be agile, strategic and disciplined

Check mutual understanding
Set goals and review progress systematically
Use what we learn to revise our ways of working.

What are your priorities?
What will you do?

Abbreviations

AI   Artificial Intelligence

AIDS   Acquired immunodeficiency syndrome

BBC   The British Broadcasting Corporation

BCE   Before the Common Era (an alternative designation to BC, Before Christ)

CEO   Chief Executive Officer

EBI   Even better if: a prompt to find ways of improving what we do

fMRI   Functional magnetic resonance imaging

HIV   Human immunodeficiency virus

INSEAD   Institut Européen d'Administration des Affaires, in Paris, France

IT   Information Technology

MIE   Minimally invasive education

NHS   The national health service in the UK.

OECD   The Organisation for Economic Cooperation and Development

Ofsted	The Office for Standards in Education, in the UK
RI	Remote Intelligence
SOLEs	Self organised learning environments
UEFA	Union of European Football Associations: the administrative body for association football, futsal and beach soccer in Europe, although several member states are primarily or entirely located in Asia.
UK	The United Kingdom
US/USA	The United States of America
WHO	The World Health Organisation

Index

Abercrombie, M. L. 'Jane' Johnson, 85, 89
Adams, Elizabeth 84
addiction 54, 58, 117, 165, 172 181, 208
Adelman, Clem 93
Ainsworth, Mary 35
Al-Khalili, Jim 34, 219
allostasis 53, 151
altruism 73, 207, 208
Amos (Comenius) 138
Arendt, Hannah 48, 63, 169, 180, 236
Armstrong, Michael 112
Austin, J. L 75
Aziz, Sheema Abdul 223

Bahns, Angela 86
Baim, Clark 15
Baldwin, Richard 184, 199
Ball, Philip 150
Barrett, Lisa Feldman 13, 25, 97
Bearwish, Moira 195
Benson, Alan 94
Bernasco, Wim 195
Bion, Wilfred 134
Blakeslee, Sandra 162
Blass, Thomas 184
body 13, 20, 23, 25, 27, 42, 47 52, 53, 76, 141, 151, 174

Bossart, Richard 233
Bowlby, John 35
Boyd, Brian 207, 208
Bradbury, Ray 156
Bradshaw, Emma 229
Brecht, Bertolt 24
Bregman, Rutger 11
Bullock, Alan 82
Bumrungsri, Sara 223
Bunting, ... 205, 206
Burgess, Tyrrell 83
Burkeman, Oliver 135

Cain, Susan 82
Cannon, Walter Bradford 222
Carnahan, Matthew 144
Carnie, Fiona 7, 57, 190
Carr, E. H. 90
Chekhov, Anton 129
Chesley 225
Churchland, Patricia 63, 73
Cohen-Hatton, ... 225, 242
Collingwood, R. G 214
compromise 74, 157, 164, 168
confidence . 19, 24, 28, 29, 30, 32, 69 78, 81, 98, 113, 126, 187, 190 193, 236, 257
Coombe, Davis 172
cooperation .. 113, 137, 149, 150, 159 167, 175, 197, 201, 209, 211, 218

Correa, Mario 144
C-PTSD Complex Post-Traumatic Stress Disorder 18
Crittenden, Patricia 15
Csikszentmihalyi, Mihaly 27, 182
Cumming, Laura 65
Cuomo, Andrew 160
Curtis, Vickie 172

Damasio, Antonio 7, 38, 52
Darley, John 184
Darwin, Charles 39, 132
Davies, Russell T 224
Day, Christopher 238
De Botton, Alain 165
DeAngelis, Tori 116
Deci, Edward 229, 244
deciding (decision-making) 52, 58 112, 140
Deisseroth, Karl 19, 38, 58, 106, 139
democracy 158, 182, 228, 235 244, 250
Dewey, John 138
dialogue 197, 209, 211, 222
Diamond, Jared 47
Dickens, Charles 166
Dillon, Dick 116
disinformation 55, 172
Dixon, Leslie 223
Domingos, Pedro 119
Donaldson, Margaret 95
Dunbar, Robin 38, 40, 231, 252
Dweck, Carol 13, 29

Eastwood, Clint 245
education 70, 71, 89, 96, 116 117, 141, 153, 154
Egan, David 143

Einstein, Albert 57
Elliott, John 92
Enoka, Gilbert 28
Escher, M. C 87
ethics 73, 185, 251, 257
extinction 51, 139, 211
Eyer, Joseph 53

Fehr, Ernst 162
Ferguson, R. Brian 48
Festinger, Leon 42
Fielding, Michael 184
Flaxman, Seth 162
Floyd, George 74, 160
Foster, Craig 211
Franklin, Benjamin 145
Frederick 225
Freud, Sigmund 35
Frevert, Ute 205
Frith, Chris 86
Fritjof 38
Fullan, Michael 245
future 11, 32, 43, 100, 126, 135 156, 172, 202, 228

Galinsky, Adam 259
Gallego, Francisco 244
Gallie, W. B 143
Gawande, Atul 259
Gibson, Stephen 184, 192
Gilbert, Sarah 105
Gladwell, ... 54
goals 28, 73, 78, 104, 119, 170 210, 220, 226, 235
Godfrey-Smith, Peter 38, 42, 43
Goel, Sharad 162
Goffman, Erving 84
Gould, Kath 215

Graafland, Johan 75, 83
Grant, Adam 133
Grant, Susannah 144
Grayling, A.C 7, 38, 55, 166
groups 39, 43, 45, 54, 65, 66, 73, 101, 172, 174, 232
Gupta, Sanjay 223

Hafez, Logaina 221
Hall, Miranda 176
Hammond, Lily Harvey 223
Hampshire, Stuart 100
Harari, Yuval Noah 38, 43
Hari, Johann 179
Harris, Alma 244
Harris, Victor 81
Harvey-Jones, Sir 228
Hastings, Reed 132, 145
Haynes, Todd 144
Heinlein, Robert 223
Heller, Marielle 146
Helmreich, Robert 255
Herzberg 225, 229, 234
hierarchy 48, 72, 159, 176, 191, 228, 235
Hoar, Peter 224
Holmes, Oliver Wendell 138
Holmes, Richard 105
homeostasis 52, 53, 151, 222
Howard, Ron 33
Huxley, Aldous 156
Hyde, Catherine 223

Illich, Ivan 39, 166, 252
immunity 20
Infeld, Leopold 57, 203
Izzard, Eddie 32

James, William 138
Jane 85, 89, 93, 120, 147, 162
Jennette 17
John 228
Johnson, Anne 219, 224
Jones, Edward 82
Jones, Michelle 244
Jürgen, Habermas 80
justice 178, 197, 221, 238, 257

Kafka, Franz 120
Kahneman, Daniel 85, 88, 104, 237, 251
Kaku, Michio 111, 129, 207
Keats, John 122
Keynes, John Maynard 174
Klein, Gary 225
Klotz, Leidy 246
Komarnicki, Todd 245
Komenský, Jan 109
Kosfeld, Michael 162
Kuhn, Thomas 144

Labov, William 95
Laland, Kevin 44
land 173, 174
Land 221
Landini, Andrea 18
language 21, 22, 48, 95, 141, 200
Lanier, Jaron 115
Latané, Bibb 184
Leder, Mimi 223
Levine, Mark 195
Lewin, Kurt 92
Li, Danielle 244
Liebst, Lasse Suonperä 195
Lindegaard, Marie 195, 203

Lippitt, Ronald 225
Lodge, Basil 111
Loos, Bjorn 75
Luisi, Luigi Pier 38

MacGregor, Neil 40, 71
Machiavelli, Niccolò 244
Macready, Tom 221, 224
Madeleine 205
making 85, 91, 100, 111, 116 126, 129
Malcolm 55
Malle, Bertram 66
Malthouse, Ian 110
Marteau, Theresa 246, 248, 259
Maulfry 140
Mayo, Aziza 82
McCold, Paul 224
McCurdy, ... 17, 34
McGilchrist, Iain 41, 94, 100, 136
meetings 91, 168, 253, 255
Menand, Louis 145
Mesler, Bill 125, 155, 249
Metzl, Jamie 58
Meyer, Erin 132
Michael 124
Milgram, Stanley 184
Millard, Kathryn 184
Miller, Alice 33
Miller, Ann 112
mind 52, 99, 122, 167, 209
Mitra, Sugata 110, 118
Monk, Ray 143
Mottley, Mia 157
Mukherjee, Ankhi 27
Muller, Gail 145
Munby, Steve 244

nature 43, 172, 205, 209, 211
need 44, 49, 64, 73, 74, 77, 80, 89, 92
Neville 145
Nishimura, Takuma 229
noise 53, 151, 230, 251

O'Connell, Bill 36
O'Connor, Cailin 122
O'Sullivan, Suzanne 13, 23
Ockenden, Ray 112
Olival, Kevin 223
Orbach, Susie 13, 41, 172, 214
Ord, Toby 43, 119, 189, 212
Orkin, Kate 246
Orlowski, Jeff 172
Orwell, George 156

paradigm 58, 132, 136, 224, 256
Paradigm 131
paradox 19, 139, 210
Parker, Steve 232
pattern 23, 24, 39, 210, 249
Paul Jnr, Bill 225
Peaty, Adam 64
Peirce, Charles 143
Perez, Caroline Criado 180, 245
Peter, Laurence 234
Phillips, Adam 71, 85, 99, 113 140, 165
Philpot, Richard 184, 195
Pickett, Kate 83
Pippa Ehrlich, Pippa 223
Polanyi, Michael 110, 124, 226
Popper, Karl 143
prediction 58, 112
protocols 69, 242, 257
Protocols 216

Racey, Greg 223
Ramachandran, V. S 156
Rao, Justin................................... 162
Raworth, Kate 164
Reed, James 223
Rees, Lord Martin 164
resilience 20, 27, 28, 29
Richard.. 83
Richards, Paul 223
Ringelmann, Maximilien 63, 78, 203, 213
Robertson, Keith 225
Rogers, Carl 63, 76
Rogers, Fred................................ 146
Ross, Gail.................................... 122
Rutter, Michael 7
Ryan.. 223
Ryan, Richard, M........................ 229

Sabrina 225
Sacks, Oliver................................. 42
Sadler, D. Royce 146
Samuel, Julia........................... 13, 19
Sanders.. 138
Sapolsky, Robert......... 13, 38, 49, 63
Schamroth, Norman 112
Schön, Donald............................. 225
Schumacher, Ernst H 188
self-efficacy 28, 101, 104
self-esteem 28, 29, 64, 114, 249
Sexton, J. Bryan 255
shame 17, 134, 214, 219, 220, 221
sharing.......... 12, 32, 44, 80, 219, 227
Shaxson, Nicholas....... 164, 175, 182
Sheldrake, Merlin................. 38, 211
Shue, Kelly.................................. 234
Sibony, Olivier............................ 237

Silvester, Phil...............................215
Siraj, Iram......................................82
Soderbergh, Steven.....................144
Somekh, Bridget...........................92
space 16, 45, 68, 113, 115, 141, 216, 240
Stephens, Lucie....................176, 182
Sterling, Peter 61
Storr, Anthony 203
Stott, Clifford..............................106
Stuewig, Jeff.......................205, 221
Sullenberger................................241
Sullenberger,...............................225
Sunstein, Cass.............................245
Sutherland, Stuart 225, 237
Syed, Matthew 85, 86, 97, 132, 168, 188
Symington, Joan 145

Tajfel, Henri 63, 66
Tangey, June Price......................224
Thaler, Richard 246, 247
Thomas, Eric...............................255
time .. 16, 17, 18, 20, 24, 26, 255, 256
Tomasello, Michael 72
tool..42
transition 46
Trombley, Stephen 82
truth 127, 135, 137
Turknett, Josh 46
Turner, John.............................63, 66

Vedantam......................................51
Vedantam, Shankar..........13, 30, 125, 155, 249
Velázquez, Diego 65
Vygotsky, Lev 139

Wachtel, Ted 224
Wagner, Betty Jane 120
war 48, 184, 192, 206, 215, 236
Weatherall, James 130, 246
Wells, Gordon 35
White, Ralph 225
Whitehead, Jack 92
Whitson, Jennifer 259
Wilcox, Daniel T 16
Wilkinson 83, 182
Wilson, Edward 137
Winchester, Simon 164
Winnicott, Donald 13, 14, 68, 140

Withers, Bill 11, 258
Wittgenstein, Ludwig 143
Witvliet, Margot Gage 134
Wolf, Martin 177
Wolf, Maryanne 110, 117
Wood, David 139
Worthington 7, 141

Yarker, Patrick 120
Young, Kirsty 255

Zac, Paul J 162
Zimbardo, Phillip 186

Ingram Content Group UK Ltd.
Milton Keynes UK
UKHW020632240523
422260UK00005B/178

The
CONSUMER
BANKING
Regulatory Handbook